Teacher Believed in Me

The Science and Heart
of Making a Difference in
Students' Positive Well-Being

Dr. David K. Hatch

Muriel Thomas Summers

Simon & Schuster

New York   Amsterdam/Antwerp   London
Toronto   Sydney/Melbourne   New Delhi

Simon & Schuster Paperbacks
An Imprint of Simon & Schuster, LLC
1230 Avenue of the Americas
New York, NY 10020

First Simon & Schuster trade paperback edition August 2025

SIMON & SCHUSTER PAPERBACKS and colophon are
registered trademarks of Simon & Schuster, LLC

For information about special discounts for bulk purchases, please contact
Simon & Schuster Special Sales at 1-866-506-1949 or business@simonandschuster.com.

The Simon & Schuster Speakers Bureau can bring authors to your live event.
For more information or to book an event, contact the Simon & Schuster Speakers Bureau
at 1-866-248-3049 or visit our website at www.simonspeakers.com.

Interior design by Joy O'Meara

Manufactured in the United States of America

10 9 8 7 6 5 4 3 2 1

Library of Congress Cataloging-in-Publication Data is available.

ISBN 978-1-6682-1039-0
ISBN 978-1-6682-1040-6 (ebook)

For
Every Teacher,
Every Student,
Every Corner

What's Inside

Teacher Believed in Me

Setting the Context—

The Why

The two primary purposes of this book are:

1. To enable students from all corners of the world to increase their positive well-being and readiness to learn.
2. To inspire, or re-inspire, teachers' passions for making a difference in students' lives.

These two purposes are timely and meant to be together, and we look forward to explaining why. But first some context.

Tommy Schmolze was struggling. He was a sophomore at the university and majoring in business. His intelligence, his talents, and his people skills were sure to lead him in many prominent corporate directions. Yet all that was going through his mind at the time was "If I have to look at one more supply and demand chart, I'm going to be sick!"

Tommy gathered the courage to call his parents: "Mom. Dad. I have decided to change my major. I don't want to go into business. I know it may take an extra year to graduate, but I'm going to do it."

Tommy waited for his parents' disappointed reply. What came instead were his mother's understanding words: "Tommy, we have been expecting this call for some time. You want to become a teacher, don't you?"

Tommy sighed, "Yes, Mother, I do."

When we asked Tommy what inspired him to want to become a teacher, he returned to his high school days. They were filled with some tough times. His family had moved from his hometown to another state. He knew no one. "It was total culture shock!" he recalled.

Then something important happened. As Tommy describes it, "My English teacher, Sarah Anderson, observed that I was struggling. She could see that I was just going through the motions. She took me aside one day, looked me in the eyes, and said, 'Tommy Schmolze, you're going to change the world.' I felt her sincere belief in me. It was an incredible feeling. From then on, I looked at life differently. If she had that much faith in me, I couldn't let her down. I owed it to her to give my best."[1]

Tommy Schmolze did go on to become a teacher—yes, a high school English teacher. And further down his life path he became Dr. Tommy Schmolze, a highly respected district superintendent.

Thank you, Sarah Anderson. And thank you to teachers in all corners of the world who make such differences in students' lives.

So what about for you? Was there a teacher in your life who made a significant difference? If you are an educator, what inspired you to become a teacher?

Our Respect for Teachers

The type of teacher we are referring to, of course, is a professional schoolteacher. Yet we hope these pages will also reach school administrators and staff, and parents, community leaders, youth coaches, and other important teachers who influence young people. Especially parents.

In our varied career roles, we have worked alongside teachers from all continents, except Antarctica. They are some of the most talented, kind, intelligent, and humble people we know. Despite the forces aligned against them, they never cease to amaze us with their resourcefulness, patience, stamina, and caring natures. We honor them.

Most teachers choose teaching as a profession because they want to make a difference in students' lives. They want to help students develop a thirst for learning, get through a challenging time, and become contributing citizens and family members. Often, teachers were themselves influenced by one or more inspiring teachers, and now they want to leave a legacy of their own. So they join the profession, seeing it as more than a paycheck. It is a passion![2]

Many teachers' passions for making a difference stay with them from their very first day in the classroom until the lights go off at their retirement parties. As they near the finish line, they do not reflect on their favorite teaching strategy or an award they received. Instead, they remember with great satisfaction the names of specific students whose lives they influenced for the better—if only in small ways. That is the good news.

Yet along with that good news comes a growing concern. If wanting to make a difference in students' lives means so much to teachers, why then do so many burn out or lose sight of their passions for teaching?

We know a high school choir director who hit such a period of decrescendo. He had been teaching for 20 years and was well liked. Yet he hit a flat note in his career and wondered why he should continue. His wife saw what was happening and, without his knowledge, reached out to his former students via social media: "Join us tonight in singing to my husband after the concert."

Word spread quickly, and more than a hundred students showed up to surprise their former teacher. As soon as the concert ended, the back doors flew open and lines of former students flowed into the auditorium singing with gusto to let their former teacher know that because of his influence they had been "changed for good."[3] That was followed by an outpouring of "thank you" messages voiced by the former students.

After absorbing the magnitude of his influence on those students, the choir director made an interesting observation. "I suppose I never really lost my passion for teaching," he said. "I just misplaced it for a while."

Do you know any teachers who have temporarily misplaced their passion for teaching?

Our Respect for Students

We also have tremendous respect for students.

Each year, the cohorts of students seem to get stronger and stronger in so many ways. As a whole, we find them to be every bit as talented, fun, clever, smart, witty, and mischievous as their teachers were when they were students. One minute they make us laugh and the next they astound us with their concerns about what is happening in the world. And that, again, is the good news.

Yet along with the good news comes another gnawing concern. Why is it that wherever we go in the world a growing number of students are experiencing stifling levels of anxiety, depression, loneliness, and other similar challenges? Why do we keep hearing of harmful acts against self or others coming from students who we would never imagine being attached to such thoughts and behaviors? Why are so many struggling to stay engaged in school?

The easiest way to respond to those questions is to point blame. We might start with social media. We know it is a hazard for some students. Or what about peer pressure, bullying, food insecurity, turmoil at home, body shaming, or a lack of sleep? Is it gaming? What about too much pampering, too many expectations, or too much pressure to pass exams? Could it be wars or crime? And what about students themselves? Shouldn't they take responsibility for some of what troubles them?

Indeed, there are as many directions to point blame for what is causing students unrest as there are students. But has pointing blame ever proven to be a successful approach to solving challenges of such magnitude? We think not. Instead, our confidence in teachers convinces us that there are practical things teachers can do within the walls of their classrooms that will enable all students to enjoy an increased measure of positive well-being and an enhanced readiness to learn.

The Science

What we have just described are millions of students who are facing significant challenges, and thousands of teachers who are passionate about making a difference in their lives. Perhaps you can see why the two groups are meant to be together.

So what can teachers realistically do to enable students to enjoy increased positive well-being and a greater readiness to learn?

To answer that question for ourselves, we first turned to the research literature. The research we examined covered multiple fields of study, including education, child development, neuroscience, family science, psychology, and leadership. It ranged from the classic writings of past thought leaders to the insights of today's top thinkers.

The research that we ultimately chose to share in these pages is not filled with a massive amount of statistics. We have written for a global audience and recognize that the statistics for one country, school, classroom, or student can differ vastly from all others. Statistics often tell the average student's story but not your students' stories. Statistics can change overnight. So we have done our best to include only statistics that represent worldwide trends that are not going away anytime soon.

One example of the type of statistics that are trending across the globe comes from the United Nations International Children's Education Fund (UNICEF) and the Gallup organization. They partnered to conduct interviews with 20,000 students and adults in 21 countries. More than a third of the students (39 percent) reported that they frequently experience worry, anxiety, or nervousness, while 19 percent said they frequently feel depressed or have little interest in doing things. For a class of 25 students, that means that 5 to 10 students show up to class each day feeling unsettled. The adults in the study were not faring much better.[4]

If there is any positive news in those numbers, it is that the larger percentage of students seem to respond to life's challenges as well as can be expected. So, in our search through the research literature, we were looking for best practices that teachers can apply with all students, not just those who might be struggling.

If you remember only one statistic from this book, we hope you cling on to this one. It comes from the National Scientific Council on the Developing Child at Harvard University and is summarized in the form of a question and answer:

> **Question:** When confronted with the fallout of childhood trauma, why do some children adapt and overcome, while others bear lifelong scars that flatten their potential?
>
> **Answer:** A growing body of evidence points to one common answer: Every child who winds up doing well has had at least one stable and committed relationship with a supportive adult.[5]

Did you catch the statistic? "Every child!" That is 100 percent. What we found encouraging about this finding is that it indicates that adults can have a positive impact on students' lives—even students who have experienced trauma—just by being a stable, committed, and supportive adult in their lives. But what specifically might they do to be that kind of adult?

The U.S. Centers for Disease Control and Prevention (CDC) provides some general but helpful direction in answer to that question. After publishing a worrisome report on the downward trends in adolescents' mental health, the CDC concluded: "The good news is that teens are resilient, and we know what works to support their mental health: feeling connected to school and family."[6]

We agree that teens are remarkably resilient and that family connections are vital to supporting students' mental health. But given that this book is intended for teachers, what most seized our attention is the priority the CDC placed on the power of school connectedness.

No profession, as a whole, is better positioned than teachers to influence students' feelings of school connectedness. Teachers have the near-daily opportunity to connect personally with students, and they also play a role in connecting students with other students. Yet as simple as that might sound, connecting with all students is not always easy. After all, it is one thing for teachers to *want to* build connections with all students and quite another *to do it*. Especially when it comes to students who might test a teacher the most.

The good news is that there is some science to it and some practical things teachers can do. And we are eager to share a small slice of the science we have gathered from the more than 250 researchers cited in these pages. Stay tuned.

The Heart

As much as we respect science, it is only useful to the extent that it can be translated into practical application. For that to happen in a classroom filled with diverse and rambunctious students requires more than science. It requires heart. Sometimes a lot of heart.

So, in addition to examining the research literature, we went to scores of teachers and administrators to get their views on what teachers can realistically do to better connect with students. A significant number of those educators come from our work with *Leader in Me* schools and districts. *Leader in Me* is a whole-school improvement model designed to teach students and educators leadership skills, build a high-trust school culture, and focus academic efforts on what is most "wildly important." To date, it is being implemented in 8,000 schools and more than 60 countries.[7] These educators have contributed tremendous insights and best practices.

To expand our collection of insights and best practices even further, we conducted numerous face-to-face interviews with adults and surveyed over 1,000 more from 12 countries (five continents) using the world-leading technologies of Qualtrics. We asked them to describe a former teacher who made a significant difference in their lives.[8] Most were at a point when they could look back and see the direct impact their former teachers have had on who they have become and what they have achieved. Eyes often moistened as they expressed comments like: "She is the reason I chose my career." Or "I planned to drop out of school until I had him as a teacher." Or "She was the one adult I trusted when I needed someone who would listen to me." One woman had scars on her arms that signaled she had been cutting herself during a dark stage of her life. She said a high school teacher had kept her from ending her life.

Each person we interviewed and surveyed had a story to tell about their former teacher. Each story was filled with heart. We look forward to sharing a portion of their stories and insights. Again, stay tuned.

Making a Difference

So what did the combination of science and people's hearts tell us about what teachers can do to strengthen students' positive well-being and readiness to learn?

When we combined the research literature, interviews, and survey responses, and analyzed the overall findings, seven clear themes emerged. What is obvious in the themes is that the teachers who were identified as "difference makers" did not demonstrate miraculous qualities or perform heroic deeds. A few may have been the "fun" or "funny" types of teachers, but that was not what made the difference. Instead, the seven themes consisted of practical skillsets that any teacher can apply.

Occasionally what the teachers did to make a difference resulted from a one-time powerful connection they made with a student. Far more often, however, it resulted from a series of small connections that did not occur overnight. They happened over time.

We delve into the seven skillsets as we progress chapter by chapter. However, as a preview they are:

My teacher...

1. Accepted me as I was.
2. Taught me about life.
3. Inspired me to see my strengths.
4. Entrusted me with responsibilities.
5. Helped me through a hard time.
6. Empowered me to do it myself.
7. Corrected me in a positive way.

Something that quickly became obvious about the skillsets is that all seven apply to all teachers, all students, and all corners of the world.

Positive Well-Being

So what is meant by positive well-being?

The reason all seven skillsets apply to all teachers, all students, and all corners of the world is that they address basic human needs.

Basic human needs are commonly divided into three categories: physical needs, intellectual needs, and social-emotional needs.

Of course, the primary role of teachers is to address students' intellectual needs. However, when students' physical needs are not being met—such as when they show up to class with empty stomachs, no sleep, poor health, or feeling unsafe—it is a tall task for teachers to fully engage them in learning. Likewise, when students' social or emotional needs are not being met—such as when they feel sad, lonely, or anxious—that, too, decreases their readiness to learn. In fact, YouthTruth, a non-profit think tank that has surveyed more than two million students and 300,000 parents in five countries, recently declared, "Feeling depressed, stressed or anxious is now the No. 1 obstacle to students' learning."[9]

What this confirms is that all three categories of needs are highly interactive. When one category is being satisfied, the others are strengthened. And when one category is not being satisfied, the others are weakened. The ideal, of course, is when all three categories of needs are being adequately satisfied. Researchers use several names to refer to this ideal state. Some call it *flourishing*. Some refer to it as addressing the *whole student*. And for the purposes of this book, we have joined other researchers in calling it *positive well-being*, as diagramed below.[10]

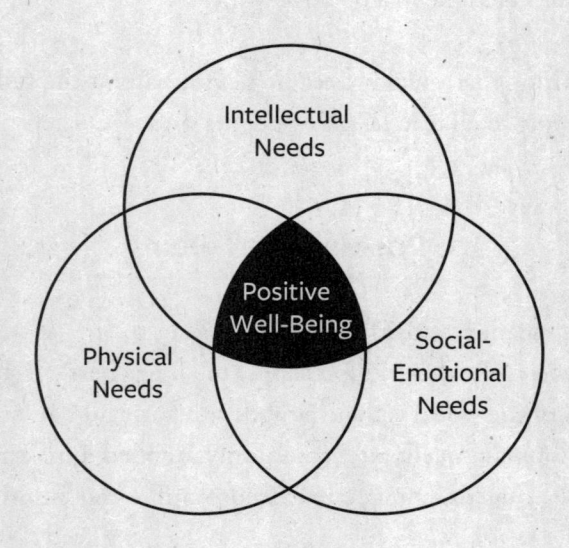

One of the more important reasons for teachers to be attentive to the positive well-being of students is that positive well-being in childhood is predictive of positive well-being in adolescence, and positive well-being in adolescence is predictive of positive well-being in adulthood.[11] It is an ongoing process of living, learning, and, hopefully, progressing.

This book touches on all three categories of needs. Of course, we were not surprised that a significant portion of people's comments about former teachers were directed toward what their teachers had done to address their intellectual needs by making their subject matter lessons interesting and relevant. In fact, nearly half of the people we interviewed and surveyed indicated that their teacher had influenced their career and further education choices. It should never be underestimated what teachers do for students' positive well-being by providing strong academics.

What did surprise us, however, was the amount of emotion people exerted when telling us about what their "difference-making" teachers had done that had little or nothing to do with academics or the subject matters that they taught. Instead, it had everything to do with what their teachers did to influence their social-emotional well-being.

A very typical example of the kinds of comments people made about their former teacher is found in the following note from a K–12 principal named Carmen:

> Growing up, I wasn't the student who thrived in the classroom. I was often in trouble, struggled to stay engaged, and felt like I didn't belong. I didn't act out because I didn't care, I acted out because I didn't feel understood. Most teachers saw me as a problem to solve. But one saw potential.
>
> That one teacher gave me my very first chance at leadership. It was a small responsibility that made a big impact on my life. For the first time, I felt trusted. I felt seen. And that changed everything. It didn't just put me on a better path, it showed me what was possible when someone chooses to believe in you.

Listening to such stories over and over was an invigorating part of our research. And the more we listened to stories like Carmen's, and like Tommy's at the start of this chapter, the more this book's focus began to take on an extra emphasis regarding what teachers do to address the social-emotional needs of students.

Within the general category of social-emotional needs is a list of more specific needs. Teachers cannot realistically be expected to address them all. However, as we began to search deeper into the research and began to write, for each skillset there was one social-emotional need that kept emerging as the most central need for that skillset. For example, the basic need for *connection*—which we have already learned is important—kept emerging as the most central need addressed by the skillset "Accepted Me as I Was." For the skillset "Taught Me About Life," the need for *meaning* kept emerging as the most central need addressed by that skillset. And so it was for all seven of the skillsets. We introduce all seven basic needs along with their matching skillset as the book progresses.

Teacher Believed in Me

To this point, we have essentially described the book's subtitle: "The Science and Heart of Making a Difference in Students' Positive Well-Being." So why choose *Teacher Believed in Me* as the main title?

The first reason for the title is that when we asked people to describe a teacher who made a significant difference in their lives, over and over we heard: "They believed in me." It was an inspiring echo.

The second reason for the title stems from the difference between the words *belief* and *believe*. *Belief* is a noun. Beliefs arise from a person's upbringing, experiences, education, and emotions. Beliefs are important because they influence what people believe.

Believe is a verb. Verbs imply action, the "doing" of something. When the people we interviewed said "My teacher believed in me," they almost instantly began listing examples of what their teacher "did" that made a difference. What teachers believe—or "do"—is important because it can influence who students *become*.

Admittedly, the seven skillsets we identified provide a rather broad view of what teachers "do" to make a difference. So, to be more descriptive, for each skillset we went back to the research literature, interviews, and survey responses, and we identified three best practices that teachers "do" to apply the skillset. We very intentionally selected only best practices that: (1) take a positive approach, (2) build connections, and (3) keep things simple.

Taking a Positive Approach

For students to enjoy positive well-being, it is not enough to remove the negatives from their lives—the things that are causing them pains or self-doubts. They must also learn to identify, develop, and nurture the positive skills, traits, and conditions that lead them to "feel good" about themselves, about school, and about life.

Whereas most traditional fields of psychology focus primarily on removing the negatives from people's lives, the relatively newer field of positive psychology focuses on developing and nurturing the positives—particularly students' strengths. While both approaches are important, we intentionally chose the positive approach. This book is NOT an attempt to "fix" or remove what isn't working in students' lives. It is a research-based effort to create the conditions that will enable students to build on their strengths and to flourish even more. The best practices apply to all students, not just those who may be struggling. Think of it as taking a tree seedling and gradually nurturing it over time until it grows to maturity.

What we hope this makes clear is that this is NOT a how-to guide for helping students deal with anxieties, loneliness, or depressed feelings. It is NOT an attempt to turn teachers into therapists. It is NOT a new curriculum to help students manage their negative emotions. It is NOT any of those things.

This is a positive approach to positive living.[12]

Building Connections

As we indicated, the need for connection will be a focus of the first skillset, "Accepted Me as I Was." But the reality is that every skillset and every best practice can be considered as a way to make a connection with students. It could be said that this entire book is about helping students feel school connectedness. In fact, given that there are three best practices for all seven skillsets, we earnestly considered subtitling the book "21 Ways to Connect With Students."

Some teachers will be relieved to know that we are not expecting teachers to build deep relationships or become lifelong buddies with students. The focus is on connecting with students in simple ways. Administrators, in particular, will also be interested to know that every best practice can also be applied to making connections with the adults in a school. Don't forget the adults!

Keeping It Simple

Teachers already have plenty to do. So we selected best practices that are practical and that do not require a lot of time or resources. Some teachers may even suggest the best practices are too simple, even commonsensical. That may be true, but common sense is not always common practice. And, as far as we are concerned, simple is a must for teachers who already handle numerous important responsibilities with limited bandwidth.

With teachers' best interests in mind, the best practices are presented in bite-sized fashion so that teachers can study and apply them one at a time and over a period of time. They can study them on their own, or as a professional development opportunity with a team, school, or district.

Important: The best practices in this book are designed for general use with all students. If you see signs that a student could be facing a mental health challenge that is beyond what you consider typical—such as isolating themselves, showing sudden mood changes, or hinting at harming themselves or others—seek the partnership of a school counselor or mental health specialist. They are equipped with strategies and tools for assisting students, and know when and how to involve parents and other professionals. Partner with them. When at all possible, do not go it alone.

You, the Leader

There is actually a third reason we chose *Teacher Believed in Me* as the book's main title. It comes from the timeless and classic story of Anne Sullivan and Helen Keller.

Anne and Helen were both products of a teacher who believed in them. For Helen, who became deaf and blind as a child, that teacher was Anne. Whereas all previous attempts by experts to work with Helen had failed, Anne quickly ignited in Helen a passion for lifelong learning and contribution. The pair ended up staying together for 49 years, much of which was spent promoting the rights of women and the blind. After Anne's passing, Helen wrote a book to honor Anne, who she always called *Teacher*. She concluded it with what might be the highest tribute a teacher can receive: "Teacher believed in me, and I resolved not to betray her faith."[13]

Isn't that every teacher's quest? To believe in students in such a way that students come to believe in themselves and resolve to do something special as a result. We call that leadership.

Our experience is that teachers receive far more training in classroom management than they do in how to lead students. Perhaps this is why many classrooms are over-managed and under-led. This book is about teachers being leaders.

Classroom leadership is about *effectiveness*—doing what is most important. It is helping students develop a vision of the bigger picture of life and how they might contribute. It is setting clear expectations. It is creating routines and systems that engage students in learning and sustain their progress. It is inspiring, entrusting, empowering, and correcting students in positive ways. It is enabling students to believe in themselves.

In contrast, classroom management is about *efficiency*—doing what is most important in a timely, quality manner. It is organizing resources, spaces, schedules, and procedures so that learning is maximized. It is ensuring that routines and systems are properly implemented and maintained. It is bringing structure and order to a classroom. It is meeting—or exceeding—expectations.[14]

Leadership and management are both essential in classrooms. Yet the people we interviewed and surveyed spoke almost entirely about how their "difference maker" teachers led and inspired them, not about how their teachers managed and controlled them. That is why we refer to them throughout the remainder of the book as the seven leadership skillsets.

When Drs. Richard DuFour and Robert Marzano opened their book *Leaders of Learning* by declaring: "Every person who enters the field of education has both an opportunity and an obligation to be a leader,"[15] they were not calling on a few superhero teachers to step up and be leaders while the rest stand back and admire. They were challenging "every" teacher to be a leader. Why? Because every classroom has students who are struggling and every classroom has students who are looking for a teacher to inspire them, a teacher to believe in them. As former teacher Rita Pierson so aptly put it, "Every child deserves a champion—an adult who will never give up on them, who understands the power of connections, and insists that they become the best that they can possibly be."[16]

That champion—that leader—can be you.

Looking Ahead

This book is organized in the following way: Chapters 1–7 each focus on one of the seven leadership skillsets and the basic need it most addresses. Each chapter contains three best practices teachers can apply to connect with students and increase their positive well-being. Each contains temperance factors—tips for finding the correct balance between doing too much and doing too little. Each concludes with a reminder that every best practice can also be applied to the adults in the school. Don't forget the adults!

Next is Chapter 8, titled "Crafting a Sustainable Plan." It may be the most important chapter. Why? Because it makes everything feel doable. There are more best practices in this book than teachers will want to attempt. Think of them as items in a healthy buffet. You do not need to consume them all, and especially not all at once. You can always come back for more. Nevertheless, Chapter 8 suggests a few approaches to consider when choosing how to best apply the leadership skillsets and best practices to your unique circumstances and students. It even suggests how to do so in as few as 10 minutes per day when spread over a school year and when using what we call *the power of 10*.

The final chapter, "Just Love 2.0 Them!," re-highlights key learnings from the book. It emphasizes the reality that teachers will be less than fully effective in applying the leadership skillsets unless students feel their teachers genuinely care about them. In the end, do we expect the seven leadership skillsets to prevent all emotional or social challenges? No. Will the skillsets stop every anxiety, sad moment, suicide, violent act, or lonely day? No. Will applying the skillsets allow teachers to create conditions for students' positive well-being to thrive? Yes!

It is difficult to write a one-size-fits-all book that perfectly addresses all levels and varieties of students and teachers. So as you study each leadership skillset, focus foremost on the principles. If you are a secondary teacher, for example, and come across a best practice from an elementary teacher or university professor, please do not regard it as irrelevant. Focus on the principle behind what is being said and find ways to adapt it to your students and circumstances. Make it your own.

Throughout the book, we refer to ourselves as Dr. Hatch, Muriel, or "we." We are the storytellers, whereas true credit for the insights in this book goes to the researchers and educators whom we honor and celebrate in these pages. While each story we share is true, the names of some students and adults have been altered to respect their privacy.

If you happen to be one of the thousands of educators in a *Leader in Me* school, you may recognize us as co-authors of the book *The Leader in Me*, along with Dr. Stephen R. Covey and Sean Covey. *The Leader in Me* and this book serve complementary purposes. Each strengthens the other. That being said, there is no need to be familiar with *The Leader in Me* to understand, apply, and benefit from the principles in this book.

Now, before moving on to the next chapter, we suppose we would not be true educators if we didn't first offer a challenge. So we invite you to read the challenge below and then begin your journey toward furthering your passion for making a difference in students' positive well-being by connecting, engaging, and leading students.

The Challenge

Don't wait for the final chapter to begin applying the seven leadership skillsets. Select one or a few students who you think will most benefit from your "stable and committed" influence. Then, as you study each chapter, make a plan to apply the skillsets with those students. Prompts are located at the end of each chapter for you to consider when choosing how you might best go about using the chapter's insights to make a difference in your students' positive well-being.

Accepted Me as I Was

Not long ago, Dr. Hatch attended a memorial service for Kristi, a former high school teacher who passed away after a long illness. She taught sign language for eight years before leaving to attend to family matters.

Though Kristi had been away from the teaching profession for 15 years, her former students had never forgotten her influence. Several attended her memorial service, and Dr. Hatch couldn't help but notice how closely connected they were. Each time one arrived, they hugged, smiled, and laughed as if they were still best friends.

As part of the service, 20 of Kristi's former students performed a tribute song using sign language. The song they chose was entitled "Friends." It was fortunate that they were singing with their hands because their vocal cords were fully choked with emotions.

What had Kristi done to unite the students? How had she personally connected with each one?

Dr. Hatch learned that much of Kristi's sign language instruction involved asking and answering questions. She started each class by signing questions to her students about their lives and interests. The students were required to use sign language to respond. The students were equally interested in Kristi's life but were again required to use sign language to ask their questions. When they lacked the correct signs to respond to Kristi's questions or to ask her a question, the students worked together to find them. In this way, much of the vocabulary building in Kristi's classes was actually friendship building.

Students came to know each other so well in Kristi's class that they ended up staying in touch over the ensuing 15 years, mostly via social media. They included Kristi in their messaging. They celebrated the births of her children. They sent her messages throughout her illness. And the more Dr. Hatch learned about all that had gone on over the years with Kristi and the students, the more it became clear that Kristi's legacy would remain alive for years to come.

The Need for Connection

What would inspire students to gather 15 years from now to celebrate your life and leadership?

Research predicts the answer to that question will largely depend on how well you connect with students and how much you accept them—as they are. It will depend on how much they feel you care about them—as they are—and how much they perceive you like them—as they are. Before they are inspired by how much potential you see in them, they want to know how much you believe in them—as they are. As the former children's television host Mr. Rogers put it, "I don't think anyone can grow unless he's loved exactly as he is now, appreciated for what he is rather than what he will be."[1]

Students use many phrases to describe their need for connection and their desire to be accepted as they are. They talk about "fitting in" or "being a welcomed member of a team" or having a ton of "likes" or "friends" on their social media site. They place extra value on the friends who they say "like me no matter what" or "don't judge me." Whatever terms they use, what they are describing is their deep desires to enjoy meaningful relationships.

Researchers likewise use multiple terms and synonyms to describe the need for connection. They write about the need for social connection, social acceptance, or social attachment. Abraham Maslow referred to the need for connection as the need for "love and belonging." In referring specifically to school connectedness, or school belonging, Carol Goodenow and Kathleen Grady defined it as "the extent to which students feel personally accepted, respected, included, and supported by others in the school social environment."[2] Regardless of the terms you prefer to use, we suggest that they include the phrase "as they are" at least in spirit.

Students' perceptions of how connected they feel at school are important for many reasons. Not the least of which is the impact that they have on academics. When students perceive they belong and are accepted at school, their engagement in class discussions rises, their perceived value of school increases, their academic performance improves, and their expectancy that they can do well academically grows. In contrast, when students lack feelings of belonging at school, they are more likely to be absent, tardy, or drop out. They are also less likely to complete homework.[3] In the words of Dr. Linda Darling-Hammond, who is one of the most respected researchers in the field of education, "When that sense of belonging is there, children throw themselves into the learning environment. When that sense of belonging is not there, children will alienate, they will marginalize, they will step back."[4]

What about the impact of school connectedness on students' social and emotional well-being? When students perceive they belong at school, they feel increased self-worth, sociability, and optimism. They possess increased resilience and greater ability to escape poverty.[5] In contrast, when students perceive they do not belong, they are more likely to experience anxiety, depression, disordered eating, and suicidal thoughts. They feel rejected and may turn to alcohol or drugs for relief and escape. They are also more likely to engage in lying and cheating.[6] Some students crave acceptance to the extent that they go to great lengths to acquire items with popular brand names—such as clothing or cell phones—thinking that belongings will bring them belonging.

A core emphasis of the research on positive well-being is the study of happiness. What makes people happy? Philosophers and poets have debated that question for thousands of years. And what modern happiness researchers have concluded is that of the many factors that lead people to be happy, there is one factor that stands well above all others. That one factor is positive relationships. Connections.

In fact, for the past 80 years, a series of Harvard scientists have been conducting what they call "the world's longest study on happiness." To date, their one overarching finding is: "Good relationships keep us all happier and healthier."[7] And virtually every happiness researcher agrees: "Connections are the key to happiness."[8] These and other research findings fully support the CDC's conclusion that one of the best ways to support students' mental health is to help them build positive relationships—connections—at school.

The Organization for Economic Cooperation and Development (OECD) has been tracking school belonging among 15–16-year-old students for more than two decades. A recent report covered 79 countries and 600,000 students, and all indicators suggest that students' feelings of school connectedness are on a slow but steady decline. Roughly a third of the world's students say they do not feel they belong at school. Students from minority or impoverished upbringings generally feel even less connectedness at school.[9]

Gallup International has also surveyed hundreds of thousands of students about topics related to school connectedness. It reports that "having a best friend at school" is one of the best predictors of student engagement. It gives students "a reason to show up, makes their days more enjoyable, and encourages positive behaviors." On the positive side, 70 percent of students indicate that they do have a best friend at school.[10] Some adults might judge 70 percent as being "good enough," but what about the other 300 out of every 1,000 students who do not have a best friend at school? Given that it puts them at risk of not being engaged in school or falling into patterns of anxiety and depression, we cannot consider 70 percent as "good enough."

Far too many students come and go from school each day without anyone acknowledging their existence. They feel invisible. Forgotten. They are longing for belonging at a time when they are experiencing what therapists are calling an "epidemic of loneliness." Many even refer to today's young people as "the loneliest generation."

The ironic thing about loneliness is that it rarely comes alone. It is close companions with anxiety and depression, and seldom does one show up in a student's life without the others coming along. Together, they are known to lead to heart disease, sleep disorders, and other physical ailments. The former two-time United States Surgeon General Dr. Vivek H. Murthy has even warned that loneliness creates a greater risk for early death than does smoking tobacco, whereas connections have the potential to heal.[11] All this puts the physical well-being of individuals at risk, and places stressors on their families and society in general.[12]

More costly in our minds is the impact that chronic loneliness can have on students' self-perceptions. Some interpret their loneliness to be an indication that something is wrong with them. Some take it to a point of feeling shame, which Dr. Brené Brown defines as "the intensely painful feeling or experience of believing we are flawed and therefore unworthy of acceptance and belonging."[13]

Of course, a worst-case scenario is for students to become so lonely or feel so shamed that they develop thoughts of self-harm or of doing harm to others. Feeling not accepted and not connected is a known contributor to thoughts of self-harm or of harming others. Some reports have even revealed that in cases of school shootings, 95 percent of attackers are current or former students of the school, and more than 70 percent report they felt persecuted, bullied, or ostracized at school.[14] Loneliness can be dangerous.

Much blame for students' loneliness is aimed at the misuse of smartphones and social media.[15] Dr. Kay Tye, a neuroscientist at the Salk Institute for Biological Sciences, explains why social media and other digital experiences—including gaming—can diminish students' feelings of connectedness. "Social media," she says, "largely consists of watching other people interact from afar, passively witnessing them making comments and responding without any real-time feedback." With social media, she adds, "You don't get eye contact. You don't get any sort of touching. You can't even laugh together. So there's no brain-synchrony connection. There's only the feeling that you're missing out. There's only the social exclusion."[16]

Indeed, when it comes to examining the research, there is not much good news for students whose primary social connections are internet connections. That being said, it is fair to acknowledge that so-cial media and smartphones have connected, re-connected, and kept connected many friendships; they have even made global connections more possible. So there are pros and cons.

So what this all tells us is that students' perceptions of connection clearly impact all three general categories of basic needs: physical, intellectual, and social-emotional. The question that then arises is: Do teachers have any influence over students' feelings of school connectedness?

Dr. Kelly-Ann Allen of Monash University in Australia has monitored the research on school belonging over the past few decades. She and a few colleagues published a meta-analysis on hundreds of research studies and identified ten factors that influence students' feelings of school belonging. The ten factors included a student's personality, peer support, parent support, teacher support, and the social and emotional environment of their school. In the end, it was teacher support that turned out to be the top predictor of students' perceived feelings of school belonging. So yes, teachers can and do influence students' feelings of school connectedness.[17]

In fact, research from the Springtide Research Institute suggests that the more trusted adults students have in their lives, the better. The institute surveyed a thousand 13–25-year-olds to examine the impact that trusted adults have on students' feelings of school connectedness. Thirty-three percent of the students reported "I feel all alone," while 36 percent indicated "No one understands me." What was most enlightening, however, was what happened when the researchers examined the data in relation to the number of "trusted adults" young people have in their lives. As the table below indicates, the more trusted adults the students reported having in their lives, the less they reported feeling completely alone and not understood.[18]

Trusted Adults in Their Lives	% reporting, "I feel completely alone."	% reporting, "No one understands me."
0	62	70
1	46	60
2–4	29	41
5 or more	9	24

So once again we see that trusted adults, such as teachers, can and do have an influence on students' feelings of connection and positive well-being. Which begs the next question of: What specifically can teachers do to enable students to feel more acceptance and connection at school?

What follows are three best practices to consider when trying to help students feel increased acceptance and connectedness at school. Each is intended to enable teachers to build connections with students, and increase their positive well-being and readiness to learn.

Three Best Practices for Accepting Students as They Are

According to the research literature and people's comments about teachers who made a difference in their lives, three best practices for connecting with students and helping them to feel increased acceptance at school are:

My teacher . . .

- called me by name.
- took an interest in me.
- voiced respect for me.

Called Me by Name

In Shakespeare's *Romeo and Juliet*, the enraptured Juliet pauses on a balcony to ask Romeo, "What's in a name?"

A teacher was talking with a former student and the name of one of their peers came up. When the teacher asked how that peer was doing, the former student responded: "He's doing great. But he thinks you never liked him." The teacher was stunned. He not only liked the student, he thought very highly of him. "Why would he think I never liked him?" he asked. "He says you could never remember his name" was the reply.

We visited a secondary school in Central America. We had been there the previous year and were hosted by a student named Karol. When, on our return visit, we happened to see Karol walking past us in a hallway, we casually said, "Hola, Karol." She was shocked that we remembered her name. Her friends were also surprised and made a big hoopla about it.

That brief exchange caught the attention of the student who was our host for that day. Three or four times throughout the day she checked to make sure we recalled her name. We could tell she was trying to ensure that, if we ever returned to the school, we would also remember her name. When a year later we did return, guess who was waiting to greet us? We could tell by her eyes what she wanted to know. So, before she could ask, we called her by name. One would have thought she had just passed her national exams. She was so delighted! It was not because we were smart enough to remember her name but because she felt that she was important enough for us to remember her name.

Muriel was checking into a hotel when the desk attendant asked her about the purpose of her trip. When Muriel indicated she would be working with schools, the attendant asked: "Oh, do you know the superintendent?" Muriel responded that she did. The attendant then raved about the superintendent. She described how her son had the superintendent as a teacher in elementary school. The son was now a senior in high school. The superintendent had been at the high school a few weeks earlier and happened to see her son. He called her son by name. The son couldn't believe the superintendent would recognize him, let alone call him by name. And on and on the desk attendant raved about the superintendent. Why? Because he had remembered her son and called him by name.

Names are one of the first things friends learn about one another. Names often have deep familial and cultural meanings. Names are a part of a student's identity. It is no accident that professional salespeople are trained to use customers' names often, particularly at the start and end of conversations. They know that customers like to hear their name in affirming ways. Students are no different.

Our colleague Gary McGuey has worked with as many teachers and students as anyone we know. He reminds teachers that when students hear their name spoken, the regions of their brains that are responsible for thought patterns and behaviors related to their identity and personality literally activate. They become more engaged.[19]

It may be difficult for secondary or university teachers to remember every student's name, given how their students rotate in and out of classrooms every hour, like passengers coming and going in an airport. However, when a teacher is not willing to attempt to learn names, it impersonalizes their connections with students and sends a clear message that says, "You are just another student." In contrast, when a teacher respectfully calls a student by name, what that student hears is: "I know who you are. I'm interested in you as a person. You are more to me than a test score."

The real key is not that a teacher remembers students' names; it is that students *hear* their names spoken in positive ways. Respectfully calling a student by name turns a casual teacher-student relationship into a meaningful connection. Students feel less anonymity and more accountability for their actions, and are more likely to behave in positive ways.

The best way to ensure that students hear their names called on a consistent basis is to create routines or systems. In the following example, what routines do you observe being used with a first grade student named Anthony?

As Anthony boards the school bus each morning, the driver says, "Good morning, Anthony." Anthony then goes and sits alone.

Upon arrival at the school, a few administrators, support staff, and students are stationed near the school's entrance to welcome students by name and provide a friendly greeting. They have a special eye out for students who sit alone or may be having a rough start to a day.

Given the mass of students arriving at the same time, Anthony may slip into the school without hearing his name. But once he arrives at his classroom, there is little chance of him going unnoticed. His teacher is standing at the door to extend a warm greeting and call him by name. Inside the classroom, the name recognition continues as Anthony's teacher, for the first few weeks of the year, begins each morning by taking attendance using the following routine:

Teacher: "Good morning, Anthony."
Class (in unison): "Good morning, Anthony."
Anthony: "Good morning, class."

Anthony's teacher then shifts to the next student and repeats the routine until each student has had a chance to hear their name spoken and learn the names of their peers. And so it is that within the first few minutes of each day, Anthony and his peers have each had the chance to hear their names spoken by a bus driver, an administrator, their teacher, their classmates, and perhaps a few other friends. He feels accepted. Connections are made.

Of course, teachers may prefer to use entirely different routines for calling students by name. Secondary teachers may prefer to greet and connect with students inside the classroom. They may chat and laugh with students as they arrive, as opposed to preparing for a lesson. They may not get to every student every day, but they will on a consistent basis because they have a routine.

Other teachers make it a routine to call daily attendance out loud, using good eye contact to let students know their teacher knows their name and who they are. The exact nature of the routine is less important than *having* a regular routine to ensure that each student is acknowledged in a positive manner.

Calling students by name can also occur in print form. We know a teacher who faithfully writes students' names on assignments when scoring papers and tests. Instead of writing "Good job!," she writes "Good job, Mary." The simple addition of her name honors Mary with a personal touch and lets her know that her teacher is aware of her.

It is equally important, if not more important, for students to hear their names being respectfully used by peers. Teachers can facilitate this. Some teachers, for example, invite students to take turns reading attendance—out loud—instead of doing it themselves. As the assigned student calls out the names of their peers—one by one—that student learns the names of their peers and their peers have the chance to hear their name being spoken by a peer. Other teachers plan get-to-know-you activities at the start of each year to ensure that students learn and use each other's names. These are but a small sampling of routines teachers can use to ensure that students hear their name.

It is important to use students' names in respectful ways. The famous Irish playwright George Bernard Shaw hated the name George, so he insisted that his teachers and friends called him Bernard. You may have students who feel similarly about their names. And, for sure, no student likes to hear their name mispronounced or made fun of, or to be given a derogatory nickname. What student wants to hear their name spoken only when they are in trouble?

So, getting back to Juliet's question, "What's in a name?," if hearing their name spoken respectfully helps students feel a greater sense of connection and acceptance, then there is enormous value in calling students by name.

What effective systems or routines have you found to be helpful in learning and using students' names?

Took an Interest in Me

Andre Deshotel is a superb behavioral coach. He works at an elementary school where a high percentage of students come from emotionally stressed backgrounds. He knows well the power of connections and calling students by name. "Connections set the stage for cooperation," he insists before adding that "If Bobby's teacher wants to make a real connection with Bobby, and hopes for Bobby to fully cooperate in class, then Bobby's teacher will not only call Bobby by name, he will also get to know the name of Bobby's pet hamster. Bobby's teacher will then see how much quicker Bobby will be inclined to work on his math assignment."

Teachers cannot fully accept students "as they are" until they know something about their interests and backgrounds—their stories. Some students' stories are full of action and adventure. Some are mysteries. Some are filled with romance. Some are horror stories. Some are fictional works—a mixture of truth and wishful thinking. Some students' stories are historical; others are hysterical. How well do you know your students' stories?

When talking with people about a teacher who made a difference in their life, a common comment we heard was: "She was interested in me as a person, not just my academics."

Traci is a school administrator and the parent of a high school student. When her daughter raved about a certain teacher, Traci couldn't help but ask: "What is so special about this teacher?" "She just gets us, Mom," the daughter replied. "She just gets us."

Clearly, the teacher had done something to show interest in her students. Contrast the daughter's experience with the following three brief accounts, beginning with this man's recollection:

At the start of my junior year of high school, my mother was diagnosed with cancer. None of my teachers knew it, and I don't remember there being a natural opportunity for me to tell them.

Mom was very weak. So my sister and I took turns with chores like cooking meals, shopping, giving her rides to the doctor, and so on. That was in addition to our schoolwork. It was a busy and emotional year.

Mom died the week before finals. On the day of her funeral, I was marked absent in all my classes. None of my teachers knew why. They were all good teachers, but I suppose I could have also marked them absent from my life that day.

How many parents have felt a portion of what this single mother expressed following a parent–teacher conference?

I was exhausted after work and only reluctantly attended my son's fourth grade parent–teacher conference. I wanted to be a good mom.

"Oh, you're Matt's mom," the teacher began while opening her gradebook. "I see that Matt is a little below average in math. He's doing average in reading and writing. Matt's citizenship is above average."

And on the teacher rambled. She was describing my son entirely based on how he compared against some class average.

I kept thinking: "Is this my Matt she is talking about? The boy who gets himself out of bed and dressed every morning on his own while I'm off to work. The boy who makes sure his little sister gets fed and safely to her classroom each morning. The boy who cheers me up when I am down. Is it my little hero she is talking about? Does she even halfway understand all he has gone through in his short life?"

I almost told her she was a below-average teacher.

Last, Dr. Hatch recalls from his middle school years a student named Steve. Steve could take a car engine apart and put it back together by himself, which is why his hands were always as greasy and black as his long hair. He seldom stayed awake in class.

Mr. Newman was the science teacher. He, too, had long hair, only his was solid white. He combed it straight back as if it was a foamy wave crashing down upon the back of his neck.

Steve saw zero value in completing Mr. Newman's homework assignments, and Mr. Newman had zero tolerance for "lazy" students like Steve. So the two did their best to ignore each other.

One day, a man from the school district interrupted our class. He had come to announce an award for a student in our class who had scored the highest in the entire district on the state science exam. With 60,000 students in the district, it was a big deal.

Suspense grew as Mr. Newman and all of us students tried to guess who that student might be. Sure enough, it was Steve.

What Dr. Hatch remembers well was Mr. Newman's face when Steve's name was announced. He was not happy. He may have even growled. That is because Mr. Newman was far more into managing students than he was into leading them. He was more into getting students to be silent than he was into discovering that there was a budding genius sitting toward the back of the room with his head on his desk.

Had Mr. Newman taken an interest in Steve, he might have discovered that Steve's widowed mother always kept science magazines on their living room table. Even before Steve could read, he would study the pictures.

Had Mr. Newman taken an interest in Steve, he might have discovered that Steve knew more about certain aspects of science than his science teacher did, and that Steve was far more bored in the class than he was lazy.

Yes, had Mr. Newman taken an interest in Steve, he might have become that one steady, committed, and supportive adult Steve desperately needed in his life.

All three of these examples point to the importance of teachers creating routines for taking an interest in students' stories. Consider a few suggestions and examples of routines and systems that we have observed teachers utilizing.

Dedicate a Specific Time for Learning Students' Stories

We were at a secondary school interviewing students about their school's fabulous culture, and the name of one teacher kept popping up. We asked the principal if we could observe the teacher in action. She agreed and came along with us.

It was a Monday. To start off class, the teacher had a student lead the other students through what they called "Monday's Highs and Lows." (Some call this "Roses and Thorns.") Within the span of 10 minutes, each student shared something that had gone well over the weekend (a *high*) and something that had gone not so well (a *low*). It was the teacher's every-Monday routine for finding out what was going on in her students' lives. "When students come back from a weekend," she told us, "they want a few minutes to re-connect with each other. If I don't give it to them, they find time in the middle of my lesson to do it. Besides, it is the one time when I learn the most about my students."

As we departed that class, the principal told us that she had learned more about the students in those 10 minutes than she had in the two previous years she had known them. She committed to creating a routine of her own to learn more about students' stories.

Ask Safe Questions

Teachers who connect with students tend to ask a high number of safe questions, such as: "What did you enjoy about your summer?" Or, "If you were not here loving my class today, what would you rather be doing?" They avoid drilling students only about their test scores or missing assignments and focus instead on taking an interest in their students' interests.

Mr. Salazar, for instance, teaches high school history. While calling attendance each day, he invites students to respond to a safe question, such as, "What is your favorite dessert?" Then, when their name is called, each student replies with a two-second answer, "Chocolate ice cream!" "Donuts." "Mom's cookies." In those brief seconds, Mr. Salazar learns something small about each student, and the entire class has fun learning about each other. It is Mr. Sal's daily routine for learning portions of students' stories.

As teachers build trust with students, they may take their questions a little deeper to discover what matters most to students, what is worrying them, or what *is* and *is not* going well in their lives. They might ask, "You haven't seemed to be yourself for a few days. How are you feeling?" Or, "On a scale of 1 to 10, what is your stress level?" Students respond; teachers listen.

Another safe way to ask safe questions is to seek students' input or advice: "I'm looking for something fun for my family to do this weekend. What fun things do your families do on weekends?" Or, "I'm on a committee and we are trying to improve the school's culture. Do you have any ideas?" In listening to the students' answers, teachers learn about their students' friends, hobbies, family life, and other interests—their stories.

The intent of asking safe questions is not to pry into students' private backgrounds but to make connections.

Meet Students Where They Are At

Our colleague Lonnie Moore was a middle school math teacher. One year at his school, there was a discussion about which teacher would be assigned to take on a student named Jimmy, who had been a challenge for teachers in the past. Mr. Moore said, "I want him."

Instead of waiting for the next school year to arrive, Mr. Moore proactively began to seek out Jimmy. He located him one day in a hallway and introduced himself. He told Jimmy that he was looking forward to having him in his class the next year. Each time he saw Jimmy from then on, he would say hello and ask how things were going. Before the summer break arrived, there was a glimmer of hope that Mr. Moore could make a difference in Jimmy's life.

When the new year arrived, Mr. Moore was quick to reconnect with Jimmy, asking him about his summer. Occasionally, they had one-on-one conversations that were not about math but about Jimmy's interests. By the semester's end, Jimmy received a B grade with zero behavioral issues. A difference was made in Jimmy's life.

Jimmy was not the only recipient of Mr. Moore's efforts to meet students where they were at. He was leaving school one day when he noticed a soccer match going on. He knew that one of his struggling students, Scott, was on the team. Soccer, not math, was what Scott cared about most, which was why he was earning a near-failing grade in Mr. Moore's class.

Mr. Moore walked over to the soccer match with hopes that he might find some small way to connect with Scott. Conveniently, within a matter of minutes Scott scored a goal. Everyone was cheering as he ran by the sidelines where he was greeted by a crowd of hands reaching out to give him a high five. Scott high-fived Mr. Moore's hand before he realized it was Mr. Moore. He stopped and looked back. "Mr. Moore! What are you doing here?"

"I came to see you play, Scott," said Mr. Moore. "I've heard how good you are and wanted to see for myself."

When Scott entered Mr. Moore's classroom the next day, he was a different student. A connection with Mr. Moore had been made on the soccer field that would not have happened in the classroom. Scott began to transfer that connection to his math studies. He wanted to impress Mr. Moore. Before long, Scott's growing confidence in math began to spill over to other subjects.

Four years later, Mr. Moore received a phone call: "Mr. Moore, this is Scott. Do you remember me?"

"Yes, Scott. I absolutely remember you," replied Mr. Moore. "How's soccer? How's life?"

"Things are going great," said Scott. "I've been selected as an honor student for graduation and was told I could invite one of my former teachers to sit in the front row to represent all the teachers who have impacted my life. Would you be that teacher for me?"

Did Mr. Moore do anything grandiose to turn Jimmy's and Scott's lives around? No. It was not much more than a "Hey, Jimmy!" or a high five followed up with some regular in-class attention. But in both cases, connections were started outside the classroom with Mr. Moore proactively meeting the boys where they were at.

Of course, teachers can also find ways to meet students where they are at within the classroom. But at times, it is helpful for teachers to get outside the classroom, to attend school events, or find other times to observe students mingling with friends and family in non-classroom ways.

Tailor Class Assignments

Regardless of the subject matter they teach, teachers can tailor existing assignments to better get to know students and their stories. English teachers can assign students to write a short essay about a favorite memory from the past year. Art teachers can invite students to draw a picture of what they like to do during their non-school hours. History teachers can ask students to write a story from their personal or family history. Foreign language teachers can assign students to write a paragraph describing their family in the foreign language: "*Ich bin eines von vier Kindern.*" Music teachers can have students compile a mix of favorite songs. And so on. Every subject matter has assignments that can be tailored to help teachers discover a portion of students' stories.

Create a System to Record Students' Interests

Some teachers create a system for recording students' interests. Ms. Michelle, for example, keeps a chart to record her elementary students' interests. She updates it each time she learns something that is of interest about a student. Then, if she notices Abby is struggling to feel included, Ms. Michelle refers to her chart, sees that Abby's favorite color is purple, and then she wears purple the next day, saying, "Abby, I wore this shirt just for you." Or, if she looks at the chart and sees what Jose's favorite song is, she plays the song as students enter the classroom the next morning and says something like, "This is Jose's favorite. Let's all dance in honor of Jose." Can you sense Abby's and Jose's connection with their teacher growing?

Plenty of teachers start a year with a student interest survey to get to know students. It is a system that works for them. The important thing is for teachers to create systems and routines that work for them.

Enlist the Village

Since "it takes a village to raise a child," why not enlist the help of the village in discovering students' interests and stories? Talking with former teachers or parents may reveal insights into students' stories that may not be discovered in any other way. Harvard's Dr. Karen Mapp suggests that teachers ask parents: "What are your dreams for your child's education and future? What capacity do you have to support your child's learning? What are your child's strengths? . . . I'm interested in learning from you about your child's interests and how your child learns best."[20] Notice that the questions are phrased positively. In many cases, parents will mention any worrisome "watch outs" they have without teachers needing to ask.

For Each "Me" Offer a "We"

For students to feel a full sense of school connectedness, they must have a "somewhere" or a "someone" to go to, a safe haven where they feel comfortable and accepted as they are. It may be a certain class or teacher. It may be as a member of the school band, a choir, a club, or a sports team. It may be in a homeroom or an advisory setting. It may be that they are part of the student council or a service group. It is somewhere where students perceive that at least one person is genuinely interested in them, understands them, and accepts them as they are.

In other words, every "me" deserves at least one opportunity to be part of a meaningful "we." For students at one high school we visited, their somewhere is in the Success Lab. Students who are at risk of dropping out, failing school, or experiencing anxiety go there. They may go there because they feel that they don't fit in or feel intimidated in the more traditional classrooms. Perhaps they have a social anxiety or a learning disability that requires them to learn in a different manner or pace. Regardless of the reason, Ms. Rogers, Mr. Rowland, and Mr. Davis are the someones who are there to welcome each student to the Success Lab. These teachers know each student's story. They work with them at their own pace. They enable them to progress well ahead of their previous levels. They offer a place for them to connect with each other, a place for them to feel success, a place for them to feel accepted. From there, the students can venture out into other classes if and when they desire. But it all starts with the caring, nonjudgmental natures of their teachers in the Success Lab who accept them as they are.

Wherever that place may be, or whoever that someone may be, at your school, every "me" deserves a chance to feel part of a meaningful "we."

So there are a few ways to connect with students by taking an interest in them. As Dale Carnegie notes in his legendary book *How to*

Win Friends and Influence People: "You can make more friends in two months by becoming interested in other people [or students] than you can in two years by trying to get other people [or students] interested in you."[21]

> *What are some routines or systems you use to take*
> *an interest in students and their stories?*

Voiced Respect for Me

We know of no better way for teachers to let students know they are accepted—as they are—than to tell them. Tell students that they accept them as they are. Tell students that they respect them. Tell students that they believe in them.

For 32 years, millions of children were greeted each morning by a sweater-clad Fred Rogers. Better known as television's "Mr. Rogers," he closed each program by saying: "You've made this day a special day by just your being you. There's no person in the whole world like you. And I like you just the way you are."[22] It was his daily routine for letting each child in his "neighborhood" know that he accepted them. It was a message of acceptance.

Too often, students hear messages of non-acceptance. Dr. Ruby Payne, author of *Emotional Poverty*, says that when students' external environments tell them they are less than, separate from, or inferior to other students, they do not feel acceptance.[23] When they are mocked by peers for any reason, such as race, economic status, religion, or academic or athletic ineptness, the message they hear is that they are not accepted as they are. They feel disconnected. They feel unwanted. Mother Teresa, who lived among the poorest of the poor, described the feeling of being unwelcomed as the most terrible form of poverty.[24]

Some teachers send "You're unwanted!" messages to students that are so subtle that even the teachers themselves are not conscious of them. For example, when a teacher always selects the same five students to help them, they send a silent message to all other students that they are being excluded. Or when a teacher always selects the same ten students' art to be displayed in the school's art show every year, it sends a subtle but real message to all other students that they are excluded as "artists." As silent and subtle as those messages may be, students hear them loud and clear, especially when the non-selected students consistently come from a marginalized group.

Think of respect as being on a spectrum. When students feel *disrespected* by peers, or even by teachers, they feel disliked, anxious, rejected, and unwanted—the opposites of respected or connected. When students are *ignored*, they feel unknown, lonely, depressed, and excluded. It is not until students are *respected* that they feel known, understood, happy, and included—connected, as illustrated in the Spectrum of Respect below.

Spectrum of Respect		
Disrespected	**Ignored**	**Respected**
Disliked	Unknown	Known
Anxious	Lonely	Understood
Revengeful	Depressed	Happy
Unwanted	Excluded	Connection

How people are treated.

How people feel.

We asked a high school senior to identify a teacher who made a difference in his life. The student's name was Ethan, and he immediately recalled his second grade teacher, Mr. Charland. Ethan was timid as a child, and one day he was late to class. It caused him to fret enormously over what Mr. Charland might do or say. In the past, Ethan had figured out that whenever he felt anxiety coming on, he could turn to his favorite source of stress relief—doodling. And he was doing a lot of doodling that day.

Ethan got the idea to write Mr. Charland a note. He took a sheet of sticky-note paper and wrote on it, "I'm sorry I was late." He added a stick-figure doodle of himself. Then, when the time came for the class to go to lunch, Ethan left the note on the top corner of his desk in hopes that Mr. Charland might pass by, see the note, and know that he was truly sorry for being tardy.

When Ethan returned from lunch, he could see from the classroom door that Mr. Charland had placed a sticky note on top of his note. It felt like a grand distance as Ethan walked slowly to his desk, all the while agonizing about what Mr. Charland had written. Ethan's entire body must have gone into full relief when he read the note. There was no scolding and no threat of punishment. Just a little stick-figure doodle Mr. Charland had drawn of himself, and one sentence: "I am so glad you are here." Ten years later, Ethan warmly remembers the feeling of acceptance, warmth, and respect he felt from those seven words.

Renowned talk show host Oprah Winfrey said, "In all my talks and understandings over the years—doing thousands and thousands of shows—I came away with the thread that runs through all our human experiences. It is that we all want to be validated, we all want to be seen, we all want to know that we matter. And the most you can ever do for somebody is to show up and allow them to know that they've been seen and heard by you."[25]

But what if a student is difficult to accept as they are? You know, that one student who tests you the most. That one student about whom you struggle to think of anything positive to say. What do you do with them?

Do what leadership expert Ken Blanchard says, which is to "Catch people doing something right."[26] If you observe closely enough, you can catch any student doing at least one thing right. Validate them for that one "right" thing. Let them know you respect them for that one "right" thing. A teacher cannot only catch students doing "wrong" and expect to make a difference in their positive well-being.

When voicing respect for a student, rather than make a general comment such as "You're a good student," use the following three elements to tell students why you believe in them:

Name Call the student by name.
Quality Acknowledge a specific positive quality of the student.
Respect Voice respect for that quality.

For example, "Hi, Edward. I noticed how you reached out to Peter and befriended him this morning. I sincerely respect you for that." Or "Nicki, I saw the way you took such good care of your mother. I respect that quality in you. I'm glad you're in our class." Such statements of respect can be uttered—or written—in a matter of seconds and yet last a lifetime. Acknowledging special events, special milestones, or significant achievements in a student's life builds connections. Voices respect.

Do not assume that students know you respect them. Let your voice be the voice that tells them you accept them as they are. Let your voice be the voice that lets them know they belong in your classroom. Let your voice be the voice that says, "I believe in you."

How do you let students know you
respect them as they are?

Temperance Factors

Temperance is finding the correct balance between too much and too little. In other words, it is possible to use students' names too often. Therefore, we suggest three cautions for avoiding taking students' need for connection too far.

Be Cautious of Social Anxieties

Have you ever boarded a thrill ride at an amusement park and within seconds you thought, "Stop! I want this ride to stop!" Some students feel that same level of fear and anxiety the moment they step onto the school campus.

For some students, just walking into a classroom filled with other students may be as much as their social anxieties can handle. Some may even resist a teacher's efforts to help them feel more connectedness. This is why it helps to do what high school teacher Evett Barham does, which is to gradually ease students into participating in activities and discussions at the beginning of a year. She starts out with a few low-stress activities like having students share their name or discuss a favorite food with a few peers. She uses those times to observe students' emotional and social comfort levels and assess their readiness to participate in a group activity or to lead a full-class discussion. If she observes certain students struggling with participation, she is careful to allow them to ease into activities at their own pace. Students feel safe and respected in her classroom.

Avoid Being Too Personal

Making connections does not require a teacher to get too personal or too knowledgeable about students' stories. It does not require physical touch or being alone. Though connecting one-on-one is encouraged, it can happen in a filled classroom, a crowded hallway, a busy school event, or in the middle of a lesson. It can happen by writing a message on a returned assignment. It does not require physical touch. This is why, for everyone's protection, we recommend not being alone with a student when possible.

Privacy laws are meant to protect students and teachers—both. Many teachers make it a best practice to not even email or text students without a parent or guardian being copied so that everything is transparent. That is because making a positive difference in students' lives includes adhering to all local legal, ethical, and professional standards.

Don't Forget the Adults!

Avoid focusing so heavily on students' positive well-being that the positive well-being of teachers and other adults in a school gets neglected. They, too, want to feel accepted as they are.

It is hard for teachers to help students feel acceptance when they, themselves, do not feel connected with other adults in the school. In fact, Drs. Robert Eaker and Richard DuFour reported that some critics characterize public schools "as little more than independent kingdoms (classrooms) ruled by autonomous feudal lords (teachers) who are united only by a common parking lot."[27]

Adults are not immune from anxiety, loneliness, or depressive thoughts. In fact, an estimated 26 percent of adults ages 25–44 report feeling moderate to severe loneliness. That number rises with age, and it includes teachers.[28] Indeed, it is common for teachers and administrators to be surrounded by crowds of students all day and yet still feel isolated and lonely. As with students, Gallup has determined that "having a best friend at work" is the best predictor of a teacher's level of engagement at school. And yet only 30 percent of teachers claim to have a best friend at work.[29]

One new teacher described eating lunch in the faculty lounge the first week of school, and not a single other teacher said hello. Another teacher spoke about being under 25 years of age and feeling not accepted by the older teachers, while a 50-year-old teacher talked about being in a school of mostly young teachers, and how she felt excluded by the younger teachers. An art teacher told us about being in a classroom at the end of a long hallway and how she seldom saw another adult throughout the day. She felt isolated. Other teachers talked about peer teachers being "cliquish." We like to assume that all of these accounts are rare exceptions. For a teacher to feel not accepted is not acceptable. Strong connections retain strong teachers.

When Muriel was principal, she made it a routine for all grade-level teams to join together each morning in a hallway huddle for 10 minutes prior to the bell. It was a chance for teachers to coordinate activities, share ideas, and take an interest in each other. It ensured that every teacher was part of a "we."

What systems do you, your team, or your school have in place to foster feelings of school connectedness for students and for each other? How well do you know the names of peer teachers and their stories? When did you last voice respect for one of them?

Concluding Thoughts

Perhaps the greatest gift that accepting students as they are has to offer to students is the gift of self-acceptance. When students perceive that others accept them as they are, that is the moment when they start to accept themselves as they are, to believe in themselves. The moment when that happens is the same moment when they start thinking more seriously about moving toward their higher potential.

Now some teachers may think that calling students by name, taking an interest in their stories, or voicing respect for them is not enough to help students feel connected at school. "It takes more than that to connect with students! That's too simple!" they may think. "Besides, I already do those things." And to an extent they may be correct. But research indicates that the school interventions that are meant to increase students' positive well-being and that get the most positive results are the interventions that stay simple.[30] And though many teachers may think "I already do these things," why then do only 22 percent of high school students agree that their teachers are interested in them beyond their academics?[31]

That being said, we absolutely agree with the teacher who thinks that there is more to building connections with students than what we have covered in this chapter. Calling students by name, taking an interest in them, and voicing respect for them are only a starting place. But they are an important starting place in light of what those best practices can do to increase students' positive well-being and readiness to learn. In fact, they are important enough that Dr. John Hattie, after extensive research on the benefits of school connections, concluded: "It is incumbent therefore upon schools to attend to student friendships, to ensure that the class makes newcomers welcomed, and, at minimum, to ensure that all students have a sense of belonging."[32]

And as a reminder, you might recall that we said from the beginning that every best practice in this book is a viable way to connect with students. So there are plenty more ways to connect with students coming in the pages ahead.

But it all starts with students feeling accepted, connected, and respected—as they are.

The Challenge

Select and do one of the following:

- Create and apply one routine or system for calling students by name.
- Set aside a dedicated time and routine for taking an interest in students' stories, beyond their academics.
- Use the three-step process to voice respect for a set of students and/or teachers.

2

Taught Me About Life

Passed down through the artisan studios of Europe comes the story of *The Italian Sculptor*. Our version goes like this.

Paolo grew up in a small village nestled in the Italian Alps. He was a budding young artist with visions of someday becoming as renowned as his earlier countrymen—legends like Michelangelo, Leonardo da Vinci, and Donatello. So, when he reached a mature age, Paolo left home and headed for life in the big city.

Upon arrival, Paolo planned to study art and begin carving out a name for himself. Imagine his grand delight when he secured an apprenticeship under the tutelage of a master sculptor. Day after day, the master assigned Paolo small square blocks of stone and taught him how to chisel basic designs—mostly half circles, straight lines, and gentle curves.

Paolo appreciated the master sculptor's ability to teach the fine skills for chiseling. However, as the days turned into months, he could feel the tasks he was being assigned growing mundane. He had no idea what the stones would be used for and felt his new skills had outgrown the basic patterns he was being assigned. He was ready for something more challenging. More meaningful.

One moonlit evening, Paolo found himself wandering the city's cobblestone streets in search of solace. Life seemed so big. Paolo felt so small.

It was then and there when Paolo spotted a tall new building under construction. What caught his keenest attention was that one entire wall of the building was being turned into a magnificent work of art. A masterpiece was in the making.

From a distance, Paolo gazed with envy at the artistry. He could only hope to someday be part of such a marvelous work instead of producing meaningless slabs of stone. "Who might the masterful artist be?" he wondered.

The nearer Paolo drew to the building, the more he could see the qualities of a master at work. However, it was what he spotted next that nearly overwhelmed him. For in examining the fine workmanship up close, he could see that the wall was formed out of nothing more than a tidy array of small square blocks of stone. Each was chiseled with a simple half circle, a straight line, or a gentle curve. The work was largely the creation of Paolo's own hands.

All along, Paolo had been part of creating a masterpiece. He had just not known it. And as he walked home that night, his every stride was filled with a new sense of vision and joy. He could see purpose in the skills he was being taught and the tasks he was being assigned.

Paolo could also see that he, too, was a master artist in the making.[1]

The Need for Meaning

Paolo's story is as relevant today as when it was originally told.

When students see no purpose or meaning behind the knowledge and skills they are learning in school, they come to view school as an endless array of mundane, worthless tasks. They start to question, "What is the worth of this assignment? Why does it matter that I go to school?"

Let's face it. Most students are relatively naive about life beyond their family, school, and neighborhood. They hear about all kinds of things that are happening in the world but are unsure of how to make sense of it all. They dream of someday being part of a masterpiece, yet the closer they get to graduation, the more they become anxious about their futures. Without a sense of vision and meaning in their lives, they feel small in a big world.

The search for meaning is not new. Philosophers have discussed the topic for centuries. German philosopher Friedrich Nietzsche summed up the thoughts of the early thinkers best when he wrote, "He who has a *why* to live for can bear with almost any *how*."[2]

It was not until after World War II that researchers began to earnestly apply scientific methods to studying the impact that a sense of meaning can have on a person's positive well-being. Much of that early research grew out of the early work of Viktor Frankl.[3] Frankl had been confined to a World War II concentration camp, along with thousands of others. Under torturous conditions, he made two observations. The first was that the fellow inmates who endured their confinement best were those who found meaning in their present days by doing kind deeds, such as giving up a prized morsel of food so that another prisoner would suffer less. The second observation was that the prisoners who could envision themselves doing something meaningful in their futures were the ones who kept their hopes of being freed alive. They were the happiest. Personally, Frankl envisioned himself working as a professor teaching students how to find meaning in their lives.

The war eventually ended and Frankl did become a university professor. And yes, he did focus his lectures on how people can fill their lives with meaning. He told students that the only thing worse than living a life *with* difficult circumstances was living life *without* meaning.

Since Frankl's time, virtually every credible theory of human motivation has emphasized the basic need for meaning. What is meaningful is also a matter of personal perception. What is meaningful to one person—such as a teacher—may not be meaningful to another person, such as a student. And what is meaningful to a person at one stage of life may no longer be meaningful at a later stage—or even the next day. It is all part of students' search for identity.

Now, at this point, you might be thinking, "My students aren't thinking about anything meaningful beyond what is for lunch today." And that may be true. Some students are not far enough along in their identity development to be thinking about life's purposes. Yet what students—regardless of age or stage—do not want to feel that what they are learning and doing in school has purpose, both for today and into their futures?

If the term *meaning* sounds too theoretical for your students, a word that is perhaps more common in the field of education is *relevance*. Students want what they are doing in school to be relevant. They want to see how it will help them succeed in the real world.

Yet there was a time not long ago when relevance seemed to be almost forgotten in education. Around the turn of the 21st century, educators were almost fixated on one objective—more *rigor*. The world was changing. Parents and business leaders were demanding that students be prepared to compete not only locally but in the larger global economy. The countries that seemed best at readying students for the new reality were requiring students to spend more time studying science, math, technology, and reading.

The problem was that in some classrooms rigor was being served in such over-sized portions that it was more than students could swallow. Their academic plates were overflowing with mounds of facts to gulp down, reams of worksheets to chew through, and pages upon pages of textbooks to digest. The weight of it all was taking a toll on students.

The more sizeable problem, however, was that students were being asked to do all the rigor without knowing the *why*. They were rigor-exhausted yet could not tell you how what they were learning and doing in school was connected to life.

Dr. Willard R. Daggett came to students' rescue. He argued that unless students can see the relevance in what they are learning in school, they cannot be expected to engage with more rigor. "Relevance makes rigor possible, and rigor makes life success possible," he insisted. And soon, teachers were marching to the cadence of Dr. Daggett's two-part mantra: *rigor and relevance*. It had a nice beat to it.

Yet something was missing. Dr. Daggett quickly recognized that if teachers are to make learning relevant for students, then they must come to know "what students—each of them—find interesting, fun, and meaningful. This is made possible only through relationships."[4]

In other words, Dr. Daggett saw more reason for teachers to take an interest in students' lives than to help them feel accepted as they are. By taking an interest in what is of interest to students, teachers can use that knowledge to make lessons more student-centered and meaningful. And that is why Dr. Daggett's new success-in-teaching formula became: *relationships, relevance, and rigor*. In that order.

Other researchers have since confirmed the need for relevance and meaning in what students are expected to learn and do at school. Mihaly Csikszentmihalyi, for example, has emphasized the role that meaning plays in students experiencing *flow*. Flow is the state of mind where students become so immersed in assignments that they nearly lose consciousness of time and their surroundings and end up performing at their highest levels. For flow to happen, however, students must see personal meaning in the assignments they are asked to complete.[5]

Angela Duckworth has similarly promoted the need to build meaning into what students are expected to do. Dr. Duckworth is a former high school teacher and a current professor at the University of Pennsylvania. She has done extensive research on the concept of *grit*. Grit, she says, is what keeps students persevering in their pursuit of projects and goals, even in the face of obstacles or potential failure. Grit consists of two parts: passion and perseverance. Passion also has two parts—interest and purpose. "Interest" suggests that a project must be of interest to the student, while "purpose" indicates that the project must be meaningful to people other than oneself, as illustrated below.[6]

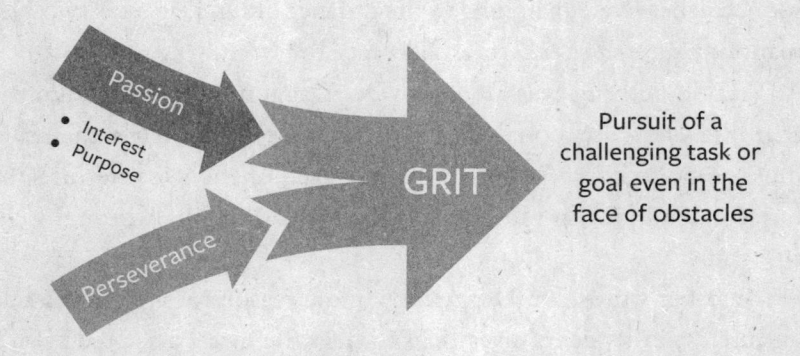

Dr. Barbara Fredrickson at the University of North Carolina is one of the most prolific researchers in the field of positive psychology. Her research confirms that the people who enjoy the most positive well-being are not just *feeling* good, they are *doing* good. They are benefitting others. Doing good does not require "doing amazing." It does not require grandiose actions to provide meaning for students.[7] Small contributions are sufficient.

What each of these researchers is suggesting is what leadership expert Simon Sinek captures in four words, "Start with the *why*."[8] If you want students to engage in school, to feel flow, to stick with assignments and goals to completion, and to do good for others, then start with the *why*. Put meaning into what they are assigned.

So where do people get their *why*, their sources of meaning? That is a question the Pew Research Center asked nearly 19,000 people from 17 countries. The responses fell into three general categories: (1) *close relationships*, such as family, friends, teachers, and other trusted adults; (2) *societal causes,* such as doing community service, helping the elderly, fighting poverty and hunger, participating in religion, joining social clubs, or saving the environment; and (3) *things they like to do*, such as their hobbies, employment, recreation, sports, exercise, or the arts.[9] The more teachers connect academic lessons and assignments with one or more of these three sources of meaning, the more students can be expected to engage as learners.

Notice that none of the three sources of meaning involve material things alone, such as wealth, clothing, cell phones, or toys. Money and things are means to an end. They may lead to happiness or to unhappiness, depending on how they are perceived and used. In fact, Dr. Tim Kasser's research on *The High Price of Materialism* suggests that the more students prioritize obtaining things, and the more they value being seen as having things, the more likely they are to suffer from depression, anxiety, and despair.[10] Adults can help students see "things" in proper perspective.

What all this suggests is that it is not too early to be giving students—even young ones, but especially those in secondary school—opportunities to think about and choose for themselves what is and what will be most meaningful in their lives. After all, this is the time of their lives when students begin developing an early vision of the masterpieces they want to be a part of in life and the contributions they want to make to society and to their families. So what follows are three best practices that teachers can apply to provide students opportunities to ponder what is most meaningful to them, and what will bring them the most happiness, both now and in the future.

What are your greatest sources of meaning?

Three Best Practices for Building Meaning into Students' Days

Three best practices for teaching students about life and helping them to see more meaning in what they are learning and doing in school include:

My teacher...

- connected academics with life.
- shared a memorable life hack.
- lived an inspiring life.

Connected Academics with Life

We cannot state strongly enough how much teachers do for the positive well-being of students by teaching them core academic knowledge and skills. As the saying goes, "Education breeds confidence. Confidence breeds hope. Hope breeds peace."

Many people we interviewed about a teacher who made a difference in their life said things like, "She is the one who taught me to love reading." Or "Not a day goes by when I don't use the skills he taught me." They made it clear that by teaching them how to read, write, communicate, and calculate formulas, or how to understand science, history, technology, and the arts, their teacher played an enormous role in bettering their life and increasing their positive well-being.

But let's be honest. Not all master sculptors are master teachers. In other words, Paolo's mentor may have been a master at sculpting and even at teaching skills for sculpting, but he was not a master at connecting the skills he was teaching with life. And so it is with all teachers. They may be subject matter experts, but are they experts at teaching students about life?

Master teachers do more than teach skills and facts. They connect the skills and facts they teach to what is meaningful to students and relevant to life. They connect skills and facts with potential careers students might want to pursue. They connect historical accounts and psychological studies with how students can be happier. They connect scientific laws with how students can solve real-world problems. They explain how skills and facts will help students become better employees, leaders, and parents.

So what might teachers do to better connect academic lessons with life? Consider a few suggestions.

Use "Real-Life" Case Studies

Consider the following case study approach used by a university professor, as described by a former student:

I was required to take a psychology class during my first year of university. I had zero interest in psychology.

Dr. Davis was the professor and a family counselor on the side. Each class period he would step up to a podium, open his notebook, and begin emphasizing key points from the textbook.

Then, after about 15 minutes of lecture, Dr. Davis would walk away from the podium while continuing to talk. "Yes, that's what the research and your textbook tell us," he would say. "Now would you mind if I step out of my professor shoes and talk plainly about what I've experienced in my counseling?"

Everyone knew that what Dr. Davis was about to say was not going to be on the exam. Yet no one tuned out as he proceeded to tell us about one of his real-life counseling cases. He presented each case like a murder mystery, pausing occasionally to invite us to discuss how we would solve the case using what we had learned from the textbook. He kept us in suspense until the very end before letting us know how the case was ultimately resolved.

For many students, Dr. Davis's stories hit directly. Either we had experienced something similar in our lives, or we knew someone who had. It all felt very real. Not all of his stories had happy endings. Yet, even on those occasions, he talked frankly with us about how to handle times when life doesn't go the way we planned.

I left Dr. Davis's classes wanting to become a professor of psychology. And I did.

By taking the contents from the textbook and tying them to real case studies, Dr. Davis brought life to his lessons in ways that allowed students to connect with him and apply the learning to their personal circumstances and positive well-being.

Invite "Real Life" to Be a Classroom Guest

An elementary teacher assigned her students to draw a picture of a firefighter, a doctor, and a fighter pilot. Of the 60 images her 20 students created, all but five depicted males.

The teacher decided it was time to rid her students of their limited stereotypes. She invited three guests to visit her classroom: a firefighter, a doctor, and a fighter pilot. All three were women. The students were surprised to see women in those roles. They left the classroom that day with a more real-to-life view of three career opportunities that are open to all students.[11]

Who is a guest you can invite into your classroom to give students a real-life perspective on the subject matters you teach?

Explore "Mirrors" and "Windows"

Grace Lin is an award-winning author and illustrator of children's books. She observed in her work with schools that many teachers use only "mirrors" to teach students. Mirrors, she says, are books that help students better understand their own ethnic cultures and interests. Mirrors are great. But if teachers only use literature sources that are mirrors, then the students who are in the majority will miss out on learning about the cultures and mindsets of the minority students.

Grace Lin recommends a blend of mirrors and "windows." Windows are books that enable students to see into other people's lives and cultures. "As much as kids need books to be mirrors," she says, "they also need books to be windows. . . . How can we expect kids to get along with others in this world, to empathize and to share, if they never see outside of themselves?"[12]

Travel the World, One Click at a Time

Samuel Clemens wrote: "Broad, wholesome, charitable views of [people] cannot be acquired by vegetating in one little corner of the earth all one's lifetime."[13] To that Maya Angelou adds, "Perhaps travel cannot prevent bigotry, but by demonstrating that all peoples cry, laugh, eat, worry, and die, it can introduce the idea that if we try and understand each other, we may even become friends."[14]

To these ends, the internet allows teachers to take students on virtual field trips to all sorts of lands and latitudes. It provides an opportunity for them to meet all kinds of people and cultures. With one or two clicks on a computer, teachers can take students to visit laboratories, factories, nature reserves, spaceships, cultural events, and so forth, and all around the world. No school bus necessary.

Honor the Heroes

Every academic subject matter has heroes, people who have done remarkable things in their field and whose life stories are filled with life lessons. Yet many teachers teach no more than those heroes' theories and formulas. Why not add to academic lessons a few insights into how the subject matter heroes exhibited grit, humility, or kindness? Why not highlight their sacrifices or stories of how they overcame a challenge in life?

Neuroscientists like Dr. Mary Helen Immordino-Yang at the University of Southern California indicate that parts of students' brains literally light up on brain scans when they are discussing hero stories, and most particularly when the hero stories involve peers their age. Hero stories help students build mental narratives around who they want to become and what meaningful contributions they might someday make in the world.[15]

Engage Students in Making Life Connections

Invite students to identify a person, a social cause, or a career interest or hobby that they personally find meaningful. Then ask the students to make their own connections between what they are learning in school and how it can be used to benefit the people, causes, career interests, or hobbies they identified.

Some students have little idea about what is most meaningful to them or what careers interest them most. They are still figuring it out, and that is perfectly normal. Teachers may need to first create assignments that challenge such students to ask themselves: Who are the most important people in my life? What causes am I most passionate about? What do I most like to do? What values will I stand by? What careers interest me the most? Once they have determined their answers, challenge them to connect their answers with what they are learning in class. Engage them in writing a personal mission statement.

This may include making time for in-class solitude. Solitude is a different place from loneliness. Loneliness is where people go to contemplate their inadequacies and count the friends they do not have. Solitude is where people go to count the things for which they are grateful, to reflect on their personal sources of meaning, and to discover their next destinations. Students are prone to spend too much time visiting loneliness and not enough time voyaging into solitude. So why not make time for them to reflect on the types of meaning they want to have in life?

No one, of course, has their future courses fully paved out for them. As the Dutch say, "*Van het concert des levens krijgt niemand een program.*" ("In the concert of life, no one receives a program.") Nevertheless, it is never too soon for students to begin connecting life with what they are learning and doing at school. It is never too soon for students to be thinking about the types of meaning they want to experience in their present and future lives, and connecting those sources of meaning with what they learn in school.

What ways have you connected
academic lessons with life?

Shared a Memorable Life Hack

There are many other topics and strategies for navigating life that students want to know about that are not covered by traditional academics. Perhaps that is the same mindset that inspired actress and comedian Lily Tomlin to say that she liked teachers who gave her something to take home and think about beside homework.

Indeed, among the common comments expressed by former students about their difference-making teacher were statements like these: "He said something one day that inspired me, and I have never forgotten it." Or "She would always share a favorite quote at the end of class, and it always made me want to be a better person." In most cases, the quote, inspiring story, or life lesson that was shared had nothing to do with the subject matter the teacher taught. Yet years later, the insights continue to influence their former students.

Brief lessons or "shortcuts" for living in more effective and efficient ways are known as *life hacks*. Many life hacks come in the form of simple and clever ways to get a stain out of clothing, prepare a food item, or improve one's health. The life hacks that this best practice is focused on are those that deal with living a more effective and meaningful life. They come in the form of an inspiring message, a time-saving tip, a short story with a moral, the lyrics of a song, or a short lesson on effective living.

Inspiring Messages

Life hacks can be shared in seconds and yet provide a lifetime of wisdom and guidance. For example, we are reminded of a teacher whose wife died and it left a lonely void in his life. Yet all who knew him would describe him as happy. When asked "How do you stay so positive on those occasions when you feel lonely?," the teacher replied, "Blossom where you are planted." Years later, the former student still relies on his teacher's five-word life hack for staying positive when he feels lonely.

One of our mentors, Dr. Blaine Lee, was fond of telling teachers, "Seek to bless, not to impress." Those six words have provided us guidance for years. Trying to impress students is stressful; trying to bless their lives is joyful.

Some of the more common life hacks are tips for saving time. A successful executive once described his mentor as a grand source of life hacks. He said, "This man who has incredible life experience tells you the best insights he has and saves you a decade or two."[16]

Time-saving life hacks include strategies for prioritizing time, simplifying life, removing clutter, being organized, and finding life balance. In fact, some of the best time-saving life hacks are those that deal with how to say no when "no" is the wise answer. As Charles Spurgeon declared: "Learn to say no. It will be of more use to you than to be able to read Latin."[17]

Do you have a favorite life hack for living a meaningful life or being an effective student that you like to pass on to students?

Short Stories with a Moral

A business consultant told us about a university course he took on Chinese culture. The only thing he remembers from the course is an ancient fable the professor shared that had a moral to it. To this day, the man reflects on the story and its moral when making tough decisions. It is no coincidence that the one thing the consultant remembers about his teacher is a short story with a moral.

Teaching stories with a moral recalls a study carried out by 33 children's doctors, neuroscientists, social scientists, and mental health specialists. Alarmed by the rising rates of depression, anxiety, violence, suicide, substance abuse, and addiction among young people, they decided to combine their diverse skillsets to see what they could do to better understand and reverse the trends.

The team was sponsored by the Dartmouth Medical School, the YMCA, and the Institute for American Values. After months of investigation, they concluded that most social and emotional disorders among young people can be traced to two sources: (1) young people feeling not connected with other people and (2) young people feeling not connected with "moral meaning."

In other words, it is more than a lack of connection with people that causes young people grief. It is also a lack of connection to principles of character, such as integrity, kindness, and courage, that is disrupting their peace. The researchers encouraged adults to do more to teach young people character-based principles and values for interacting with people in ethical ways, though they left it to parents and other local adults to define what those character principles would be.

The researchers named their report *Hardwired to Connect*.[18] What is ironic is that their report was literally fresh off the presses when a rock band released an album titled *Hardwired to Self-Destruct*. Hundreds of thousands of copies were sold to young people. Its lyrics were filled with general themes of pessimism, the rejection of moral principles, and the belief that life is meaningless. So, while the *Hardwired to Connect* researchers were voicing the need for young people to feel more connected with moral meaning, the *Hardwired to Self-Destruct* rockers were drumming into their brains the message that life has no meaning and that who they are as individuals is of little importance. We are convinced that teachers can send better life messages than that to students.

Lyrics of a Song

Inspiring music has the power to connect people and motivate them to greater heights.

In the Disney movie *Frozen II*, a main character, Anna, finds herself in the darkest depths of a dismal cave. Lost, anxious, lonely, empty, numb, grieving, and directionless, she fears all hope is gone. Just when she is ready to succumb, a tiny voice whispers into her mind a little life hack: "Just do the next right thing." Inspired, Anna begins to see her challenge as reachable and starts climbing her way out of her cave of despair.[19]

No sooner was that song released than young people by the thousands began describing how they connected with Anna's situation and how those lyrics—that musical life hack—inspired them to go on in life, one right step at a time.

Many choir teachers select songs for students to sing that are filled with inspiring lyrics. Some of their former students then keep those inspiring lyrics stuck in their heads for years. Teachers who are less musically inclined can play inspiring background music as students come and go from class or as they work on projects.

Short Lessons on Effective Living

The reality is that teachers have been teaching lessons on effective living for as long as teachers have been teaching. Early on, the lessons centered primarily on teaching *character* traits, such as honesty, integrity, patience, courage, empathy, fairness, and kindness. The lessons were in full harmony with Dr. Martin Luther King, Jr.'s declaration, "We must remember that intelligence is not enough. Intelligence plus character— that is the goal of education."[20] Or as Angela Duckworth observed, "To help chronically low-performing but intelligent students, educators and parents must first recognize that character is at least as important as intellect."[21]

Then, as the 21st century arrived, the emphasis shifted to teaching skills for personal, interpersonal, and team effectiveness.[22] The global economy was becoming highly competitive, and if students wanted to compete in the new reality, then they needed to possess the skills to get along with others, to work in teams, to communicate, to lead their own lives, and the like.

As one example, for the past two decades at *Leader in Me* schools, we have had the privilege of teaching life and workforce readiness skills to students based on Dr. Stephen R. Covey's acclaimed book *The 7 Habits of Highly Effective People*, which has been on international bestseller lists for nearly 40 years and taught to leaders all over the world. From pre-K to university students, we have watched them confidently use familiar phrases such as:

- **Be Proactive.** "I take charge of my life."
- **Begin With the End in Mind.** "I have a plan."
- **Put First Things First.** "I do what matters most."
- **Think Win-Win.** "I balance courage and consideration."
- **Seek First to Understand, Then to Be Understood.** "I listen first."
- **Synergize.** "Together is better."
- **Sharpen the Saw.** "I renew my body, mind, heart, and spirit."

Each of the seven habits is a life hack. Each is full of life and career tips on how to be effective personally and how to connect with others. Each is based on timeless principles of effectiveness that apply to people of all cultures and backgrounds.[23]

In recent years, with so many students struggling with emotional and social challenges, extra emphasis has been given to teaching students skills for identifying and managing negative emotions, such as anger, frustration, anxiety, and grief. Many schools are currently implementing such curriculums on their campuses, including university MBA programs.

An even more recent trend has been to teach skills for how to be happy. These skills for happier living have been particularly popular with university students. For example, when Dr. Tal Ben-Shahar of Harvard (author of *Happier*)[24] began teaching principles of happiness to students, his course quickly became the most popular class on campus. Dr. Sonja Lyubomirsky at the University of California at Riverside (author of *The How of Happiness*),[25] Dr. Barbara Fredrickson of the University of North Carolina (author of *Positivity*),[26] and Dr. Laurie Santos of Yale University (founder of *The Happiness Lab*)[27] have received astonishing interest from students who enroll in their happiness courses. Happiness content is now trickling down into K–12 schools, including in some countries where their governments now provide a happiness curriculum for their students.

All seven leadership skillsets and the best practices contained in this book—such as calling people by name, taking an interest in people, and voicing respect—are also great life hacks for students to learn about for connecting with their peers. A student named Jon, for example, was feeling lonely when he began high school. He had been taught the importance of calling people by name, so he decided to start saying hello to every student he knew in the hallways, and to say their name if he knew it. He soon realized that he had more friends than he thought. His loneliness evaporated. Similar benefits come to students who learn and apply all seven leadership skillsets and their best practices.

A broad glimpse of the types of personal, interpersonal, and team effectiveness skills and character traits that are taught in schools is captured in the diagram on the next page. Notice how the character traits provide a foundation for the effectiveness skills. When people possess skills but lack character, their overall effectiveness diminishes and people are less sure they can be trusted.

Shorter lessons on effective living have the most lasting impact, so long as students do not view them as "preachy."[28] And don't be surprised if students prefer topics that are positive. They are so saturated with "negative news" that they will often prefer "positive news" for a change.[29] One father described how his daughter was reading her literature homework one night when she suddenly blurted out, "I wish my teacher would assign anything besides this junk to read." Her teacher had decided that it was her professional duty to expose students to real

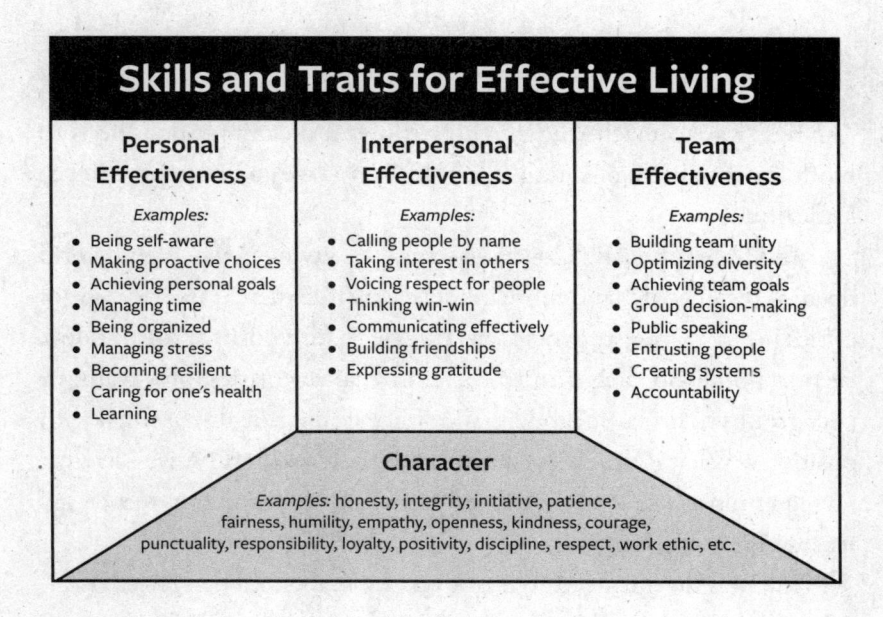

Skills and Traits for Effective Living

Personal Effectiveness

Examples:
- Being self-aware
- Making proactive choices
- Achieving personal goals
- Managing time
- Being organized
- Managing stress
- Becoming resilient
- Caring for one's health
- Learning

Interpersonal Effectiveness

Examples:
- Calling people by name
- Taking interest in others
- Voicing respect for people
- Thinking win-win
- Communicating effectively
- Building friendships
- Expressing gratitude

Team Effectiveness

Examples:
- Building team unity
- Optimizing diversity
- Achieving team goals
- Group decision-making
- Public speaking
- Entrusting people
- Creating systems
- Accountability

Character

Examples: honesty, integrity, initiative, patience, fairness, humility, empathy, openness, kindness, courage, punctuality, responsibility, loyalty, positivity, discipline, respect, work ethic, etc.

life, and "real life" for her meant literature that was filled with drugs, swear words, deep poverty, violence, crime, abuse, and broken families. That teacher had not respected that the students might prefer or benefit from knowing that not all life is as negative as is often portrayed in the media or top songs. Sure there may be a need to find a balance between the positive and the negative, but as the late news journalist Charles Kuralt declared: "It does no harm just once in a while to acknowledge that the whole country isn't in flames."[30]

A visual way for teachers to share their favorite life hacks with students is to place them on classroom walls. We have seen numerous colorful posters and wall murals in classrooms that display teachers' favorite quotes and life hacks. Some teachers post a new quote each week and use it as a "Theme of the Week." Their classroom walls speak continuous inspiration to students without the teachers saying a word.

If you could share one single-sentence life hack or inspiring quote for students, what would it be?

Lived an Inspiring Life

The best way to teach students how to live a meaning-filled life is to model how to live a meaning-filled life. It is a "we go first" approach to leadership.

As Dr. Stephen R. Covey was fond of saying, "What the world needs is fewer critics and more models."[31] While there is no shortage of critics in the world, students may struggle to find positive role models, even at home. So they turn to social media, celebrities, musicians, or peer groups to find role models. Who they find is not always filled with positivity. What if they turned instead to their teachers? A well-known saying reminds us: "I am indebted to my father for living, but to my teacher for living well."

Teachers do not need to leap over skyscrapers to be viewed as inspiring role models. Three George Mason University professors partnered with Pearson Publishing and asked 13,225 stakeholders from 23 countries to identify what they thought were the most important qualities of an effective teacher. Six stakeholder categories were represented in the responses: students ages 15–19, teachers, principals, parents with children in school, researchers, and education policymakers. All six stakeholders—all six!—identified the ability to develop trusting, productive connections as the most important quality. Second in importance was a patient, caring, and kind personality. Third was a teacher's professionalism (e.g., being respectful, honest, punctual, etc.). The fourth quality was a teacher's subject matter knowledge. Each of these qualities is important for teachers to model.[32] Notice how the qualities include both character traits and skills.

We, of course, encourage teachers to model all seven leadership skillsets and best practices found in this book. Doing so will model for students how to connect with others; it will also increase students' and teachers' positive well-being.

Two specific qualities we highly encourage teachers to model are the will to overcome and the joy of learning.

The Will to Overcome

Mr. Bezzant was repairing a roof when he fell and landed on a cement pad. The accident left him paralyzed from the waist down and wheelchair bound. He could have justifiably spent the remainder of his life bemoaning his misfortune, but he chose instead to pursue a new personal motto: "Happy no matter what!"

After extensive physical therapy and a lot of grit, Mr. Bezzant miraculously returned to the classroom. During his previous 25 years of teaching, he had always towered over his fourth grade students due to his tall stature, broad chest, and bulging muscles. But under his new conditions, he sits eye to eye with them. The new angle leads him to view students with a new degree of empathy.

Several of his students have already experienced difficult circumstances in their young lives. Others are sure to encounter their own unique set of trials and obstacles. So Mr. Bezzant makes time to share with his students examples of how he has found ways to overcome challenges. But mostly he teaches by example.

Indeed, Mr. Bezzant doesn't need to say a single word to teach his students a life lesson about overcoming challenges. Simply by showing up in his wheelchair with his big smile he has already taught a great life lesson. His life is a living textbook on how to find positive ways to approach life's obstacles.

What if your life was the only textbook your students ever read on overcoming life's challenges? What would the chapter titles be? What might the final words be?

The Joy of Learning

Dr. Daniels was a university professor who had his ways of modeling the joy of learning. As told by a former student:

> Dr. Daniels was nearing retirement and yet he never stopped loving to learn and sharing his latest discoveries. At points during the semester,

he would pause in the middle of a sentence, put on a huge smile, and exclaim, "I love learning about this stuff!" He would then do a little dance and laugh for joy.

We cannot confirm that Dr. Daniels's students ever agreed that dancing is the best way to model the joy of learning. But they never doubted that he loved learning. More natural ways to model the joy of learning might be to say, "Let me tell you about this history book I'm reading." Or "I took a course this summer that was fascinating." Or "I watched the most interesting documentary last night." Or "I have reduced my social media time and replaced it with learning a new hobby. I love it."

Teachers model the joy of learning by being well-rounded learners. Bill Gates, co-founder of Microsoft and one of the wealthiest people in the world and a contributor to education, says that he makes it a point to read newspapers, magazines, and books from cover to cover so that he learns about many topics, not just his existing areas of expertise.[33] Since teachers are likewise some of the most well-rounded people we know, this may be an easy quality for them to model.

A question to ask in determining if you are a role model for the joy of learning is: As a teacher, do I have ten years of experience or one year of experience ten times? If you have been teaching from the same lesson plans for the past ten years without updating them, then you most likely have one year of experience ten times. If you are consistently updating your lessons and applying new strategies for teaching, then you more likely have ten years of experience and are a model of lifelong learning. As the saying goes, "Wisdom comes with age, but sometimes age comes alone."

All this raises a question: How will students know you are an inspiring role model if you never share the inspiring things you have done or are currently doing in life?

One person we interviewed told of a teacher who was very knowledgeable about his subject matter but had a rough time connecting with students. Ten years later, the interviewee learned the teacher had been a top-ranked national athlete and was inducted into his university's Hall of Fame. "Who would have guessed?" said the former student. "I would have enjoyed hearing his stories, the challenges he faced, and the sacrifices he made."

Students like to know what achievements their teachers have experienced, what obstacles they have overcome, what hobbies they enjoy, and what they find meaningful. They like knowing that they share things in common with their teachers. In fact, one research study suggests that academic scores increase for lower-income minority students when they discover they have things in common with their teacher.[34] But how will students know they have things in common if their teacher never shares their stories?

Morgan Harper Nichols, an autistic artist, poet, musician, and motivational speaker, encourages teachers to "Tell the story of the mountains you climbed. Your words could become a page in someone else's survival guide."[35]

What inspiring life qualities might you model for students?

Temperance Factors

Like the other leadership skillsets, teaching students about life can be taken too far. Three cautions are:

Beware of Toxic Positivity

Yes, it is possible to be too positive when teaching lessons of life. This is called *toxic positivity*. When teachers or parents teach as if everything in life is entirely lovely when students know it is not, it doesn't serve to relax students. It breeds stress and anxiety.

Students tune out adults who talk about life in overly glowing and unreasonable terms. They prefer straight talk—a positive yet realistic view of life.

Consider Parental Views When Choosing Life Topics

Perhaps you smile as we did at the pre-school teacher who declared, "I share very private things about myself with my students. I've gone so far as to tell them that I have a mother and two cats."

In contrast to that careful teacher, some teachers have been known to share portions of their lives that are better kept private. Some even try to use their teacher stage to promote their political views, address controversial social issues, or critique school policies in front of students. This is unprofessional and has potential to stir the ire of parents.

More than 90 percent of parents favor students being taught skills for personal, interpersonal, and team effectiveness.[36] However, they also want the comfort of knowing that the content being taught to their children fits within their family values. So, in a spirit of caution, if parental resistance to a topic is a possibility, involve parents up front in determining what might be taught and how best to teach it. Where there is no involvement, don't expect commitment from parents.

Don't Forget the Adults!

Adults share the need for meaning. They, too, want to feel that what they are doing at school is meaningful and relevant. They, too, want to be part of a masterpiece.

Teachers enjoy learning life hacks from each other and like to be inspired by one of their mentors or as role models. But what they like even more is to see that they are making a difference in students' lives. When they see that they are bringing meaning to students' lives, it magnifies the amount of meaning they feel in their own lives.[37]

Yet seldom do teachers see the end products of their efforts with students, including the careers they choose, the families they raise, and the persons they become. When they are unable to see they are making a difference, teaching can easily shift from being a passion to being a job—a tough job.

That is why, when Muriel was an elementary school principal, one of her favorite routines was to bring back former students who were about to graduate from high school. She invited them to give tips to graduating fifth graders on how to succeed in their secondary school years. The tips were great, but what teachers enjoyed most was to see how their former students were doing, and how they as teachers had influenced those students' lives for the better.

Concluding Thoughts

In thinking about the best practices in this chapter, we are reminded of Helen Keller and the moment Anne Sullivan entered her life. Of that day and moment Helen wrote:

> Have you ever been at sea in a dense fog, when it seemed as if a tangible white darkness shut you in, and the great ship, tense and anxious, groped her way toward the shore with plummet and sounding-line, and you waited with beating heart for something to happen? I was like that ship before my education began, only I was without compass or sounding-line, and had no way of knowing how near the harbor was. "Light! give me light!" was the wordless cry of my soul, and the light of love shone on me in that very hour.[38]

Helen is not the only student ever to feel like they are living in dense fog or groping for direction, or sailing through life without compass or sounding-line. How good it must feel for such students when a stable and committed adult enters their life and brings light and meaning by teaching them about the bigger picture of life and how to find positive well-being.

By connecting academics with life, sharing memorable life hacks with students, and living an inspiring life, teachers can bring added light and meaning to students' lives. And if a teacher does nothing more than to help a solitary student see meaning in their present and future lives, then that teacher will have made a significant difference in that student's positive well-being and readiness to learn.

The Challenge

Select one. Make and implement a plan for how you will

- connect lessons with the bigger picture of life,
- share a life hack that will inspire students to better deal with life's challenges, or
- model either the joy of learning or how to overcome challenges in life.

3

Inspired Me to See My Strengths

Jorge worked in a deli as a teen. He performed duties with such quality and pleasure that it was not unusual for customers to notice.

What was unusual was the day a man entered the deli, ordered a sandwich, carefully observed how Jorge prepared it, and then, after paying for the sandwich, threw it into the trash as he exited. Jorge was puzzled.

Imagine Jorge's surprise when the man returned a few days later and repeated the same routine. He again ordered a sandwich, watched Jorge prepare it, paid for his food, and then casually tossed it into the trash on his way out. Now Jorge was really puzzled.

Envision Jorge's disbelief when the man returned a third time and followed the same routine. Only this time, Jorge was bold enough to catch the man before he departed: "Sir, may I ask why you are trashing the sandwiches? Am I doing something wrong?"

"Oh, no," replied the man. "I own a restaurant, and I'm not interested in the sandwich. I'm interested in how joyfully you go about your work and how you treat customers. I've been teaching my employees what I have been learning from observing you. If you ever want to work in a restaurant, talk with me." Then he left.

Jorge took pride in the man's positive comments. As he thought about it, he really did enjoy making food and working with people. He decided to enroll in a foods and nutrition class at his high school. The teacher quickly spotted his interest in cooking and began mentoring him. "She made me feel intelligent," Jorge said. "She complimented my cooking and encouraged me to follow my passions. At one point, she connected me with some chefs in our area and I was able to learn some cooking tips from them."

Today, Jorge is known as Chef Jorge. He is an award-winning chef and owner of multiple restaurants. When reflecting back on his life, he told us, "I will always be grateful to those chefs for their cooking tips. But the reason I am who I am and doing what I am doing today is because of my teacher and that man in the deli who pointed out strengths that I had never recognized in myself."

The Need for Hope

The challenge this chapter presents for teachers is to view students through the lenses of their strengths, not their weaknesses, and for students to do the same for themselves. When students are viewed for their strengths, they tend to behave better and to have more hope.

One of Dr. Hatch's early career roles was to create leadership assessments for top corporate, education, and government leaders. Each assessment contained feedback from the leader's boss, peers, and direct reports. The feedback was then provided to the leaders in the form of a multi-page report. Almost without exception, upon receiving their feedback report, the leaders began searching for what people identified as their weaknesses. Some leaders never even looked at what people said were their strengths.

Observing this, Dr. Hatch changed the action planning process so that the leaders were almost forced to first review their strengths. Yet, despite his efforts, the leaders persisted in skipping the strengths portion of their report to get at what others identified as their weaknesses. They then created an action plan to eliminate the weaknesses.

Why is it that people are so quick to focus on their weaknesses—and the weaknesses of others?

In 2001, Marcus Buckingham, Donald Clifton, Tom Rath, and the

Gallup organization released the book *Now, Discover Your Strengths*, along with a *StrengthsFinder* self-assessment tool that only identifies leaders' strengths. Their goal, they said, was "to start a global conversation about what's right with people." They declared, "We were tired of living in a world that revolved around fixing our weaknesses. Society's relentless focus on shortcomings had turned into a global obsession. What's more, we had discovered that people have several times more potential for growth when they invest energy in developing their strengths instead of correcting their deficiencies."[1]

Around the same time, Dr. Martin Seligman of the University of Pennsylvania was serving as president of the American Psychological Association. He was also renowned for his research on learned helplessness, and much of his research included doing therapy with young people. The methods he used were based on what he later referred to as a *disease model*, since they were designed to diagnose what was "wrong" with young people and to then try to "heal" them. He began, however, to wonder if there was a more positive, preventative approach to helping young people. After sifting through mounds of research, he concluded:

> What progress there has been in the prevention of mental illness comes from recognizing and nurturing a set of strengths, competencies, and virtues in young people—such as future-mindedness, hope, interpersonal skills, courage, the capacity for flow, faith and work ethic. The exercise of these strengths then buffers against the tribulations that put people at risk for mental illness. Depression can be prevented in a young person at genetic risk by nurturing her skills of optimism and hope. An inner-city young man, at risk for substance abuse because of all the drug traffic in his neighborhood, is much less vulnerable if he is future-minded, gets flow out of sports, and has a powerful work ethic. But building these strengths as a buffer is alien to the disease model, which is only about remedying deficits.[2]

Notice how Dr. Seligman's methods shifted from diagnosing and remedying what was "wrong" with young people—their *deficits*—to discovering and nurturing what was "right" with young people—their *strengths*. He later confirmed that "Raising children . . . was far more than just fixing what was wrong with them. It was about identifying and amplifying their strengths and virtues and helping them find the niche where they can live these positive traits to the fullest."[3]

Dr. Seligman's conclusions gave birth to positive psychology as its own field of research. His findings have since been supported by thousands of research studies. Yet after visiting hundreds of classrooms in the past few years, we worry that many teachers are still stuck on using weakness-based methods to identify and "fix" students' weaknesses rather than seeking out and nurturing their strengths.

When, for example, was the last time you saw a school improvement plan that was built around identifying, developing, and amplifying staff members' strengths, not their weaknesses? When was the last time you personally received training on how to identify and optimize students' strengths?

William James observed: "That which holds our attention determines our action."[4] Or as the saying goes, "Where your attention goes your energy flows." If all that holds teachers' attention is students' weaknesses, then those weaknesses are what will drive teachers' strategies in working with students. In contrast, if what holds teachers' attention is students' strengths, then those strengths are what will drive teachers' strategies.

Research tells us that when teachers become more aware of students' strengths, they have more respect and compassion for those students and become more likely to see them as being in the process of "creating" or "rebuilding," as opposed to being "broken" or "failing." They are also more likely to be patient with them and to try new strategies if one doesn't work.[5] The more teachers focus on nurturing students' strengths, not just removing weaknesses, the more teachers view their own roles as being classroom leaders.

Most students are overly aware of their weaknesses. Some even define their identities by their weaknesses. Some high-performing students suffer from what is referred to as *impostor syndrome*. Despite their many strengths and successes, they see those strengths and successes as being not fully legitimate.[6] They view themselves as frauds, impostors, unworthy of their status among peers.

To be clear, what we are referring to are strengths, not superpowers. Some students think erroneously that a strength only qualifies as a strength when they can do it better than anyone else. A father told us a story about his daughter who competed in a county swim meet. The county had a population of over 500,000, and the daughter came in second place in her event. She walked away thinking she was a failure. Why? Because she didn't win first place. Second place out of thousands in her age group is not a failure. It is a strength!

Buckingham and Clifton suggest that for a strength to be considered a strength, it needs to be something a person can do consistently—that's what separates a strength from one-time luck.[7] As we see it, any skill, knowledge, character trait, or experience becomes a strength the instant students use it to benefit their own well-being or the well-being of others. By either definition, a thousand students can share the identical strength and still consider it to be a strength.

One of the most fundamental assumptions of this book is that every student has strengths. Plural. Call them gifts, talents, strong-points, intelligences, unique experiences, marketable skills, or whatever you want to call them, but please do not label them as strengths only when a student does them better than everyone else.

An important reason for students to become self-aware of their strengths is that it helps to satisfy their basic need for hope. Hope is more than optimism or positive thinking. Hope requires a realistic path for how to be happier. But unless students can see they have skills and strengths to progress on that realistic path, they will not have hope. They will walk in despair, which is the absence of hope.[8]

Dr. Charles R. Snyder spent years at the University of Kansas developing a theory of hope. He viewed hope as even more than a basic need. He also viewed it as a skill.[9] So when teachers inspire students to see and develop their strengths, they are teaching them a skill.

Compared with students who score low on hope assessments, students who score high on hope assessments

- show higher academic performance.[10]
- enjoy stronger interpersonal relationships.
- view stressful situations as challenging, not threatening.[11]
- show lower levels of depression and anxiety.[12]
- persist further when pursuing long-term goals.[13]
- are more likely to graduate from college.[14]
- experience more overall life satisfaction.[15]
- are more resilient and have higher self-esteem.[16]

Hope enables students to see beyond their shortcomings and into their futures. But for hope to continue to grow and to remain vibrant in students, it must be continuously fed and nourished with new learning and inspiring messages. Hearing teachers acknowledge their strengths and then develop those strengths will go a long way to inspiring young people to put "hope in their brains and not dope in their veins."[17]

What are your two greatest strengths as a teacher?

Three Best Practices for
Inspiring Students to See Their Strengths

Three best practices for inspiring students to view themselves through their strengths, not their weaknesses—and to give them a greater sense of hope—are:

My teacher...

- communicated my strengths and potential.
- turned a stretch into a strength.
- saw my differences as strengths.

Communicated My Strengths and Potential

Don't be surprised if the students you lead are tired of living in a world that revolves around fixing their weaknesses.

Marie was the fifth child in her family to attend her local high school. Teachers knew her siblings well because each had excelled academically. So when Marie arrived, the teachers assumed she would fit the family mold. What they did not know was that Marie had sustained a traumatic brain injury as an infant and could not process information as quickly as her siblings. Without knowing this, teachers wondered why she was not performing academically as well as her siblings.

When word got around about Marie's injury, the teachers lowered their expectations. They gave her sympathy. They gave her extra attention. They gave her more time to take tests. What they did not give Marie was the recognition that she had impressive strengths of her own.

Marie had earned "Outstanding Student of the Year" awards in both elementary and middle school in honor of her work ethic. She may not have been able to process information as quickly as other students, but she was smart in her own right and worked hard to compensate for her slow processing. She was also excellent at befriending students who were lonely or struggling. She particularly connected and empathized with students with special learning needs. These were just a few of Marie's strengths. Yet all her teachers seemed to see were her academic weaknesses in comparison to her siblings. One day, frustrated and crying, she asked her parents, "Why do teachers keep comparing me with my siblings? Why can't they see me for who I am?"

Now, switch scenes to an elementary school where teachers took us to see their school's data room. It was a vacant classroom set aside as a place for teachers to track the progress of students who were struggling academically. All four walls were dotted with photos of struggling students. Beside each photo was a chart indicating the academic areas where the student was weak.

On the one hand, the room was impressive since it enabled teachers to familiarize themselves with the students' intellectual needs. On the other hand, there was nothing to indicate anything positive about the students. There were no indicators of their strengths, success stories, or positive qualities. Only their weaknesses were on display. They could have called it their Hall of Shame.

Like the behavior of the teachers in Marie's case, the data room evidenced a culture focused on identifying and fixing students' academic weaknesses. The intentions were noble. But how might things have been different if equal wall space in the data room were focused on highlighting and developing students' strengths? What impact might that have had on students' positive well-being? On their intellectual well-being?

Now consider a strengths-based example.

Mr. Santos was teaching at a school designated for students with special learning needs, including 14-year-old Glen. Glen could not read, write, or do math beyond a second grade level. He was a likeable young man with solid verbal skills, but as soon as it came time to do any type of schoolwork, Glen's countenance changed from happy to gloomy. He hated feeling like a failure.

Mr. Santos was leaving home for work one unusually rainy day and his car would not start. Moisture had gotten into the unit that housed the car's spark plugs, which prevented them from starting the engine. Later, Mr. Santos was explaining to a fellow teacher what had happened, and Glen was nearby. At some point, Glen interrupted: "Mr. Santos, did you spray Bactine [a brand of antiseptic medicine] on it?"

Mr. Santos assumed that Glen was thinking that the medicine would heal things, including car engines. So he asked, "Glen, why would you spray medicine on the engine?"

Glen responded, "Because it has alcohol in it. It evaporates faster than water. It will dry the spark plugs quicker."

Mr. Santos and the other teacher glanced at each other in disbelief. Did those words truly come out of Glen?

It turned out that Glen's mother worked multiple jobs and was seldom home. His father was an alcoholic who lost job after job. So he stayed home fixing people's cars. Glen had nothing to do after school besides hang around his dad, which is where he learned about cars—a lot about cars. In fact, a few days later, Mr. Santos and Glen were in front of the school and Glen started identifying the make and model of nearly every car that passed. Mr. Santos turned to Glen and said, "Glen, you're smarter than I am about cars!"

Glen grinned big to think he was smarter at something than Mr. Santos. And that was the moment something started to happen inside of him. No, Glen did not suddenly turn into an academic genius. However, as Mr. Santos used car examples to teach Glen about the alphabet and to solve simple math equations, Glen began to relax when it came time to do schoolwork. Progress started to happen. But that progress didn't start to happen until Mr. Santos communicated to Glen that he had a strength, a strength that Glen didn't know was a strength.

Leadership expert Peter Drucker observed that "most people do not know what their strengths are, and when you ask them, they look at you with a blank stare."[18] We interviewed one man who certainly had that view of his strengths when he was in high school. In his words:

By the time I left high school, I had already been fired from ten jobs. Why? Because I fired myself before I was hired.

I needed a part-time job, but each time I saw a job opening I would think to myself, "They will never hire me. I don't have any experience washing dishes in a restaurant." Or "I'll never get hired to stock shelves in that store because I can't reach the tallest shelves." On I went firing myself before I filled out an application.

Now that I am older, I look back and think, "Employers would have been thrilled to hire me!" I was honest. Punctual. Good with people. Drug free. A quick learner. A hard worker. I was willing to do jobs that others would not do.

How was I to know that those were strengths that employers were looking for? How was I to know that those were strengths that adults saw in me? I needed someone to point those things out to me.

How might things have been different for that young high school student if a teacher who saw his strengths had communicated those strengths to him?

A high school student told us how a teacher commented to her one day, "You are good at math and have strong conceptual skills. You might enjoy being part of the engineering club. We need a few more people." She had never heard of the engineering club, but the teacher seeing a strength in her was enough to spur some interest. She attended a club meeting where she learned the club was building a solar-powered vehicle and would be traveling out of state to compete with it against other schools. Building things, traveling, and meeting other students were all interests of hers. She joined the club. In the process, she also got interested in flying. The engineering club advisor learned of that interest and arranged an opportunity for her to fly in a small engine plane. She loved every second of it. Today, she is well on her way to earning a college associate's degree while in high school, and she proudly declared that she will have her commercial flying license two years after graduation. All because a few teachers spotted her strengths and interests and offered her opportunities to explore them and put them to use.

Unless their strengths are communicated, students may never see them in themselves. This is the essence of Dr. Stephen R. Covey's favorite definition of leadership: "Leadership is communicating people's worth and potential so clearly that they are inspired to see it in themselves."

It is not easy to spot strengths and potential in every student. Some students' strengths are unseen to the common eye. Being able to spot strengths and potential in students has a lot to do with a teacher's overall beliefs about students in general. Which of the following beliefs best represents your general view of individual students?

1. This student has weaknesses (half empty glass).
2. This student has strengths (half full glass).
3. This student has seen and unseen strengths (full glass).

Teachers who have a knack for spotting seen and unseen strengths and potential in students tend to be intentional in doing so. They are on the active lookout for strengths. And when they spot a strength or see potential in a student, they communicate it: "I see a strength in you!" As Robert John Meehan wrote: "When you see something beautiful in a student, let them know. It may take a second to say, but for them it could last a lifetime."[19]

Christie is a former teacher and principal who is masterful at seeing strengths and potential in students. We were guests at a second grade assembly one day and the students were all huddled into a swarm to sing a song. Christie was with us and the very instant the song ended she bolted out of the audience and headed for one of the students—a twig of a boy. We wondered what he possibly could have done wrong.

Christie exclaimed to the boy, "I love the way your eyes light up when you sing. Every muscle in your body moves in rhythm with every beat! You love music! Don't you?" The boy's face didn't know how to respond. But eventually a shy smile cracked through his look of shock. "Yes, ma'am," he answered. "I do love music."

The boy had not done anything wrong. He had revealed a strength, and it caught Christie's attention. There must have been 20 other adults in that room that day and not one of us spotted the musical prodigy that Christie spotted in the boy. She was not his teacher. It was not her school. Yet she could not resist bursting out of the audience to recognize a budding star's musical strengths. The key, however, was not that she had spotted talent in the boy but that she *communicated* to him what she saw.

Christie's example makes another important point, which is that not all strengths are tied to core academics. As the research of Dr. Seligman and Mihaly Csikszentmihalyi demonstrates, courage, future mindedness, optimism, work ethic, honesty, perseverance, and the capacity for flow act as buffers against mental illness.[20] So why not also communicate those types of non-academic strengths when you see them in students?

Teachers cannot afford to let academic measures be the only measuring sticks they use to assess students. Some students have gifts for being peacemakers or for being kind. Some have other admirable character traits, including:

Adaptable	Focused	Open-minded
Ambitious	Forgiving	Optimistic
Articulate	Friendly	Organized
Authentic	Future-minded	Patient
Brave	Generous	Persistent
Calm	Grateful	Polite
Caring	Happy	Positive
Cheerful	Hard-working	Proactive
Considerate	Helpful	Protective
Cooperative	Honest	Punctual
Creative	Humble	Resourceful
Curious	Humorous	Respectful
Decisive	Leader	Self-confident
Dependable	Listener	Self-directed
Detail oriented	Loyal	Sociable
Disciplined	Multi-talented	Supportive
Efficient	Obedient	Unselfish
Empathetic	Observant	Well-rounded

Consider what a teacher recognizing a non-academic strength did for the following successful executive:

I was in fifth grade when my class was competing against another class in a game of kickball, and an argument broke out. My team was yelling that a player on the opposing team was "out" at second base, while the opposing team was yelling that the player was "safe."

Mrs. Smith came to see what was happening. Players from both sides screamed their views until she had heard enough. "Stop shouting! Everyone be quiet!" she snarled.

Once the noise had silenced, Mrs. Smith did something totally unexpected. She looked directly at me and said: "Robert, I know you are honest. Was the player safe or out?"

I knew the other team's player was safe, but admitting it would put me in conflict with my teammates. Yet I had just been labeled as "honest" in front of everyone. What else could I do but be honest?

Fifty years have passed since Mrs. Smith put that "honest" label on me. It took her five seconds to put it on me and I have spent the past fifty years trying my best to live up to it.

Placing strength labels on a student, like "You are honest," has the potential to nurture that strength for a lifetime. Placing weakness labels on a student, like "You are lazy," has the potential to thwart all ambition.

Sometimes, all it takes to discover students' strengths is to ask. At one school we work with, whenever an event was held where adult guests were invited and students were given the opportunity to showcase a talent—such as playing a piano piece, giving a speech, or singing a song—the same group of students was typically selected to perform their same set of talents. They wondered if there might be other students who wanted to showcase different talents. It was decided to ask all the students if there was a talent they wanted to share at the next event, and they were stunned by the outpouring of positive responses from the students and also by the variety of talents the students were eager to share. Over a hundred students volunteered to share their soccer skills, dance skills, cooking skills, basketball skills, guitar talents, handmade crafts, swimming awards, and so forth. To their credit, the teachers found ways for all of those students to showcase their talents at the next event. As this example shows, sometimes teachers do not need to work all that hard to discover students' strengths. They only need to ask.

For many teachers who are accustomed to seeing students through the lens of their weaknesses, and to trying to "fix" those weaknesses, discovering students' strengths is one of the most difficult best practices for them to master. The best way we know to change such thinking is to create a new system or routine for identifying and communicating students' strengths. That is what Rita Pierson did. If a student missed 18 items on a 20-item math quiz, instead of using her old routine of giving the student a negative score of -18, Rita started a new routine of giving students only positive scores, in this case a score of +2. It became her built-in routine for viewing students through the lens of what they did correctly. From there, she could find ways to build upon the students' successes, however modest.[21]

Communicating to students their strengths and potential makes them feel good about themselves, and it gives them hope.

When did you last communicate a strength to a student?
How did the student respond? How did you feel?

Turned a Stretch into a Strength

Several people we interviewed shared stories about how a teacher helped them turn what previously was a weakness into a new strength, a new source of hope.

Dr. Hatch was the beneficiary of such a teacher. As a doctoral student, he was honored to join the University of Maryland's European Division faculty for a one-year position in Germany. It meant pausing his studies for that one year. He loved the experience and all too soon, it was time to return to the U.S. to finish his degree.

It is common for doctoral students to be assigned to a professor as a research assistant. There were eight professors to which Dr. Hatch could be assigned, but only three had research interests that matched his. So he sent a message to the department requesting that, if possible, he be assigned to one of the three. That didn't happen.

The professor to whom he was assigned specialized in research methods and statistics. Those were weaknesses for Dr. Hatch. Nevertheless, he soon found himself attending the professor's introductory statistics lectures and tutoring beginning students. It was not his idea of fun, but he was learning insights from the professor that he had not learned from previous statistics professors.

Aside from his university duties, the professor consulted with several clients. With time, he invited Dr. Hatch to assist with one of his client projects. Dr. Hatch was thrilled because the project fell more in line with his strengths.

A month into their working together, the professor said to Dr. Hatch, "I suppose you are wondering why I fought to get you as my research assistant." That was the first time Dr. Hatch heard that the professor had "fought" to get him. The professor continued: "The faculty was meeting, and the three professors you requested were each making their case for why you should be assigned to them. That's when I pounded my fist and insisted that I get you."

At that point, Dr. Hatch was thinking, "Why did you do that to me? I wanted to work with one of those professors."

The professor went on: "I have observed you throughout your time in the program, and I believe you can be successful in this field. However, I have noticed that you have intentionally avoided developing your statistics and research skills. If you are to reach the potential I see in you, then you need to have a basic understanding of research methods. That is why I fought hard to get you."

Dr. Hatch was stunned. He immediately recognized that the professor had made a sacrifice. It would have been easier for him to choose a student who was better skilled in research methods. And that is when Dr. Hatch's thoughts shifted from "Why did you do that *to* me?" to "Why did you do that *for* me?"

Over the next two years, the professor involved Dr. Hatch in more client projects. Each required learning new research skills. When the time came to graduate, Dr. Hatch still did not consider himself an expert in research methods, but he left the university with tangible skills that have since engaged him with clients around the world. All thanks to the professor who believed in him and helped him turn a stretch into a new set of strengths.

Notice how Dr. Hatch's professor did not make school easier for him. He didn't allow him to live in his complacency. He knew that the place where students feel most comfortable—most content—is not always the place where they and their potential belong.

We have had the privilege of working with Dr. Elizabeth Murphy. She is a premier expert on students' personality types and learning styles. She has ingrained in us the preference to refer to "weaknesses" as "stretches." In students' minds, stretches sound more hopeful than weaknesses. It gives them the hope that, with effort, they can turn their stretches into strengths.

How does a teacher help students turn a stretch into a strength? Consider a few suggestions:

Clearly Communicate Strengths, Stretches, and Potential

Dr. Hatch hadn't seen a need to improve his skills, and he didn't fully engage with the professor until the professor was frank with him and communicated a vision of what he saw as his strengths, his stretches, and his potential. Had the professor remained silent, done the easy thing and allowed the other professors to have their say, Dr. Hatch never would have become open to the professor's leadership and mentoring, and never would have stretched his weaknesses into a strength to the extent he did.

Present a Vision of Why the New Strength Is Important

As the professor explained why the research skills would be important to be successful in his career, Dr. Hatch could see that the professor was correct. He did not need more convincing. The more students can see how developing a new strength will help them succeed in life, the more likely they are to put effort into stretching toward the new strength.

Start from a Secure Base

According to journalist David Brooks, "All of life is a series of daring adventures from a secure base."[22]

To help students turn a stretch into a strength, start from a secure base—their *comfort zone*. Then, move with them into their *growth zone*. In Dr. Hatch's case, the professor essentially said, "Given your current level of skills in statistics and research methods, let's start you with my introductory statistics class and beginning students." That for Dr. Hatch was a secure place from which to start. From there the professor worked with Dr. Hatch on additional assignments that gradually afforded him the opportunity to develop additional research skills.

Take Small Steps

Daniel Pink, in his book *Drive*, declared, "The best moments in our lives are not the passive, receptive, relaxing times. . . . The best moments usually occur when a person's body or mind is stretched to the limits in a voluntary effort to accomplish something difficult and worthwhile."[23] But such moments often come in small steps.

Whenever you hear a story about a student who made amazing overnight progress, what that typically means is that the person telling the story is either hiding something or missed all the effort and the many small steps that went on behind the scenes. In the words of Anne Sullivan, "People seldom see the halting and painful steps by which the most insignificant success is achieved."

In Dr. Hatch's case, the professor taught him research skills over a period of several class lectures, several projects, and multiple clients. It took numerous small steps, not one giant leap.

Avoid the Fear Zone

Another university professor was impressed with a certain student and gave her opportunities to expand her abilities, including presenting in front of groups. He felt he was doing her a grand favor by showcasing her abilities. Then, one day, he invited her to present to a group of professors and, instead of being excited or grateful, she pushed back: "Why do you keep doing this *to* me? Presenting in front of people scares me. It causes me to lose sleep at night."

All along, instead of doing the student a favor, the professor had been pushing her into her *fear zone*, causing much stress. Very little learning goes on when students are thrust into their fear zone. So it pays to learn what falls within a student's growth zone and what falls within their fear zone. The answer will differ for different students. The objective is to inspire them to stretch, not to snap, as shown in the table below.

Comfort Zone	Growth Zone	Fear Zone
A secure place. No stretching. **Start here.**	Where stretches turn to strengths. **Move to here.**	Where little learning occurs. **Avoid here.**

Acknowledge New Strengths

Students do not always recognize their progress or notice a new strength they have developed. The more teachers help them to see tangible "before and after" snapshots of their progress, the more reward-ing their new strengths will feel, increasing their feelings of hope. We know a high school teacher, for example, who gives students the same test four times a year. He does it so students can see and celebrate how much they are progressing.

So there are a few suggestions for helping students turn stretches into strengths. Helping a student to turn a stretch into a strength has the potential to create a new fountain of hope.

One reason it is important to intentionally think about each stu-dent and which of their stretches can be turned into strengths is that we have seen situations where a student is identified early on as having a par-ticular strength. Let's say they are identified as being "the best" at sing-ing. They are then given every opportunity to sing at special occasions from an early age all the way until the time they graduate. What they are not given is the chance to develop strengths in new areas, including areas that might make them more career or university ready. Meanwhile, a stu-dent who wants to turn their singing ability from a stretch to a strength is not given an opportunity because the opportunities are always given to the student who is "best" at singing. In the end, neither student devel-ops a stretch into a strength. As the saying goes: "The woods would be very silent if no bird sang but the one that sang best."[24]

> *Can you think of a time when you helped a student*
> *to turn a stretch into a strength? How did you do it?*

Saw My Differences as Strengths

Great leaders know how to optimize everyone's best *me* to create a bet-ter *we*.

When the word *differences* is mentioned in schools, people often think of *respecting* the different cultures, belief systems, and lifestyles of others. We applaud such thinking. However, there is an even higher quest that goes beyond respecting differences, and that is to see those differences as strengths. We compare it to climbing Mount Everest, the world's highest peak.

It takes a physically fit and fully equipped hiker about eight days just to get to the base camp of Mount Everest, which sits at 17,000 feet above sea level. About 40,000 people reach it each year. Yet every climber knows that beyond base camp is an even higher quest, the 29,000-foot summit. Fewer than 1,000 climbers achieve that level each year.

Similarly, getting to where differences are respected takes a lot of work. Like reaching base camp, it is no small feat. Yet beyond it is a higher summit. It is where people's differences are not just respected, they are truly valued, utilized, and celebrated. It is beneficial to say to a student, "I respect your different strengths and views"; it is an even higher way of believing in them to say, "We not only respect your differences, we are stronger because of your differences. We can learn and benefit from each other's differences."

So what does it look like for a teacher to see students' differences as strengths? A man named Kirk shared:

I graduated with a degree in psychology and began a master's degree in political science. For the first time in my life, I felt like I was a flunking student. There were so many terms and facts I did not know, whereas the other students all came from undergraduate majors in political science and knew all those things.

One of my professors the first semester was Dr. Hollist. Much of our class hours were spent critiquing each other's research papers. Some of the students were brutal in their critiques, especially when it came to critiquing my novice ideas.

One day, after the other students had finished tearing apart my paper, Dr. Hollist took his turn. I braced for the worst. He said to the class, "In terms of political science knowledge, Kirk has the least. But there are things I really like about Kirk's work. He is the best writer in the program. I love that he has a psychology background. He has lived abroad and looks at things from an entirely different view than the rest of us. I find his views refreshing. They cause me to think differently."

Dr. Hollist's one suggestion for me was that I needed to look for more ways to bring my psychology background into class discussions. "It will make our discussions better," he insisted.

That did wonders for my confidence!

Had Dr. Hollist focused solely on respecting Kirk's differences, he would have been patient, understanding, and considerate of Kirk's diverse skills and background. But he did more than that. He let the students know that he felt the class was stronger because of Kirk's differences. He encouraged Kirk to utilize his diverse strengths more frequently to improve class discussions. And, according to Kirk, Dr. Hollist did the same for all students. He made the entire class feel like a team of diverse strengths that were unitedly helping each other to learn, as opposed to a bundle of independent learners who were competing for the top grades.

Seeing and utilizing students' differences as strengths produces *collective intelligence*.[25] Collective intelligence is when two or more people combine their strengths and experiences in ways that lead to better decisions and better outcomes. It is the opposite of *groupthink*, which is when two or more people work together in ways that lead to weaker decisions and weaker outcomes.[26]

In nature, collective intelligence is known as *symbiosis*. It is when animals work together to optimize each other's strengths and minimize each other's weaknesses to survive. In businesses and sports, it is called teamwork or synergy. In fact, the best businesses and sports teams tend to be those that intentionally recruit team members and players with different strengths that complement each other.

Since the larger part of students' lives will be spent working in groups and teams—including families—it is important for students to learn how to work with people who are different from them.[27] This requires more than just teaching them how to tolerate each other or coexist peacefully. It is truly a matter of teaching them how to optimize people's strengths and minimize their weaknesses.

The spirit of achieving collective intelligence is found in Doug Floyd's statement, "You don't get harmony when everyone sings the same note."[28] It is found in Ray Kroc's declaration that "None of us is as good as all of us."[29] And it is found in Maya Angelou's declaration that "It is time for parents to teach young people early on that in diversity there is beauty and there is strength."[30]

So how does a teacher create collective intelligence in a classroom that is filled with wildly diverse students? The answer is hidden in what Tom Peters and Bob Waterman referred to as *essential dualism*.[31] It stems from the dual reality that people want to be part of a unified team while at the very same time they want to be fully recognized for their individual talents, knowledge, and contributions. For this to happen, teachers must simultaneously utilize and celebrate "me" and "we." Both!

Celebrate "Me"

You may have heard quotes like "There is no 'I' in team." Or "To be a team player you must forget yourself for the good of the team." But has that been your actual experience?

The best teams do not hide, bury, or minimize individual contributions. Instead, they almost go out of their way to respect and honor the individual strengths that each member brings to the team. That is because being part of a successful team does not require that a person give away their sense of individuality. As Piglet once remarked to Winnie the Pooh: "The things that make me different are the things that make me, me."[32]

To not recognize students for their individual contributions is akin to asking them to give up their identity—who they are. To become almost anonymous. In fact, when taken to a negative extreme, a student can become so submerged into the culture of a group that they lose their unique identity and risk becoming *deindividualized*.[33] In worst-case scenarios, they become aggressive, violent, or crude—traits they would not exhibit when alone and acting on their own judgment.[34]

So instead of trying to hide or mute students' strengths to create collective intelligence, teachers like Dr. Hollist do their best to create opportunities to recognize and utilize the individual strengths of each student in ways that make the class better as a whole. They find ways to truly acknowledge, value, utilize, and celebrate each person's unique "me."

Celebrate "We"

The other half of essential dualism is to apply and celebrate the power of "we."

Sherelin is a university student who learned the hard way to value collective intelligence and the power of "we." When assigning students to make a class presentation, her professor gave students a choice: "You can do the presentation on your own or you can work in small groups." Sherelin could only think about what a hassle it would be to try to accommodate everyone's diverse schedules and opinions. So she quickly chose the "I'll do it by myself" option.

Sherelin put much time and effort into her presentation. When the day came to present, she felt her presentation went very well, until she saw the group presentation. It was better than good. One student in the group was talented at graphic design; the group's slides looked professional. Another student was skilled at public speaking; he captured the audience with his humor and poise. Another student was a strong writer; he did most of the written portion. And so forth. The group had optimized its members' strengths and made their weaknesses irrelevant. Individually, they spent less time working on their group presentation than Sherelin had spent working on her own. And once it was over, the group members all went out and celebrated. As for Sherelin, she vowed to take the group option if ever given the chance again.

Not all students are given opportunities to experience the power of "we" because not all teachers offer students opportunities to work in teams. In fact, some common systems and routines appear intended to deny the power of we. Students, for example, are seldom allowed to work together on tests or research projects, and commonly used grading policies often pit student against student as competitors vying for the top scores.

We were visiting a school in a foreign country and the guests were all chatting excitedly as they watched a group of students working as a team to solve a challenge. We had no idea what the guests were saying since we didn't understand their language. We asked our interpreter what the guests were discussing, and she responded, "Oh, they have never seen students working in teams to solve a problem." We were stunned. Hopefully, the days of students not working together in a spirit of learning together are long gone in today's classrooms.

Teachers play a large role in uniting groups of students who have diverse strengths and backgrounds. We have visited classrooms where students have very different cultural backgrounds and yet students have bonded as a tightly unified team. They respect each other's differences and they even have routines that are designed to celebrate the diverse talents, beliefs, cultural traditions, foods, holidays, and other strengths of class members. The teachers understand and teach students that oneness does not require sameness. In a world where divisiveness is an unfortunate reality, the teachers in these classrooms are able to both optimize what their students have in common and to also find ways to beautify the class by not just respecting their different strengths but also celebrating them. They plan and create opportunities for students to experience that together really can be better.

In contrast, we have also visited highly diverse classrooms that lack any resemblance to being a unified group. They are filled with chaos and contention. What is the difference? It starts with the way the teacher views and celebrates differences. When teachers consistently talk about how they love the diverse strengths of students, then students regularly talk about how they love each other's diverse strengths. When teachers find ways to optimize and celebrate students' different strengths, then students find ways to optimize the different strengths that their peers bring to the classroom. When teachers model the importance of listening, of having the courage to voice one's opinions, of not always having to be "right," and of solving conflicts in win-win ways, students begin to think and behave that way, too.

So, when attempting to see students' differences as strengths and build collective intelligence, teachers are best to start with themselves. First, become a better model of celebrating differences yourself. There's always room to improve! Then create routines that allow the entire class to utilize and celebrate both "me" and "we."

What are some ways you can optimize and
celebrate students' different strengths?

Temperance Factors

When attempting to inspire students to discover their strengths and to feel increased hope, remember that:

Not All Weaknesses Are Meant to Be Ignored

Does this chapter suggest that teachers ignore students' weaknesses? No. Especially not when students have weaknesses that prevent them or others from making progress. To ignore weaknesses creates a false sense of hope. Our suggestion instead is to make sure that weakness is not the main lens through which teachers view students, or through which students view themselves.

Strengths Can Become Weaknesses

Suppose a student is very good at studying. That is a strength. But what if the student becomes so fanatical about studying that they neglect all other aspects of their life, such as important relationships or their physical needs? Are that student's study habits still a strength? It is still a strength, but they have gone too far with their strength to the point that it has also become a weakness.

Similarly, a strength in one situation may not be a strength in another situation. And when students use a strength to harm the well-being of others, that strength has again become a weakness.

Don't Forget the Adults!

Adults also want to be viewed through the lens of their strengths. They want opportunities to turn their stretches into strengths. They want their different strengths to be valued and utilized. They want to feel hope.

What might happen if teachers' annual personal development plans were designed to develop one of their strengths instead of to "fix" one of their weaknesses? Or what might happen if teachers' strengths were more frequently showcased for students? At one school we were shown a large display case filled with paintings, woodwork, quilts, and other beautiful crafts. All were the creations of the talented teachers, and most had nothing to do with the subject matter they taught. At another school, we watched a teacher play his electric guitar in front of all the students. He had the students rocking. Why not do more to celebrate teachers' diverse strengths?

Concluding Thoughts

Some time ago, Dr. Hatch was interviewed by a national Colombian newspaper. The journalist asked, "What do you give students?" The journalist was thinking in terms of materials, yet Dr. Hatch's response was focused on the students' positive well-being. "We give them hope," was his reply.

Similarly, when we asked one teacher what subject she taught, without hesitation she responded, "I teach hope."

When all that students hear about is their weaknesses, their gaps, their loss of learning, it is very difficult for them to see hope. In contrast, when teachers communicate to students their strengths, when they help students turn a stretch into a strength, and when they celebrate students' differences to create collective intelligence, those teachers are teaching them hope. That is leadership.

The Challenge

Select one. To enable students see more hope in life, make and implement a plan for how you will

- communicate their strengths more often,
- turn one of their stretches into a strength, or
- utilize and celebrate their diverse strengths.

4

Entrusted Me with Responsibilities

Oprah Winfrey is among the most influential people in the world. Through her talk shows, podcasts, and global philanthropy, she has blessed many lives, including the lives of many students.

One of Oprah's strengths is her ability to bring out the best in her talk-show guests. One day, however, a surprise guest appeared on her show, someone who always brought out the best in Oprah. It was Oprah's fourth grade teacher, Mrs. Duncan. The instant Oprah spotted Mrs. Duncan, tears began streaming down her face. Oprah explained how she had run home from the first day of school, shouting to her father that she had "the best teacher ever!"

What had Mrs. Duncan done to deserve that grand title after just one day? Mrs. Duncan had invited Oprah to be responsible for leading the class in morning devotionals. The devotionals were meant to start each day with a positive, inspiring thought. Oprah felt so honored to be entrusted with that responsibility. She absolutely could not wait to get home to tell her father all about it.

As that school year progressed, Mrs. Duncan invited Oprah to take on other important responsibilities, even grading assignments on occasion. Oprah credited those early experiences with helping her to feel of worth and to become the confident, poised, and influential person she is today.[1]

The Need for Self-Worth

In the words of Booker T. Washington, "Few things help an individual more than to place responsibility upon him and to let him know that you trust him."[2]

A basic assumption of this book is that all students are inherently of worth. They do not need to do anything special or out of the ordinary to be of worth. But not all students perceive their worth, so one of teachers' roles is to help them to discover their worth. One way for that to happen is to offer them opportunities to take on responsibilities that they perceive to be of worth. As students successfully complete responsibilities that they perceive to be of worth, the easier it will be for them to perceive and to feel their own worth.

Another basic assumption of this book is that students attend school to gain intelligence. But what is intelligence? The Oxford English Dictionary defines intelligence as "[t]he ability to acquire and apply knowledge and skills."[3] The key word in that equation is *apply*. Intelligence results when students learn how to apply the knowledge and skills they acquire. This, of course, is referring to real intelligence, not artificial intelligence. In fact, we know of no better way for students to learn how to apply the emotional and social knowledge and skills they acquire in school than to entrust them with meaningful responsibilities. Let them learn by doing.[4] This develops both their EQ and their IQ, and increases their feelings of self-worth.

Like connection, meaning, and hope, the basic need for self-worth is a matter of personal perception. Peers, family members, and teachers can each see great worth in a student, but if the student does not see it in themselves, they will not perceive their self-worth fully.

Students rely on two sources of evidence to assess their self-worth: *extrinsic* and *intrinsic*. Extrinsic sources of self-worth come from outside the students, such as:

- how other people view them and their appearance
- who they know and befriend

- their possessions, such as a cell phone
- their family's status in society
- comparisons with others
- awards and positions they attain
- the number of social media followers they have

When Dr. Jennifer Crocker at the University of Michigan asked university students how they measured their self-worth, 80 percent revealed that they base their self-worth on their academic grades, 77 percent mentioned the amount of family support they get, and 66 percent said they base their self-worth on how they compared with others. A solid 70 percent of female students indicated that their physical appearance plays a large role in how they measure their self-worth. All are extrinsic measures of self-worth.

Dr. Crocker further reports that students who base their self-worth almost entirely on extrinsic measures

- are prime candidates for depression and anxiety;
- express lower levels of happiness;
- are more likely to view themselves as a failure;
- struggle more with making academic progress;
- report more stress, anger, and interpersonal conflicts;
- have higher levels of drug and alcohol use; and
- are more prone to eating disorders.[5]

Not all extrinsic sources of self-worth are detrimental to self-worth. In fact, extrinsic sources that are positive can be extremely beneficial for students, particularly those with low intrinsic self-worth. There may even be times when compliments from others are the only things that keep a student with low intrinsic self-worth from falling apart emotionally. Never underestimate what good a kind remark can do.

Nevertheless, intrinsic sources of self-worth, which come from inside students, are extremely important. They are students' internal beliefs about their present and future value. Research from Terry Clark-Jones of Michigan State University indicates that young people who feel a strong internal sense of self-worth are more likely to

- stand by their convictions and not be easily swayed,
- hold the belief that they can be successful in life,
- try new things and take healthy risks,
- handle disappointments and failures in a stable manner, and
- set ambitious goals and achieve them.[6]

Self-worth theory proposes that intrinsic self-worth is primarily the result of a person achieving a steady series of successes, even small successes.[7] Terry Clark-Jones builds on this idea, reporting: "Successful experiences boost our sense of competency and mastery and make us feel just plain good about ourselves. Don't just tell a teen that she is of worth and valuable, help her to believe it by giving her every opportunity to succeed."[8]

Students feel of most worth when they perceive that they are doing things of most worth. Ironically, what gives students the greatest sense of internal worth are projects that get them thinking external to themselves. As Dr. Martin Seligman declared: "We scientists have found that doing a kindness produces the single most reliable momentary increase in well-being of any exercise we have tested."[9]

Whereas numerous therapists attempt to cure young people's low sense of self-worth by delving into their deepest inward thoughts and emotions, Drs. Susan Nolen-Hoeksema and Sonya Lyubomirsky have compiled evidence to suggest that an equally effective, if not more effective, first approach is to get them thinking externally to themselves and serving others. They warn that when students dwell on or over-analyze their innermost feelings, it often "sustains or worsens [their] sadness, fosters negatively based thinking, impairs [their] ability to solve problems, saps motivation, and interferes with concentration and initiative."[10] So there may be a valid argument to consider giving students responsibilities to do kindnesses for others as a first aid remedy when attempting to resolve their low feelings of worth.

Entrusting students with meaningful responsibilities to serve others provides several additional noteworthy benefits. It gives them the opportunity to make responsible decisions. It gives them the chance to feel the pride that comes from contributing to the betterment of others. It gives them the chance to connect with other students and adults and to feel they are a valuable part of a team. In fact, in many ways, it gives them added chances to feel more connection, more meaning, and more hope in their lives, which in turn adds to their feelings of self-worth and readiness to learn.

> *What personal successes in your life have*
> *most increased your feelings of self-worth?*

Three Best Practices for Entrusting Students with Responsibilities

We now suggest three best practices to consider when exploring ways to entrust students with responsibility and to increase their feelings of self-worth. They are:

My teacher...

- gave me a chance to lead.
- involved me in service learning.
- appreciated my contributions.

Gave Me a Chance to Lead

Roland S. Barth declared, "A school should be a community of leaders—not just a principal and a lot of followers. The principal, teachers, students, and parents should all be first-class citizens of that community."[11]

When we interviewed a vibrant 90-year-old woman named Janice, she credited three teachers with helping her to become the happy, confident person she is today. During her childhood, her family moved year after year, which meant she changed schools year after year. When she arrived at what would become her final new school, it was the middle of the year, and she had no friends. She felt alone. Her fourth grade teacher noticed her loneliness and also recognized that Janice was very good at drawing.

At the time, the class was studying farm animals. So Janice's teacher retrieved a long roll of poster paper that ran nearly the full width of the classroom and asked Janice to sketch the outlines of several farm animals. Before long, Janice had the entire length of the paper covered with horses, goats, cows, chickens, cats, dogs, and other farm animals.

The teacher next gave the other students a set of crayons and assigned them to color in the various animal outlines. "The teacher had me be the leader and give the other students directions," Janice recalled. "It made me feel special. All the students came to know who I was and to accept me as their friend. The teacher didn't know how shy I was before she gave me that assignment."

The other two teachers that Janice mentioned gave her meaningful opportunities to lead, too. Three-quarters of a century later, she is still praising all three teachers for the trust they extended to her.

We sat beside a father during a middle school assembly. His family had just moved into the school's boundaries. He told us he was worried about how his daughter would adjust to the new school since she had been extremely shy and anxious at her previous school. When he heard that she had been asked to lead an activity during the assembly, his worry doubled. What if she panicked? Yet there she was standing in front of all the students and confidently telling them what to do for the activity. The father kept repeating, "I can't believe this is my daughter."

Afterward, the father told his daughter how proud he was of her and how surprised he was that she would do it. Her reaction was smirky. "Dad!" she replied. "This is what students do at this school."

It turned out that when the daughter arrived at the new school, she observed students doing things that only teachers did at her previous school. She saw students greeting students at the main entrance each morning. She saw students handing out homework assignments. She saw students leading morning announcements. She saw students setting up technology. It was as if students were leading the school. She wanted to be part of it. And she was.

In each of these two cases, we find shy students rising to the level of trust that the teachers established for them. When students feel a teacher's belief in them, they often find a way to rise to the level of their teacher's belief in them. This is known as the Pygmalion effect, or the teacher expectation effect.[12]

Entrusting students with meaningful responsibilities will often cause them to elevate their behaviors. Take fifth grade student Lee, for example. Lee struggled academically and sought out attention in ways that distracted his classmates from learning. One day, his teacher became fed up with his antics and sent him to the principal. Lee's family, which struggled with issues ranging from poverty to drugs to domestic violence to gangs, offered him very little support. He had been sent to the principal's office multiple times before, so what was the principal to do?

When Lee returned to the classroom, his teacher was eager to learn what consequence the principal had given him. "She gave me a speaking responsibility for the Leadership Day program," Lee said while trying hard to hide a smile. It meant he would be speaking in front of more than a hundred adult guests. He'd never been entrusted with that level of responsibility before. However, it came with the expectation that he show responsible behavior in class, or else the responsibility would be offered to another student.

Privately, Lee's teacher had hoped the principal would give him a harsh consequence. So her first reaction was incredulous: "What? She gave him a reward for his bad behavior?" Nevertheless, she put on her "be patient" face and watched to see what would happen.

In the days that followed, Lee talked frequently about his upcoming speaking opportunity. He talked about what he would say and what he planned to wear. What he didn't do was exhibit poor in-class behavior. The principal had put her trust in him, and he was resolved not to betray that trust.

The same approach may not work for all students. But in many cases, the best thing a teacher or principal can do for a struggling student is to offer them a chance to taste success, to be a leader. And then step back and observe what that trust does to improve the student's behavior and feelings of worth. Does it always work? No. But it does often enough to be worth a try.

To entrust students to be leaders does not mean to give them a task, tell them exactly what to do, and constantly check up on them to make sure they follow directions exactly. To entrust means "I put my trust in you." It means giving students the opportunity to own the responsibility and to decide how they will get it done.

Too often, the opportunity to be a leader is reserved only for the same ten remarkable students who fill the same ten remarkable student leadership roles year after year. When students are never entrusted with responsibilities to be leaders, it essentially guarantees they will graduate as followers.

One of the easiest ways to entrust students with meaningful responsibilities is to offer them opportunities to utilize and further develop their strengths. Recall the second grade boy in the previous chapter who was singled out for his rhythm and passion for music. Four months later, his teachers were putting his musical talents to use by giving him a chance to lead the school choir in singing one of its concert songs. He may have looked like a small tree among the forest of his much taller fifth grade peers, but self-worth was splattered all over his face.

Some of the most touching examples we have seen of students being leaders are those that involve students with special learning needs. They hide no emotions when showing how thrilled they are to be contributing in important ways as leaders of their class or school rather than always being the ones to receive support.

Of course, teachers must be careful not to throw students into leadership responsibilities where they are likely to fail. If a teacher has doubts that a student can stretch to meet a responsibility, it is best to let the student practice in a less visible or low-stress situation. Or partner them with a sure-to-be-successful peer or a member of an action team before placing them on a bigger stage all alone.

When entrusting students with a responsibility, always provide the *why*. Why is the responsibility important? Who is it benefitting? Having a compelling *why* can turn an otherwise meaningless task into a responsibility that builds self-worth.

When thinking of possible opportunities for students to lead, two questions to ask as a teacher are: What am I currently doing that a student can be entrusted to do? And which of my students are in need of increased self-worth and can successfully take on this role?

Some of the responsibilities that build the most self-worth in students involve opportunities to apply the leadership skillsets highlighted in this book. Students can be invited to call out students' names while handing out homework or to lead "get-to-know-you" activities for taking an interest in students' stories. Students can be assigned to identify and celebrate other students' strengths. Indeed, all seven leadership skillsets and their best practices can be turned into meaningful opportunities for students to lead.

Responsibilities to lead do not need to be large to give students feelings of being successful and of worth. Sandra Gasca-Gonzalez of the Annie E. Casey Foundation's Center for Systems Innovation says that while students need opportunities to stand out and be trusted, it can be as simple as giving them the responsibility to be at the head of the line.[13] In fact, some of the most important leadership responsibilities students take on may be anonymous, such as being asked to be a peacemaker, to befriend a lonely student, or to let the teacher know if a student is feeling overwhelmed.

In the end, what a student wants to hear from their teacher are the words *I trust you*. It may be only a small responsibility they are entrusted with, but hearing their teacher say they trust and believe in them may be the most important words a student hears that year. Indeed, if you are inclined to put a positive label on a student, then label them a "leader." Watch their smile grow a little wider and their positive well-being stand a little taller.

> *What meaningful responsibility are you*
> *currently doing that a student can take on instead?*
> *Who is the student in need of increased*
> *self-worth that can successfully take it on?*

Involved Me in Service Learning

Simply referring to students as leaders can give them a feeling of self-worth. But students do not need to be "the leader" to feel self-worth. Small and quiet acts of service for others will do.

The Mayo Clinic confirms that doing service for others improves students' physical and mental health, provides a sense of purpose, teaches valuable skills, and builds connections.[14] As Professor Booker T. Washington observed more than 100 years ago: "I began learning long ago that those who are happiest are those who do the most for others."

Opportunities for students to serve are all around. They can be found in the classroom, in the school, and in the community.

In the Classroom

A grand place to start is with students doing service for their teacher. Why not start there?

Teachers are natural helpers. But sometimes, the best way they can help students feel self-worth is to ask them for help. An elementary teacher we interviewed was spending 10 to 15 minutes after school each day closing her classroom. This involved shutting window blinds, placing chairs on desks, turning off computers, straightening shelves, and so forth. Each task delayed her from getting home to an elderly parent.

Then the teacher realized that students could do all those tasks. So the next day, she described her situation to her students and involved them in brainstorming ways they could help. From then on, what had previously taken her 10 to 15 minutes to do after school, the students were doing in less than three minutes before the departure bell rang. What was once a source of stress for the teacher had become a source of joy for the students. They were happy to be making life easier for their teacher and felt they were doing something of worth.

We have seen other elementary and secondary teachers entrust students with all kinds of opportunities to serve and make life easier for their teacher. The opportunities can be assigned to an individual student or a group of students, or on a rotating basis. For example, students can be invited to serve as the classroom

- **Technology Specialist:** Sets up technology for lessons.
- **Attendance Monitor:** Tracks attendance.
- **Celebration Coordinator:** Recognizes positive events.
- **Photographer:** Makes slide shows of activities.
- **Horticulturist:** Cares for classroom or school plants.
- **Mediator:** Makes first attempt at resolving disputes.
- **Motivational Speaker:** Starts class with a motivational quote.

- **Class DJ:** Chooses and plays music as students arrive.
- **Organizer:** Gets supplies ready for lessons.
- **Humorist:** Starts the week with a joke or riddle.
- **Computer Tech:** Troubleshoots peer computer problems.

And the list goes on. Be careful not to underestimate what even the youngest students or the most challenging of students can and will do for their teacher.

Other times, it may be a classmate who is in most need of receiving service. Students in one classroom were shocked to discover that one of their classmates was homeless. The students didn't just accept that as a fact of life, nor did they assume that adults would take care of the matter. They, on their own initiative, went to work finding ways to help their classmate get school supplies and needed clothing items. The effort was entirely student driven and teacher supported. Doing service for each other was a natural part of that teacher's classroom culture. It was something the students had talked about and wanted as a class.

In the School

Many opportunities to do service are available outside of the classroom but still on a school's campus.

A middle school student named Evan struggled academically. School was always a source of embarrassment for him. Then, one winter day, he noticed a few students who were waiting for a bus without coats. He sensed their families could not afford to buy coats, so he gave his coat to one of them. Evan didn't stop there. With the permission of his teacher, he rallied his classmates to organize a school-wide coat drive. Several coats were collected and given to students in need. But perhaps the best outcome of the event was that school became a place where the young man felt respected by his peers for his kindness and initiative. He had come up with the idea on his own and had owned the idea all the way to completion. Students are more inclined to own the ideas for service and feel of most worth when the ideas are their own.

One of the most practical ways for students to learn as they serve in a school is through peer teaching and mentoring. Older students, for example, can be assigned to read with or tutor younger students in various academic subjects. Preparing to teach requires the older students to more thoroughly study and think about the content. In the end, the students who do the peer teaching often end up being the ones who learn the most about the subject matter, while also gaining skills in leadership and empathy and building self-worth.[15] Just being a positive peer influence can have great benefits.

Some of the most impactful forms of service are when students are asked to mentor peers who struggle with low positive well-being. Numerous schools have peer mentoring groups, such as Hope Squads, where students are trained to look out for and befriend peers who might be lonely, depressed, or considering self-harm.[16] Though the intent is for the peer mentors to help their peers, it is the peer mentors who insist that they benefit most from the experience.

One of students' favorite forms of peer mentoring is when they are given the chance to serve students with special learning needs, including those who are on the autism spectrum or are children with Down syndrome. Such students often connect with their peers in ways that they do not connect with their teachers. For example, Bridger is a peer mentor who has personally faced physical setbacks in life due to a genetic heart defect. When he was invited to mentor students with special learning needs, his past physical struggles afforded him much empathy for helping other students with their struggles. He is very kind and gentle with them. They love working with him. But Bridger will insist that the students he mentors have done more to teach him about how to be happy and overcome physical limitations.

In the Community

Memorable opportunities for students to serve and learn are found in their communities. For example, the annual "Leading with Love Week" at A.B. Combs Elementary gives students the chance to serve members of their community, such as first responders. One year, students honored a police officer who had been shot in the line of duty. He and fellow officers were served breakfast and given a chance to speak to students about what it means to be a leader. Another year, an author of children's books was honored. Students lead the events from start to finish. They suggest who to honor. They plan the food. They do the invites. They write the thank-you notes. And so forth. All planning is left to the genius of students, with the shadowing support of parents.

Doing service-learning projects as a class brings the added benefit of building unity and making connections. Working together to serve others can even help class members set aside conflicts that exist between students, as they turn their focus toward a unified, superordinate goal.[17] It can also take students' minds off their own concerns, as they orient their minds and hearts toward the concerns of others.

One high school we work with requires every graduating student to participate in a community service project during their senior year. Students choose the activities and work in teams to plan and complete their service project on a school-wide day of service. They then present their projects for students in younger grades, so they, too, can be inspired, benefit from the older students' learning, and begin thinking about service ideas they can do when their turn to do community service arrives.

So there are a few examples of service learning opportunities in the classroom, school, and community. Students can also be encouraged to pursue service opportunities in their families and neighborhoods and report about their service to their class. In the process, they may discover that when they feel sad or anxious, rather than seeking advice in the "Self-Help" section of the library, they might be better off looking for remedies in the "Help Others" section, if there is such a shelf.

What are some ways your students can serve
others and build their self-worth?

Appreciated My Contributions

William James is credited with being the father of American psychology. He was a professor at Radcliffe College (now part of Harvard), where he identified several principles of human nature. At the end of one semester, a few students wrote a thank-you note and gave him a flowering potted plant as a gift of gratitude. No students had ever done anything like that for him before. What surprised him most, however, was how much the gift meant to him. The feeling of being appreciated ultimately led him to declare: "The deepest principle in human nature is the craving to be appreciated."[18]

Like professors, students crave to be appreciated. When teachers voice appreciation for a student's contribution, it sends a message that says far more than "Thank you." It says: "I value you. You are helpful to me." The student experiences success. Self-worth is built.

One elementary student was entrusted to be the tour guide for a group of adult visitors to her school. Muriel was included. As the tour ended, members of the group heartily thanked the girl. She beamed as the group complimented her people skills and listed specific ways that she made them feel like honored guests. The girl smiled as she waved good-bye and skipped happily back to class.

The group learned later that their tour guide's grandmother had passed away that morning. When her parents told her she could stay home from school and be with family, she said, "I need to go to school. Important guests are coming, and my teachers are counting on me."

Thankfully, the guests did not let the girl down, as they had been genuine in telling her how much her service was appreciated. It gave her a boost of self-worth on a day when her heart needed it.

One man we interviewed is in his 60s. He has battled mental health issues since the age of six. It was at that age when he began to be bullied at school. Some boys threw him to the ground and when he got up, they threw him down again, all while laughing and mocking. The bullying persisted into his middle school years when one of the bullies secretly taped a note to the back of his coat that said "Kick me." The other bullies then took turns kicking him. Anxiety, loneliness, and depression have been the man's constant companions ever since.

When we asked the man about a teacher who made a difference in his life, he immediately spoke of his fifth grade teacher. She had phoned his mother one day to say, "Your son is a gift to our class." She went on to tell his mother all the things she appreciated about him. Fifty years later, the man still vividly remembers what that phone call did for his self-worth and his willingness to stay in school.

Dr. Chip Heath of Stanford and his brother Dr. Dan Heath of Duke University refer to the teacher's phone call to the bullied man's mother as "breaking the script," which entails finding out-of-the-ordinary ways to say and do things to let people know they are appreciated.[19] Perhaps it is a sad commentary on society to think that making a phone call to express appreciation has become a matter of breaking the script.

Expressing appreciation to students does not need to be complicated or awkward. It can be done in two simple steps:

Honor the Gift: Express sincere appreciation for the *gift*—whether it be a tangible gift or an act of service or compassion—and what it means to you and others.
Honor the Giver: Honor the *giver* by stating how their kindness impacted you and others, and complimenting their fine qualities.

For example, a teacher might say, "Peter, thank you for helping to calm the class yesterday. It calmed me, too. You are a person the other students respect—a natural leader." Or "Thank you, Sarah, for organizing the shelves. It was such a relief for me to have it done. You are so responsible." It is that simple, and it is an incredibly impactful way to connect with students and build their self-worth.

> *When was the last time you expressed*
> *appreciation for a student? What did you say*
> *and how did it make the student feel?*

Temperance Factors

Teachers can go overboard when entrusting students with meaningful responsibilities. Common cautions to consider include:

Avoid Overloading Students

Many students already have much to do aside from schoolwork. Giving them "one more thing" to do may cause them more stress than it builds self-worth. So resist giving students responsibilities that are beyond their bandwidth or growth zone and risk placing them into their anxiety zone.

Keep It Simple

Some teachers set up complicated systems, such as colorful "job charts," to organize student responsibilities. This is an effective and efficient way to track which students have been given which responsibilities and to ensure students get equal turns to be entrusted. We praise and recommend such charts.

However, when efforts to track responsibilities become too complex, they end up being more of a nuisance than a help. We have listened to numerous teachers with frowns on their faces say things like,

"Oh no! I forgot to switch the chart again." Or "It's easier to do the job myself." When entrusting students to take on leadership or service responsibilities, or when creating a job chart, keep the responsibilities and the charts simple.

Don't Forget the Adults!

Surely teachers' greatest source of self-worth comes from the intrinsic self-worth they feel when they know they are making a difference in a student's life. But it also doesn't hurt every now and then for a student, a parent, a peer, or an administrator to provide some extrinsic sources of self-worth in the form of appreciation.

One teacher wrote: "My first year was incredibly difficult. I lasted three months before I decided to quit. I thought everyone disliked me—students and teachers. After I announced I was leaving, a few of my most difficult students came up to me in tears. 'Why are you leaving?' they asked. They didn't want me to leave. I never, never would have guessed they felt that way." Teachers must not be forced to quit before they are told they are appreciated.

A teacher we interviewed described how she had received a letter of appreciation from a former student at the beginning of a new school year. She said, "That one letter was enough to inspire me through the entire school year." Another teacher shared how she had moved from one school to the next. The two schools were doing the same curriculums and programs, so she couldn't figure out why she felt so much better at the new school. She eventually realized that at the new school she was consistently being told by the principal and assistant principal what a good job she was doing. The difference between the two schools was not the workload or the students, it was the appreciation she felt. And when she was offered higher pay to teach at another school, she turned it down. She wanted to stay loyal to where she felt valued and appreciated.

Concluding Thoughts

In our work with the 8,000 *Leader in Me* schools, we work from the foundational paradigm that every student can be a leader. Attempts are made to allow opportunities for all students to lead, to serve others, and to be appreciated. It makes a powerful impact on the school culture.

Students can be cruel to themselves, wallowing in self-doubt and low self-worth. So, when entrusting students with responsibilities, don't think of it as giving them a job. Think of it as giving students the gift of self-worth.

Yes, there always seems to be a handful of students who appear on the surface to have an overabundance of self-worth. They are constantly bragging and boasting about themselves. And a teacher may even be tempted to try to humble them. But don't be fooled. Students who constantly boast about themselves may, in fact, be low in intrinsic self-worth and desperately seeking attention from extrinsic sources. They may be the students who are in most need of being entrusted with a leadership responsibility, in most need of being given an opportunity to do service learning, or in most need of being told they are appreciated.

Which brings us to a good place to re-highlight the interactive nature of the leadership skillsets and their matching basic needs. When students are given opportunities to be leaders, to participate in service-learning opportunities, or to be told they are appreciated, they not only feel increased self-worth, they also feel greater connection, meaning, and hope. That is because the basic needs we have highlighted are constantly interacting in ways that build self-worth and strengthen overall positive well-being.

The Challenge

Select one. To help students feel more self-worth, create and implement a plan for how you will

- provide them with meaningful responsibilities,
- involve them in doing service for others, or
- express appreciation for their leadership and service.

5

Helped Me Through a Hard Time

This may be the most impressive story in the book.

Laura was in her 90s and facing her third bout with cancer. Her husband had passed away 27 years earlier, and it had been a battle for her to go solo for so long.

One night, Laura was awakened at 2:30 a.m. by the sound of loneliness whispering all kinds of discouraging thoughts into her ears. They caused her to doubt her physical and emotional capacity to endure another series of treatments. Calmness refused to come to her rescue.

Then something interesting happened. The lyrics of a song began to echo back and forth within the chambers of Laura's disheartened mind. "Be happy, happy all day long," repeated a phrase from the chorus.

The lyrics reminded Laura of times in her life when she was happy. The more she reflected on those happy times, the more her body relaxed. The more her body relaxed, the more the peace she so desperately sought returned.

So did her sleep.

The Need for Resilience

Laura's story is a simple one. It ended peacefully that night. So why might it be the most impressive story in the book?

What is so remarkable about Laura's story is that it was her second grade teacher who taught her that song. Nearly a century later, Laura's long-deceased teacher was still helping her through hard times. No one knows the full length of a teacher's influence.

Today's students have their own emotional battles to wage at all hours of the day and night. Difficulties making friends. Inequities. Body image issues. Poverty. Broken relationships. School pressures. Family conflicts. Violence. Homework. Worries about the future. Passing exams. Balancing all the expectations placed on them. And so on. Some challenges deal with what happens *to* students; others deal with what happens *within* students. Perhaps the greatest challenge students face is believing in themselves.

Not all hard times are equal. Some hard times are trivial, others are tragic. There is a clear difference between students who are having a tough day and students who are having a tough life. Being sad because you missed the start of a movie is not the same as being sad because you are chronically depressed. Furthermore, not all students are equally resilient. What is trauma to one student is a mere annoyance to another.

The main focus of this chapter is on the types of challenges that most people would consider minor, or an everyday part of life. In fact, the best practices in this chapter apply to any students, including those who are not facing hard times. However, before we delve into those best practices and the more minor issues, it is important to highlight a few of the more major mental health challenges that some students face. Why? Because while we do not encourage teachers to try to be therapists, we do encourage them to have a basic understanding about mental health matters.

Something that makes helping students with mental health challenges difficult is that many of them go to great efforts to hide their woes and worries. In a recent survey of 1,500 U.S. students ages 15–19 conducted by the National 4-H Council and the Harris Poll, 79 percent of students indicated that they wished there was a safe space in school for them to talk about mental health issues. Yet, 67 percent said they feel pressure to keep their emotions to themselves. So instead of talking with a trusted adult, they rely on social media as their main source for learning about mental health issues.[1]

But how might teachers respond if they notice a student appearing to have a mental health issue? Or what might teachers do if a student *does* want to talk about an emotional challenge?

On one end of the spectrum are the teachers who try to take on the role of therapist and "fix" students. At the other end are the teachers who say "Mental health is not my job!" and do nothing. Neither end of that spectrum is ideal.

When asked to identify the biggest challenge her 40,000 students face, Dr. Astrid Tuminez, president of Utah Valley University, replied, "Definitely mental health. This is an epidemic across the nation that keeps me up at night." That is why she insists that mental health is the job of everyone. She tells her faculty that while mental health may not be the job they were hired to do, they are on "the front line" and must observe and be alert to students' emotional states.[2]

Fortunately, it is an increasingly rare educator who thinks that a teacher should have no role in addressing students' positive well-being.[3] But how big of a role should teachers play? In reflecting on how to answer that question, a saying comes to our minds: "You may not stop all the storms of life or pause the roaring seas, but you can help to calm the sailors."

When attempting to calm the sailors, it is helpful for teachers to be familiar with two areas of mental health research: adverse childhood experiences, often referred to as ACEs, and the interpersonal theory of suicide. Why? Because global estimates indicate that one out of every six students will at some point struggle with a challenge that is related to one or both of the research areas.[4]

Adverse Childhood Experiences

It is said that trauma has a memory. Adverse childhood experiences (ACEs) are traumatic experiences that have negative effects on students' well-being and, if not addressed, may remain with them into adulthood. Examples of ACEs are:

- economic hardships (tied for the "most common")
- divorce or separation of parents (tied for "most common")
- emotional, physical, or sexual abuse
- exposure to alcohol or drug abuse at home
- exposure to mental illness or suicide at home
- a severe illness or accident
- witnessing violence inside or outside the home
- the death of a loved one
- a natural weather disaster
- homelessness
- a harsh health issue, epidemic, or pandemic
- bullying or discrimination[5]

ACEs may be buried for years, only to be triggered later in a student's life. This can lead to mild flashbacks, headaches, and loss of sleep and cause toxic stress reactions in children, such as intense fear or helplessness. ACEs can even stunt normal physical and mental development and increase the risk of students struggling with alcoholism, drug abuse, suicide, depression, and obesity.[6]

The higher the number of ACEs a student experiences, the more likely they are to struggle in school and the more likely they are to face emotional or behavioral challenges in adulthood. Data from 50,000 participants in a National Survey of Children's Health (NSCH) indicate that one out of five U.S. students have experienced two or more ACEs. Some races and ethnicities experience more ACEs on average than others.[7] And not all students are equally affected by ACEs. So it would be inappropriate to assume that teachers respond to all students with the same strategies.

What we already know is that teachers have at least some potential to help students survive trauma. There are several strategies that teachers can apply to help prevent, reduce, or heal the negative effects of ACEs, including the best practices in this chapter. None is more powerful than having a supportive connection with one or more stable adults![8] Positive adult connections help turn toxic stress into tolerable stress. Nevertheless, if a teacher suspects a student has experienced multiple ACEs and is struggling, that teacher is, again, advised to seek the guidance of a school counselor.

Interpersonal Theory of Suicide

This next area of research is highly sensitive and must be treated as such. Each case and circumstance is unique.

Though a student dying by suicide is still relatively rare, suicide is now the second leading cause of death among adolescents in developed countries and the fourth leading cause worldwide. Female attempts outnumber male attempts three to one, though male attempts are four times more likely to be fatal.[9] One suicide is too many. We want students thinking about how to enjoy and optimize life, not about how to end it.

The roots and routes to suicide are complex. One of the most substantiated theories that attempts to explain the *whys* of suicide is the interpersonal theory of suicide proposed by Dr. Thomas Joiner.[10] At the risk of oversimplifying such a personal topic and nuanced theory, the following diagram is our attempt to capture major components of the theory.

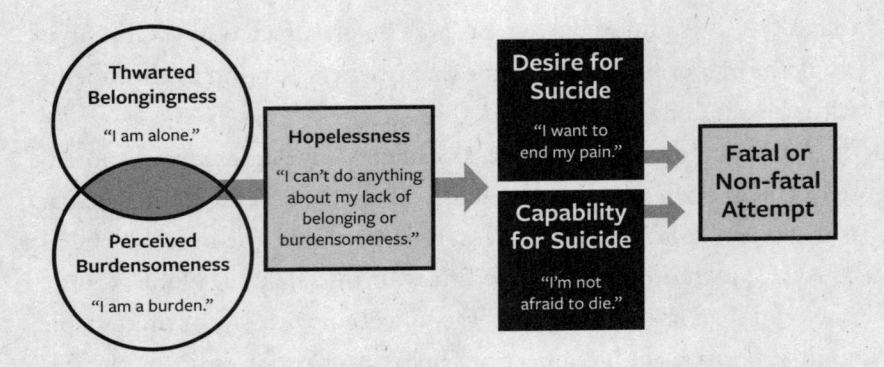

As highlighted by the black boxes, students are most at risk of attempting to take their own lives when they have both the *desire* <u>and</u> the *capability* for suicide.

The Desire for Suicide: Students do not generally think one day "I want to end my pain and take my life," and then immediately attempt to do it. It is far more likely that they have been thinking about suicide as a way to escape their pain for some time, whether it be social, emotional, physical, or even intellectual pain. This is sometimes referred to as *suicide ideation*.

According to the theory, a student's desire for suicide typically arises out of three beliefs:

1. **Thwarted belongingness.** *("I am alone. People don't like me.")* Of the risk factors that lead to suicide attempts, thwarted belongingness is the strongest. It comes from students' beliefs that they are not a valued part of a family or circle of friends. They feel lonely and unaccepted and may gradually separate themselves from social situations to escape feelings of rejection. Students can have numerous loving family relations and friends and still perceive themselves as isolated and not connected.

2. **Perceived burdensomeness.** *("I am a burden. People are better off without me.")* Perceived burdensomeness comes from students' beliefs that others would be better off without them

being around. A serious physical illness, ongoing family conflict, incarceration, chronic shame, and self-hate are common factors that fuel students' belief that they are a burden. Once again, this belief can occur even when other people do not perceive the student to be a burden.

Note: In most cases, neither thwarted belongingness nor perceived burdensomeness will be sufficient on its own to get students thinking about suicide. Rather, it is the combination of the two that increases the risk, as is represented by the overlapping shaded portion of the two circles in the diagram.

3. **Hopelessness.** (*"I cannot do anything about my thwarted belongingness or my perceived burdensomeness."*) As powerful as thwarted belongingness and perceived burdensomeness may be, if young people can see hope that they can do something about their lack of belonging or their perceived burdensomeness, they will not have a desire to die. This is why one of the best things a trusted teacher can do for a despondent student is to offer consistent words of hope that relief from their pain is possible. They are not helpless.

The Capability for Suicide: For every student who attempts suicide, it is estimated that 20 more will have thought about it without acting on that thought. One reason is because they lack the capability or courage to follow through. People will more naturally do anything to live.

So why do some students act on their desires and most don't? Once again, there is typically not only one reason. It is more likely a combination of risk factors that contribute to a student having the capability to act on their desires. Common factors include:

- access to lethal means, such as guns;
- adverse reactions to medications;
- chronic mental disorders, especially mood disorders;
- severe physical illness or disability;
- frequent family conflict, yelling in the home;

- abuse of alcohol or other drugs;
- a connection with someone who died by suicide;
- being part of a marginalized group;
- a lack of access to mental healthcare;
- loss of a close relationship;
- a history of being bullied;
- excessive social media use, especially in females; and
- a greater fear of social embarrassment than physical death.

Note that many of the risk factors that increase a student's capability for suicide are far beyond teachers'—and even parents'—influence or control. Note also that very often there is no logical reason or outward explanation for why a young person considers suicide. However, when a young person has previously attempted suicide, there is a legitimate concern that they will gradually grow less fearful or numb to the physical pain that comes with an attempt. That is why previous attempts at suicide are among the best predictors of future suicide attempts. So do not become complacent if a student has made one attempt but now seems to be doing fine.[11] And be extra vigilant when one student dies by suicide because the potential for copycat suicides is real, even among students who did not know the deceased student.

It is common for teachers or parents to see absolutely no warning signs of suicide. Others may see signs and go to great, great lengths to prevent a suicide from happening. Tragically, sometimes even their Herculean efforts are unable to prevent the tragedy. And to be on the safe side, do not downplay a casual comment from a student, such as "I'd be better off going to sleep and not waking up." One teacher spotted a student's doodle that contained an image of a tombstone with the caption, "I'd be better off dead." That teacher did not dismiss the doodle as a joke but rather sought the help of a counselor. It likely saved the student's life.

So there are two areas of research with which teachers are advised to have some familiarity. Again, the intent is not for teachers to take on the role of a therapist. Rather, it is to see their role as being on the front line, observing students' needs, and seeking help for any who may require professional attention. It is to help calm the sailors.

As indicated, the primary focus of this chapter is to help students to better deal with their more minor hard times. As teachers apply the following best practices, students will become even more resilient than they already are. The more resilient students are, the more hope they have, the more able they are to rise to challenges, and the more appreciative they are of their blessings.[12] And, from an academic perspective, the more ready they are to learn. For as Dr. Linda Darling-Hammond observes: "If you're fearful, if you're anxious, if you're distracted about something that's happened to you, you literally can't learn. Your brain shuts down. So it's essential to give kids social and emotional tools that allow students to recover from the challenges that they have experienced."[13]

What follows are three best practices that teachers can utilize to help students better deal with their more minor hard times and to grow their resilience. When applying the best practices, remember that each student's situation is unique and deserves to be treated as such. And once again, remember that the best practices in this book and in this chapter apply to increasing the positive well-being of all students, not just those who are struggling.

What were some of the hard times you experienced
while in school? How did you overcome them?

Three Best Practices for Growing Resilience

According to the research literature and the comments from the teachers and former students we interviewed, three positive best practices teachers can *do* to help students through their more minor hard times and to expand their resilience are:

My teacher . . .

- listened with empathy.
- helped me see the good in my world.
- made time for fun and relaxation.

Listened with Empathy

A vital step in helping students through a difficult time is to help them to feel understood. This requires listening.

A new student named Thomas was sent to Muriel's office by a substitute teacher. The substitute had attempted to correct Thomas's misbehavior in a way that he felt was too harsh. He took offense and yelled, "That's not how teachers talk to students at our school!" He then called her an idiot.

By the time Thomas arrived at Muriel's office he had spun himself into a frenzied fit of anger. Muriel could see he needed a cooling down period before a meaningful conversation could be held, so she invited him to help her sort some materials. He agreed.

After sorting for a while, Thomas turned to Muriel and said, "You don't know my real father, do you?"

Muriel replied, "No. I've not met your real father."

Thomas went on. "My real father got mad one day and jumped in front of a train. It killed him." Thomas witnessed it. Muriel didn't quite know what to say. She listened some more.

Thomas next blurted out, "You also don't know my real momma, do you? My real momma held a knife to my throat and said she would kill me if I didn't do what she wanted." He used hand motions to demonstrate how his mother had pretended to slit his throat. "So these people," Thomas went on, "came to our house and said it was not safe for me to be with my mom. They took me and put me with the parents I'm with now."

Can you imagine how Muriel's thoughts of how to best take corrective action were evolving with every sentence?

With some investigation, Muriel learned that Thomas started having issues with separation anxiety after being removed from his home. The mere fact that he was dealing with a substitute teacher was hard on him. When the substitute spoke harshly to him, it was more than he could handle. That was when he lost it.

Consider another example. A student was caught stealing food from the cafeteria. Muriel had every right to suspend her. But first, she gave the girl the opportunity to explain her behavior. The girl talked. Muriel listened.

By the time the girl was finished telling Muriel about how she hadn't had any food at home for two days, and about some of her other home experiences, Muriel was in tears. She couldn't condone the stealing, but she also couldn't condone the fact that she and her staff were not more aware of the girl's dire need to be fed or her desperate need to be understood.

In both cases, any teacher or principal would have been justified in immediately scolding and disciplining the students. But would that have resolved the situations or just festered them? Would Muriel have ever gotten to the root of the issues? Not likely.

Many teachers worry about how to best talk with students who have emotional and social concerns. They want to know the exact right words to say, when what the teachers really need to know is how to best listen.

We attended a conference for administrators on the topic of suicide prevention and will not forget the opening statement made by a medical professional. "Let me begin by taking a burden off your shoulders," she said. "When a student approaches you with a heavy emotional issue, such as contemplating suicide, don't worry about the right words to say. Just listen! Don't try to fix the problem. Just listen! Then do your best to engage the student with a school counselor. Leave the diagnosis and solutions to them."

Listening may not be the panacea for all social or emotional woes, but at times it may be the only treatment a student needs. At a minimum, listening may be the only way a teacher will detect that a student is struggling.

It is not always easy to spot a student who is going through a hard time. After examining a string of four university student suicides, Stanford University researchers coined the term *duck syndrome*. It refers to how a duck appears when gliding across a pond. Above the surface, the duck's progress seems effortless. Below the surface, however, its feet are paddling frantically.[14] Each of the four university students who died by suicide had projected above-the-surface appearances that portrayed them as enjoying the best times of their lives. Yet beneath the calm, happy surface, each had been paddling with all their might to stay afloat.

It is easy for teachers to assume that everything is okay with top performing students, and to put their focus on students who are low performing. Don't be fooled. Top students are among the best at putting on a wide smile in public when, in reality, they are gasping for emotional air amid all the weighty expectations heaped upon them.

In most situations, all teachers need to do to satisfy a student's desire to be listened to and understood is to practice active listening skills. This includes making good eye contact, not interrupting, and signaling with body language that they are giving undivided attention. However, in cases when teachers sense there is something in a student's behavior that signals a highly emotional issue, then a higher form of listening is appropriate. It is called *empathic listening*.

A variety of experts have offered practical steps for empathic listening.[15] Consider the following three.

Step 1: Find truth in what the student is saying.

Even when you are convinced that what a student is saying is unreasonable or not entirely true, find some common agreement with what the student says. You do not need to agree with all the student says, just point out the areas of common agreement. Dr. David Burns refers to this as a *disarming technique* because it helps to calm the student and defuse emotions. It signals that you are willing to listen without any intent to judge or prove the student wrong.[16]

Step 2: Listen for content and feelings—both.

Empathic listening is your best attempt to place yourself figuratively in another person's shoes so you can see the world through their eyes, not your eyes. Through their thoughts, not your thoughts. Dr. Burns identified two types of empathy: thought empathy and feeling empathy.

> **Thought empathy:** Thought empathy focuses on the *content* of what is said. It involves listening to what a student says, then restating in your own words the main content of what was said. For example, if a student says, "I have three tests this week and I don't know how I'm going to prepare for all of them," you might reply: "It sounds like you have a lot of studying to do and you don't know how you can do it all." This involves listening with your ears to gather facts.
>
> **Feeling empathy:** Feeling empathy focuses on the student's *feelings*, their emotions. It involves listening to what students say and then reflecting back to them the feelings you think you heard them express. It requires listening with your ears for content and voice tones, with your eyes for body language, and with your heart for emotions. So, to the student who is worried about taking multiple tests, you might simply add to your original response, "You seem overwhelmed."

With both content empathy and feeling empathy, you are not evaluating what the student is saying. You are not giving them advice. You are not trying to top their story with your story by saying something like, "You think that's bad. I had one week with five tests!" You are not interrupting their story to give them your premature solutions.

When students hear their contents and feelings received and reflected, they feel understood. But to correctly capture both content empathy and feeling empathy is not always easy or efficient. It may require some effort and time to get below the surface of what a student is thinking and feeling. The conversation might go something like this:

Student: "I have three tests this week, and I don't know how I'm going to prepare for all of them."

Teacher: "It sounds like you have a lot of studying to do, and you don't know how you can do it all. You sound overwhelmed."

Student: "I really don't know how I can do well on all the tests. I'm worried I might fail them all."

Teacher: "You seem worried that you won't do well on all of the tests."

Student: "I am worried. After all, it's the same week my mom needs my help around the house."

Teacher: "So in addition to the three tests, your mom is needing your help. And that, too, is causing you stress?"

Student: "Yeah. She's having some medical tests done, and I am more worried about her tests than I am about my tests."

Teacher: "You're really worried about your mother's health."

Student: "Yeah. She and my dad are acting strange. It seems like something is wrong and they're not telling me the whole story."

Teacher: "It sounds like you are worried that there is more to your mother's medical issues than your parents are telling you."

Student: "Well, I've noticed Mom crying a lot lately. She and my dad are fighting more, too. So it could be that something besides her medical issues is worrying her."

Teacher: "The arguing and crying seem to be the thing that worries you most."

Student: "Well, some of the fighting and crying relates to me. Sometimes, I feel like such a burden to them. I think everyone might be better off if I wasn't around."

And on the conversation continues. In fact, the conversation may go on for some time. But notice how the teacher did not jump in with her own stories or advice. She could have immediately given the student tips on how to study for multiple tests or could have said something like, "Don't worry. All parents argue at times." And yet the teacher never would have learned what was truly worrying the student, since the student would have never been given the chance to express her worry about being a burden on her family.

Step 3: Ask clarifying questions.

When you have done your best to listen empathically yet are still not certain that you understand the contents or the feelings of what a student is saying, ask *clarifying* questions. For example, "It sounds like you are (name the feeling) because of (say the content). Is that correct?" Or "If I understand you correctly, you feel (name the feeling) that (say the content). Is that what you are saying?"

Refrain from asking *judgment* questions like, "Why did you do a silly thing like that?" Avoid *probing* questions such as, "Were you this difficult as a child?" Your role at this point is not to evaluate, analyze, or critique the student. You are simply trying to clarify what you have heard and ensure you understand correctly.

If in your listening you hear, "Sometimes I feel like a burden. Everyone would be better off if I wasn't around," the student may be joking. But do not assume it. It may be a sensitive topic but it is fully appropriate to be very direct and ask: "Are you thinking about taking your life?" Asking about suicide can be a crucial step toward getting the student the help they need. If the student's answer has any hint of "Yes," give them hope that things can be mended. Assure them that they are not a burden. Try to persuade them to go with you to get help.

Again, all that is required for most conversations is active listening skills. Empathic listening is only needed when a student is emotional, when deep feelings are being expressed, or you don't feel you understand.

The reality is that most students will not approach a teacher with an emotional concern. They will prefer a friend, parent, or other trusted adult. And that is okay. However, to be at least viewed as approachable, consider the following suggestions.

Be a Trusted, Caring Adult

Connect with students early on so they come to see you as a trusted, supportive, and approachable adult. Students care more that you care about them than they care that you correctly follow the exact steps of empathic listening.

Create Opportunities for Listening

Create moments before, during, or after class to walk around and listen to what students are talking about. What is on their minds? Ask how things are going. Leadership experts Tom Peters and Bob Waterman call this "Management by Wandering Around."[17] Of course, we prefer "Leadership by Wandering Around." Others refer to it as going on a "Listening Tour."

A middle school teacher shared: "This is a tough stage of life for students. So, as students are completing assignments, I wander about the classroom. Inevitably, a student or two will try to talk with me. Through those short conversations, students come to trust me."

We have observed elementary teachers using tools or routines such as having students close their eyes and give either a thumbs-up or thumbs-down signal. Thumbs-up lets the teacher know things are okay. Thumbs-down indicates they are not doing well and could use a chat. Other teachers use other listening routines and systems to let students know they care about more than their test scores.

Our good friend and colleague, Dr. Lesley Eason, shared the following recollection of teaching high school English literature and listening to a student who was going through a hard time of life:

> I figured out very early on that my students would probably never love William Shakespeare as much as I did. But I also figured out that if I took an interest in my students and what they had to say, then they might take a little more interest in who William Shakespeare was and what he had to say.
>
> Johnny was one of those students. It was clear from the beginning that he had little interest in Shakespeare, or in school itself.
>
> One day, Johnny's chair was empty. About 15 minutes into class, I received a message saying that he had gotten into a fight and was being suspended from school for three days. I was asked to send materials for him to work on during the suspension.
>
> Rather than just dropping the materials off at the front office, I went in search of Johnny. When I found him, he looked embarrassed to see me. He kept looking down. But we began to talk.
>
> Johnny lived in a tough neighborhood. That morning, he'd had a terrible argument with his parents. Money was hard to come by in their family, and that morning, Johnny had learned they were being kicked out of their house. On top of that, his little brother was being fussy, and Johnny almost missed his bus.
>
> The only thing I could do for Johnny that day was to listen. I didn't try to correct him or figure him out; I just listened and let him know there were people in the school who cared about him.
>
> When Johnny returned to school following his suspension, I could see he was still not too impressed with William Shakespeare. However, he lingered after class and approached me. He told me that he

appreciated that I had sought him out and listened. "I want to thank you for seeing me through that tough time," he said.

Dr. Eason takes pleasure in knowing that Johnny is currently employed as the media specialist in a middle school library. Students know him as one who is always there to encourage them and to listen. None of that would have likely happened had she not gone in search of Johnny and listened to what he had to say without judging him or filling him with advice.

Avoid Trivializing Even Small Concerns

When students voice even the smallest emotional concerns, do not respond with words such as "Oh, that's no big deal" or "Don't be so weak." Students may be testing you to see how you handle a small matter before revealing a deeper matter. Likewise, if they hear a teacher mock other students' challenges as being trivial, they will not approach that teacher with their challenges.

Hold Your Remedies and Advice

Resist rushing in with solutions before you truly understand the underlying concern. As Henry Wadsworth Longfellow once wrote:

Every heart has its secret sorrows,
which the world knows not,
and oftentimes we call a man cold,
when he is only sad.[18]

Often, the emotion that is being outwardly expressed by a student is anger. But as a general rule, anger is never the first emotion. Anger is what Dr. Marshall Rosenberg calls "an alarm clock for an unmet need."[19] So when students approach you and say they are angry, assume from the beginning that something else exists beneath their anger, whether it is a different negative emotion such as sorrow, loneliness, hopelessness, discouragement, fear, frustration, jealousy, or grief, or a different unmet basic need, such as a lack of sleep. Listen empathically to the student until you get at least one layer beneath the anger. As neuropsychologist Dr. Jerome Schultz of the Harvard Medical School puts it, "If you can read the need, you can meet the need."[20] If the need appears more than trivial, hold your advice and consider involving a school counselor.

Educate Yourself About Mental Health

Not all students know how to express their emotions with words, so they end up expressing them with their behaviors. Thus, teachers must learn how to listen with their eyes and to proactively reach out to students who show signs of need. A first step is to become familiar with common warning signs, such as:

- withdrawal from family or friends;
- unusual changes in mood, sadness;
- persistent irritability, conflicts with friends;
- changes in eating patterns;
- hints of feeling worthless;
- struggles concentrating;
- not wanting to do fun things;
- threats of violent acts against self or others; and
- warnings from worried friends or family.

Warning signs typically come in combinations. They don't look the same in every student. So it is important for teachers to be trained on what the warning signs are and how to respond to the best of one's ability. It is also important for teachers to remember that, as Dr. W. Edwards Deming cautions, "It is not enough to do your best; you must know what to do, and then do your best."[21]

These suggestions for being more approachable as a listener remind us of the teacher who wrote: "Some students go through hell in their lives. For as long as I can be the one who is there to listen when they need it, I will be damned if I ever quit teaching."

When was a time you listened
empathically to a student?

> **Important!** Given the reality that most students are reluctant to approach a teacher or parent to ask for emotional help, all students deserve to be informed about crisis lines or counselors who they can turn to for help and say, "I need to talk with someone" or "I am worried about a friend." The intent is to get the student to a professional who is trained to assess and assist, and for teachers to be familiar with school policies regarding such situations.

Helped Me See the Good in My World

People seldom find happiness if all they are doing is waiting for it to come to them. They must proactively search out happiness and do their part to make it happen.

In general, more positive events happen in students' daily lives than negative events. Yet the negative events demand so much of a brain's attention that it takes a remarkable amount of concentration for their minds to attend to the positive events. Therefore, one of the best things a teacher can do for students is to create routines and opportunities for students to pause and see the good in their world.

But before we get into how a teacher might help students see the good in their world, let's first acknowledge that not all negative emotions or events are "bad" for people. Negative emotions provide valuable defense mechanisms that save people from danger. Negative events provide valuable growth opportunities in which students learn to mature and develop empathy.

It is likewise important to acknowledge that seeing the good in the world requires more than just smiling and acting positive. No students who are depressed or feeling lonely want to hear their teachers tell them, "Just put a smile on your face." No students who are being bullied want to hear their teacher suggest that they "just choose to be happy." Happiness does not come from ignoring reality or denying negative emotions.

Yet, while acknowledging those things, we must acknowledge that psychologists like Emily Esfahani Smith report that "Having a positive outlook is the most important predictor of resilience." She explains that people "who are resilient tend to be more positive and optimistic compared with less resilient folks; they are better able to regulate their emotions, and they are able to maintain their optimism through the most trying circumstances."[22] Dr. Martin Seligman adds that teaching students skills for optimism can safeguard them against depression—cutting the rates in half—and help them feel more able to control their destiny.[23] And Dr. Barbara Fredrickson notes that positivity not only makes people feel good, it changes how their minds work and opens their minds to learning. In this way, it can even transform their futures.[24]

So how do teachers balance the need to be both realistic and positive when helping students see the good in their world?

Three doable things teachers can choose from to help students see more good in their world are to provide opportunities for students to express gratitude, recall positive childhood experiences, and use positive self-talk.

Expressing Gratitude

Positive psychologists report that gratitude is vital to living a happy life. Dr. Robert Emmons of the University of California, Davis, is a world-leading expert on gratitude, and he defines gratitude as "a felt wonder, thankfulness, and appreciation for life."[25] The gratitude he refers to is genuine, and not just positive hype.

The Mayo Clinic, a leading medical institution, notes that if there existed a single pill that provided all the benefits that gratitude provides, everyone would be taking that pill daily.[26] As a few examples of gratitude's benefits, people who are consistently grateful are

- more energetic and hopeful;
- more likely to enjoy positive relationships;
- less likely to be depressed, anxious, lonely, or envious;
- better able to cope with stress and trauma;
- less likely to experience frustration and regret;
- less prone to anger and bitterness;
- more inclined to help others; and
- known to sleep better, exercise more, and live longer.[27]

Opportunities for students to express gratitude can be enjoyed through many simple in-class activities, such as:

- writing or texting a thank-you letter to a friend, family member, teacher, or role model;
- keeping a gratitude journal and recording three good things that happened each day for an entire week or more; and
- forming students into circle groups and having them go around their circle as many times as possible in five minutes, taking turns expressing things they are grateful for that week.

The more the opportunities to express gratitude are turned into routines rather than one-time events, the better. It often helps to narrow the gratitude topics for students. Instead of asking "What is one thing for which you are grateful?" ask a more specific question, such as: "What are you most thankful for about your family?" "What are you most grateful for at school?" "What are you most grateful for about one friend?" As the saying goes, "Creativity loves constraints."

Recalling Positive Childhood Experiences

Negativity breeds negativity. Positivity breeds positivity. A person cannot feed a negative mind and expect to feel and enjoy positive well-being.

This is why one of the most effective ways for students to counter-attack adverse childhood experiences (ACEs) is for them to recall positive childhood experiences (PCEs).[28] PCEs are memorable experiences that at one point in their lives brought the students joy.

When inviting students to recall and share positive experiences from their past—even small ones—it is again helpful to narrow the topics. As examples, invite them to share a time when they

- achieved a personal goal or milestone,
- participated in a positive school or community event,
- helped someone in need,
- did well on a difficult school assignment,
- apologized and felt good about it,
- were part of a team that achieved an honorable feat,
- created something of which they were proud,
- sacrificed so another person could benefit, or
- succeeded in learning a difficult skill or talent.

Opportunities for students to recall and share positive childhood experiences can be enjoyed in one-on-one conversations, small group or class discussions, or written assignments. The important thing is to get students recalling and sharing positive experiences on a consistent basis so they can see that they have within them what it takes to overcome hard times.

Using Positive Self-Talk

Students seldom encounter harsher critics than the one they see in the mirror. That is why helping students see the good in their world includes helping them see the good in themselves.

In the classic movie *The Sound of Music*, the main character, Maria, is shown leaving her role as a nun in a convent to become the governess for a strict military captain and his seven mischievous children. Worry is all over Maria's face as she wonders what her day will be like. What will her future be?

To calm her anxious nerves, Maria sings. Through the lyrics, she reminds herself that she has always held a longing for adventure, she has always wanted to do things she's never done, and she has always wanted to be out in the world and to be free. She confesses, however, that she is still seeking the courage she knows she lacks.

The more Maria sings, the more she instills in herself positive self-beliefs, like the intention to do better than her best. She insists that in a short time, those seven children will all look up to her. Eventually, her positive self-talk reaches a crescendo when she belts out that the world can all be hers. And by the time she arrives at the family's mansion, her positive self-talk has given her enough courage to mute her anxieties and ring the doorbell.[29]

Oscar Hammerstein II, who with Richard Rodgers wrote the songs for *The Sound of Music*, declared, "It is a modern tragedy that despair has so many spokespersons, and hope so few."[30] Nowhere is that truer than with self-critical students. When students' self-talk is consistently negative—"I'm terrible at math," "I'm horrible at making friends," "Nobody invites me to parties," or "The teachers all hate me"—over time, the students begin to accept those thoughts as facts. Their negative thoughts become their identities, their stories.

One of the best remedies for negative self-talk is for students to re-frame their stories into positive self-talk. For example, therapists who work with students recovering from trauma will often ask them to think back on a traumatic experience from their past and re-frame it through the lens of being a survivor, not a victim. As the young person thinks and talks positively about what they did well to overcome a past trauma, they recognize that they already possess strengths and strategies that can help them overcome their present trauma.

Making time for students to talk about what went well in their past—and why—is a strength-based, positive self-talk activity that can be done in pairs, in small groups, or as a class on a weekly or monthly basis. As each student responds to: "What went well in school today and why did it go well?" or "What went well this weekend?" and "What made it go well?" they come to see good in their world, and, more importantly, they come to see good in themselves.[31]

Positive self-talk must be realistic to be effective. Positive self-talk must not encourage students to deny reality or pretend they have no challenges. Positive self-talk will not spare students from all their hard times. But positive self-talk can be used to calm the sailors and remind them of strategies that will help them get through some of the storms they face in life.

In short, teachers teach critical thinking. Teachers teach creative thinking. Why not teach positive thinking by helping students see the good in their world?

> *What benefits do you see in giving*
> *students a chance to see the good—*
> *the positive—in their world?*

Made Time for Fun and Relaxation

Throughout the book we have cited multiple instances that demonstrate how students' social-emotional needs interact with their intellectual needs. What we have shared less of is how students' social-emotional needs interact with their physical needs.

Physical needs and social-emotional needs are highly interactive. For example, when students (and teachers) are battling an emotional or a social challenge, it can cause variations in their heartbeats, muscle pain, headaches, fatigue, panic attacks, and loss of sleep. Under heavy pressure, some students turn to alcohol, drugs, or disordered eating habits, each of which diminishes their physical well-being and may lead to addictions. In contrast, when students' social or emotional needs are being satisfied, they feel and perform better physically, even to the point of living longer.

Similarly, students' physical well-being impacts their social-emotional well-being. When students are healthy, safe, fed, and sufficiently rested, they feel better about their self-worth, enjoy more positive emotions, maintain stronger relationships, and are more pleased with who they are. On the other hand, when students' physical needs are not sufficiently satisfied, they feel increased anxiety, burdensomeness, sadness, and hopelessness. These are but a few examples.

As much as teachers might encourage students, they cannot force students to get enough sleep, eat their vegetables, or exercise regularly. Nevertheless, there are parts of students' physical well-being that teachers can influence, such as making time for students to give their brains a rest and to enjoy some relaxation and fun.

Dr. William Glasser was a medical doctor and psychiatrist, and one of the first researchers to emphasize the impact that relaxation and fun have on a person's positive well-being. He went so far as to declare that fun is a basic need.[32] Nowadays, virtually every neuroscientist, physician, physiologist, nutritionist, and psychologist proclaims that making time for fun and relaxation is not just a *nice* thing to do, it is a *vital* thing to do. It reduces negative emotions, lowers stress hormones, and increases feelings of joy.[33]

With all respect to secondary educators, most people agree that elementary educators are better overall at making time for students to enjoy fun and relaxation. Elementary students enjoy multiple outside recesses, and they take naps, sing lots of songs, and play all kinds of games. Toys are placed throughout their classrooms. Spaces and pillows are reserved for anxious or angry students who need or desire quiet time to calm themselves. Music often plays. Happy colors are splattered across their classroom walls. Some have pets.

And then, suddenly, the students transition to secondary school, and it is as if the time and resources for relaxation and fun—for giving students' brains a rest—evaporate. Classroom walls go dull. Students are told to stop talking and laughing in class. And very few teachers are caught singing songs or reading books to students.

Of course, some secondary teachers and classrooms are very engaging and pop with joy. In fact, looking back, many adults describe their secondary years as being one of the most fun times in their lives. Nevertheless, most would agree that more can be done at secondary levels to offer students a chance to relax and enjoy some fun.

Consider a few strategies that teachers at elementary and secondary schools use to offer students a little fun and relaxation.

Mindfulness

Taking breaks to relax throughout a school day helps to relieve stress, ease tension, and lessen worries for students (and teachers). Even 10 minutes can be enough to calm the mind and body. The 10 minutes can be optimized through use of mindfulness activities, such as brain games, breathing exercises, or meditation strategies.

In her book *Emotional Poverty*, Ruby Payne shares several brain activities for relaxing students. Examples include having students look at the ceiling, massage the nerves in their neck, think of a happy story about their future, stand and breathe deeply, pat their heart and stomach, or do tapping. She says that one of the fastest ways to calm a stressed or angry student is to have them drink a cup of cold water.[34]

Mindfulness activities also include experiencing small moments of "awe," such as taking a walk and noticing the beauties of nature. Getting outside of a classroom, stretching the body, and smelling fresh air can be re-energizing, especially when done with a friend.

Respect that not all students will dive into all mindfulness activities. They may need options or to take things slow. One person we interviewed talked about a psychology professor who had students do meditation exercises at the start of each class. The student found it agonizingly weird. Thirty years later, he has long forgotten the professor's lectures, yet he still uses the meditation techniques to help him relax or fall asleep.

Play and Exercise

Jonathan Haidt in his bestselling book *The Anxious Generation* uses several statistics to demonstrate that much of the dramatic rise in young people's anxieties occurred at the very same time when young people were transitioning from a "play-based childhood" to a "smartphone-based childhood." Instead of playing outdoors with friends and learning how to get along with each other, it seems that almost overnight students across the world began sitting in chat rooms interacting with faceless chat buddies. Instead of learning how to resolve disputes, take risks, or deal with friends who are different from them, they were learning how to be rid of them with the click of a mouse. He suggests that teachers allow time for students to become more "play-full" by providing more times to play together, whether in informal activities or structured games.[35]

Laura Huerta Migus, Executive Director of the Association of Children's Museums, says: "When we play, we are at our happiest, and we can withstand incredible hardships. When we play, we are engaging in complex interactions with each other, and we are building our brains. And when we play, those social interactions become relationships."[36]

Exercise is also essential to students' positive well-being. Physical exercise helps students be healthier and fight off depression, anxiety, and negative moods, particularly when the exercise involves doing something students like to do and doing it with friends.[37] Such activities can include dancing, biking, running, yoga, weightlifting, swimming, or other physical activities that get the body moving. Team sports also provide excellent opportunities for students to develop character traits and build skills such as teamwork, goal setting, leadership, and communication.

And let's not forget that learning itself can be a form of play. For some students, working on a class project in groups and with friends is all the fun they need to get them through a day. We have seen some major dances of joy happen when a student excels on an assignment or test. Many students build into their class schedules a few classes that they deem to be fun. It is all part of the joy of learning.

This is not meant to say that every class needs to be a party. But it is to say that students do need to be able to have some fun in what they are doing as part of growing their positive well-being. As one high school teacher told us: "My students work very hard, so I try to give them at least one Friday a month to do something fun in class—such as watch a movie—to remind them that school isn't all work and no play!" The students look forward to such days and usually offer fun ideas for what to do.

Music, Arts, and Reading

Inspirational music can help to calm the sailors.

As a principal, Dr. Beth Sharpe played calming music in the hallways for students before and after school and between classes. It visibly settled students' nerves and reduced their rambunctious behaviors. Some teachers play soothing music as students arrive to class or work on projects, while other teachers prefer to play upbeat songs with inspirational lyrics. Note that what is inspirational and relaxing music to one student may not be to another student, so teachers are wise to involve students when building a playlist.

Many students find relief from stress by doing crafts like woodworking, baking, ceramics, painting, or biking. The options here are nearly endless. One woman in her 70s told us about her middle school art teacher, Mr. Anderson. He taught her how to mix paints, sketch a landscape, and properly clean a brush. To this day, oil painting is her go-to source of stress relief. Whenever she gets tense, she grabs her brushes and loses herself on a piece of canvas. Mr. Anderson can rest in peace knowing that he has brought much relief to this woman over the years, and he can find joy in knowing that she still cleans her brushes precisely as he taught her to six decades ago.

School librarians and bibliotherapists argue that reading books will give students' brains more rest than watching a movie, listening to music, or visiting an art exhibit.[38] That assumes, of course, that students are reading books they enjoy.

Humor

We are reminded of the joke about the teacher who was leaving home to go to work one day. A neighbor called out "Have a happy day!" to which the teacher replied, "Thanks, but I have other plans."

We have never known a teacher who shows up to school with a plan to be unhappy. However, we have known teachers who show up happier than others. And it is our experience that the teachers who smile and enjoy a bit of humor are the same teachers students prefer to hang around. Humor drip-feeds students droplets of happiness throughout a day. Research even shows that the simple act of smiling provides stress relief for both sender and receiver.[39]

One man we interviewed shared how his high school chemistry teacher was within months of retirement and yet he had miraculously retained his sense of humor. He put fun into assignments and preparation for exams by having students memorize poems and clever phrases such as:

Once there was a chemist,
A chemist there is no more,
For what he thought was H20,
Was H2SO4.

The chemistry teacher also encouraged his students: "Be like protons. Be positive." Years later, the former student swears that H_2O (water) and H_2SO_4 (sulfuric acid) are the only two compound formulas he remembers, and he has never forgotten that protons are positive. So humor can not only have calming effects, it can also help a mnemonic device stick.

Some teachers tell jokes; others attempt riddles and puns. Some share funny videos; others tell funny stories. Any form of humor that is positive can have calming effects, whereas humor that mocks people, or is crude or cynical, does more harm than good, even if it may draw muted laughs from a few students.

Of course, some teachers are naturally funny, while others are not. If you are naturally not, consider entrusting a student, or a team of students, with the responsibility for being leaders of good humor. Invite them to share a funny joke, story, or video to begin a day.

The Physical Environment

One principal told us that her teachers used three methods of teaching: direct lessons, modeling, and placing messages on walls. The school's walls and ceilings were filled with positive messages of connection, meaning, hope, self-worth, resilience—and, yes, fun. Much of what was displayed on the walls was made by students. Students could feel better about themselves and uplifted just by being in the physical environment. Her school was enlightened by plenty of natural light to keep students engaged and alert.

What is your favorite way of giving students' brains and spirits a rest and allowing them to enjoy a little fun?

Temperance Factors

Even helping students through a hard time and building resilience can be taken too far.

Hard Times Are Laboratories of Learning

Adversity is a master teacher. It produces character, empathy, competence, and resilience in ways no other teaching strategies can.

Stress that is good for students is called *eustress*. It is the opposite of *distress*. When parents or teachers step in and try to resolve every challenge for students, they may prevent them from experiencing eustress and developing resilience. As Angela Duckworth observed: "I . . . worry about people who cruise through life, friction-free, for a long, long time before encountering their first real failure. They have so little practice falling and getting up again."[40]

Allowing students to struggle and figure out (within reason) their own strategies for building resilience is often the most empowering thing parents and teachers can do for students.

Not All Is Up to the Teacher

The ultimate responsibility for helping students through a hard time rests foremost with students themselves and their families. That includes the rare cases when a student chooses to resort to violence or self-harm. After such a tragic occurrence, it is common for teachers, friends, or family members to place blame on themselves, to feel guilt, or to think, "What could I have done? What could I have said?" Such attempts at self-blame are non-fruitful paths. It is better to ask, "What can I do today to make life easier for those who are in grief and dealing with the pain?" Or "What might I do to help prevent this from happening with other students in days ahead?" It is a positive, forward-thinking way of making life better for others, as opposed to a negative, backward-looking way of clinging to regret and remorse.

Don't Forget the Adults!

Teachers are natural helpers. But who is helping the helpers?

What teacher doesn't benefit from a friend who listens empathically to them, who helps them see the good in their world, or who brings a little fun and relaxation into their life?

While empathy and compassion are noble qualities of teachers, too much of either can cause a teacher to experience *compassion fatigue*. This leads to burnout, anxiety, and physical exhaustion. Doctors say that from birth to three months, the most important person to monitor is not the new baby but the new mom. Could this also be true for new teachers? From the first day of school to the end of the first term, might the most important people to be monitoring be the first-year teachers, not the first-year students?

And don't forget the seasoned teachers. One teacher was talking with us about mental wellness and accidentally referred to it as mental "hellness." It was a total slip of the tongue. Yet the more we listened to what was happening in her family life, the more *mental hellness* seemed the appropriate term. Even the most seasoned teachers experience hard times. Everyone can use some care.

Concluding Thoughts

As authors, we have experienced our own hard times in life. We have felt grief, trauma, loneliness, health challenges, heartbreak, and struggles of other types. We both lost parents to death during our early school years. We know something of physical and emotional pain. And we in no way treat lightly what so many students are going through, much of which is far worse than what we experienced.

No one is exempt from hard times. That is why the best practices in this chapter are meant for all students, not just those going through a major challenge. Each best practice contains positive skills for positive living. Each builds connections. Each strengthens resilience.

Resilience begins with the belief that broken things can be mended and the acceptance that not all things will be mended. Some students may feel they are so broken that they cannot imagine how their challenges can be overcome. Such times are when students benefit from the support of a trusted teacher. As the Center on the Developing Child at Harvard University reminds us: "Resilience requires relationships, not rugged individualism. . . . Despite the widespread yet erroneous belief that people need only draw upon some heroic strength of character, science now tells us that it is the reliable presence of at least one supportive relationship and multiple opportunities for developing effective coping skills that are the essential building blocks for strengthening the capacity to do well in the face of significant adversity."[41]

So, when the storms of life hit, hopefully students will connect with a supportive teacher who knows how to listen empathically, who gives students opportunities to see the good in their world, and who provides opportunities to relax and have a little fun. A teacher who believes in them and helps them to believe in themselves.

Important!

We have repeatedly emphasized that the seven leadership skillsets described in these pages are meant to help students deal with minor hard times, not major mental health challenges.

However, all seven leadership skillsets and their best practices do have the potential to prevent or minimize some of the more major mental health challenges. For example, think back on the three beliefs that contribute to a student having a desire for suicide:

Thwarted belongingness: *"I am alone."*
Perceived burdensomeness: *"I am a burden."*
Hopelessness: *"I can't do anything about my situation."*

Now, think of the leadership skillsets we have covered thus far. The first skillset focused on helping students to *feel belonging*, or what we referred to as connectedness. The next three skillsets focused on helping students to find meaning in their lives, to see they have strengths, and to be entrusted with worthwhile responsibilities. All three of those skillsets strengthen students' personal beliefs that they are *not a burden*.

The focus of this chapter and the next two skillsets center on helping students to build resilience, to develop self-efficacy, and to help them see their growth. These three skillsets help students to dismiss their feelings of hopelessness and see that they can do something about their challenges. In this way, the leadership skillsets and their best practices work together to turn negative beliefs into positive beliefs, as shown in the table below.

We'd be unrealistic to claim that these skillsets and best practices will remove or relieve all hard times for students or prevent all acts of self-harm, but all seven leadership skillsets have the potential to work

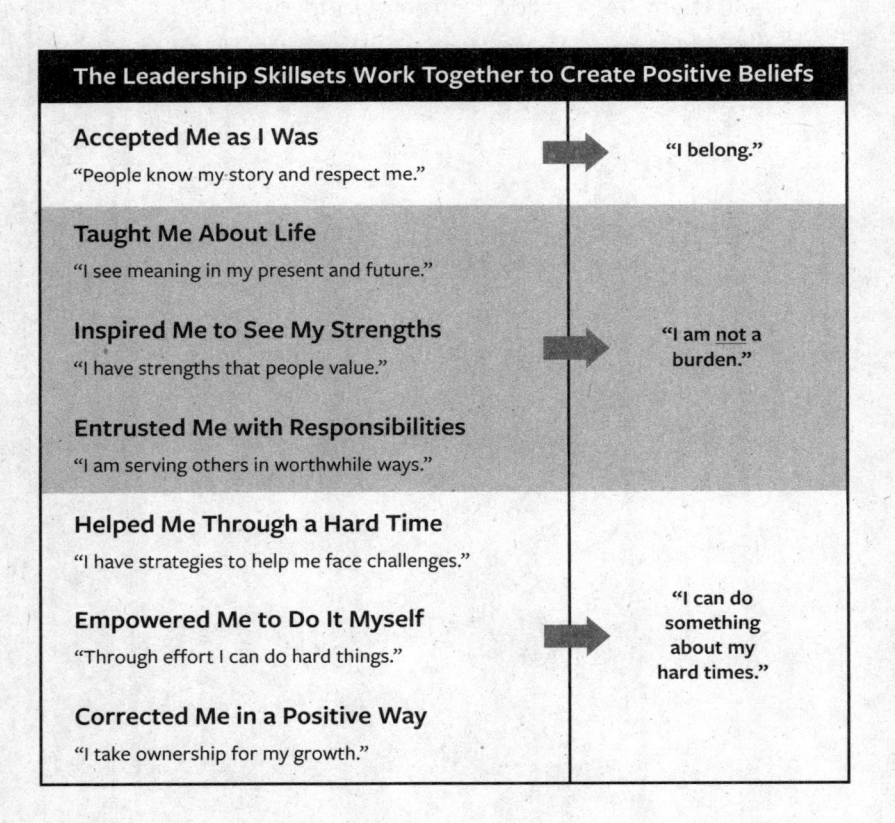

The Leadership Skillsets Work Together to Create Positive Beliefs	
Accepted Me as I Was "People know my story and respect me."	"I belong."
Taught Me About Life "I see meaning in my present and future."	
Inspired Me to See My Strengths "I have strengths that people value."	"I am **not** a burden."
Entrusted Me with Responsibilities "I am serving others in worthwhile ways."	
Helped Me Through a Hard Time "I have strategies to help me face challenges."	
Empowered Me to Do It Myself "Through effort I can do hard things."	"I can do something about my hard times."
Corrected Me in a Positive Way "I take ownership for my growth."	

together to prevent—or at least minimize—some of students' most difficult challenges and negative thoughts.

Again, they may not stop all the storms of life or pause the raging seas, but each has the potential to calm the sailors.

The Challenge

Select one. To enable students to develop more resilience, create and implement a plan for how you will

- listen with empathy,
- help them see the good in their world, or
- provide time and activities for fun and relaxation.

6

Empowered Me to Do It Myself

Alliteration is the repetition of words that start with the same letter and are placed next to or near each other in a sentence, such as "Peter Piper picked a peck of pickled peppers." We had some alliterative fun in creating our version of *The Fable of the Gullible Gulls*.[1]

In the village harbor lived a frolicking flock of seagulls. Each morning, they were awakened by the wobbly wakes of the bobbing boats heading out to salty seas. Their dandy decks were filled with friendly fishermen who worked willfully to feed their faithful families.

The gulls, too, had been born to be fine fishers. But contrary to their natural natures, they had been taught to do nearly nothing. Nearly nothing, that is, but to wait and wait as they dizzily dozed on the shimmering shores of their happy harbor.

For as with prior generations, the gulls were gullibly waiting to be served a delightful dinner of savory seafood. Why? Because every evening the same parade of bobbing boats with friendly fishermen would reliably return with a hefty harvest of fatty fish.

It was with great sympathy that the friendly fishermen tossed their slimy scraps of icky innards to the gullible gulls. And it was with pleasure that the gullible gulls gleefully gulped every slippery swallow.

And all was well for the gullible gulls!

Yes, all was well until the dreary day when the bobbing boats and friendly fishermen did not reliably return. A serious storm had woefully wrecked their happy harbor, and the friendly fishermen had dreadfully disappeared. Off they had gone to a new peaceful port.

What did the gullible gulls do? They did exactly what they had been taught to do. Nearly nothing! Nearly nothing, that is, but to wait and wait. For none had been taught to fish or hunt on their own.

So there the gullible gulls did dizzily doze in hungry hopes that the bobbing boats would reliably return. That day never came.

The Need for Self-Efficacy

Like friendly fishermen feeding gullible gulls, there are friendly parents and teachers who think they are doing things *for* students when they are actually doing things *to* them.

Though this book focuses on what teachers can "do" to help students increase their positive well-being, it is equally important to consider what teachers and parents ought not to "do" for students. After all, the ultimate objective is for students to learn how to help themselves when facing difficulties in their relationships, emotions, and daily lives. As the ancient saying goes, "Give a man a fish and you feed him for a day. Teach a man to fish and you feed him for a lifetime."

Researchers use the term *self-efficacy* to describe students' beliefs that they can do things on their own. The American Psychological Association defines self-efficacy as "an individual's belief in his or her capacity to execute the behaviors necessary to produce specific performance attainments."[2] Self-efficacy enables students to think: "If I put in the effort, I can do this by myself. I can do hard things."

Students high in self-efficacy perform better academically, are more likely to take steps toward preventative health, are better at managing stress, and are more likely to say no to negative peer pressure and put more effort and grit into pursuing goals. These are only a few of the benefits students with self-efficacy enjoy.[3]

Some parents are so intent to see their child excel in life that they do things for their child that lessen the child's self-efficacy. They hover over their child to ensure that they make correct choices. They remove obstacles from their lives instead of teaching them how to overcome obstacles. They are essentially saying to their child, "I do not believe you can learn to do things on your own." The tragedy is when the child comes to believe those messages for themselves.

Constantly rescuing students from challenges produces helplessness, not self-efficacy. Neuropsychotherapist Britt Frank says: "Children who have overprotective parents can develop depression and anxiety disorders, struggle in relationships, and have trouble with self-esteem and self-confidence. While the damage may be unintentional, the impact is undeniable."[4] Young people's self-efficacy is not strengthened when adults do for them what they can do for themselves.

Some teachers roll their eyes in disgust when seeing parents hover over their children, only to then, as teachers, hover over their students. They go soft when grading assignments because they do not want students to be sad or parents to be mad. They make constant exceptions to rules rather than holding students accountable. They reduce the amount of rigor they require because they want students to view them as one of the "fun" teachers. Such actions may please students in the short term, but in the long term they give students a false sense of self-efficacy. That false sense of self-efficacy is certain to be crushed when students come upon difficult exams, rigorous career demands, or other stiff adversities.

In defense of students, many try to take the initiative to do things on their own and try to take charge of their lives, only to experience one failure or rejection after another. When time after time their efforts to do well in school, to make friends, to excel in sports, or to overcome challenges end in failure, they want to give up. When they cannot see a connection between their efforts and their outcomes, they start to think, "Why even try? Nothing I do matters." They grow into a state of *learned helplessness*, which is the opposite of self-efficacy.[5]

So how does a teacher help students develop self-efficacy?

An important first step is to teach students about the power of their choices. And a good starting place for that is to give them a brief overview of the history of psychology and, more specifically, the question of: "What causes people to think and behave the way they do?"

Over the years, three prevailing explanations have emerged in response to that question:

A. Biology. "It is my genetics, my brain, and my health that cause me to think and behave the way I do. This is just the way I am. I was born this way. There is nothing I can do about it. I am a product of my *body*."

B. Environment. "It is my upbringing, parents, neighborhood, and things that happened to me that cause me to think and behave the way I do. I am a product of my *circumstances*."

C. Choices. "It is the choices I make that cause me to behave the way I do and to achieve the outcomes I do. My destiny is determined by my decisions. I am a product of my *choices*."

Which of the three explanations do you think is correct? Is it: A. Biology; B. Environment; or C. Choices? If you answered, "D. All of the above," you are both creative and correct.

One of the clearest examples is found in the research that attempts to answer one of life's other central questions: "What makes people happy?" Researchers estimate that roughly 50 percent of a person's happiness is due to biological and genetic sources, 10 percent is due to causes in their environment, and the remaining 40 percent is due to their intentional choices, as illustrated in the happiness pie chart below.[6]

What determines happiness?

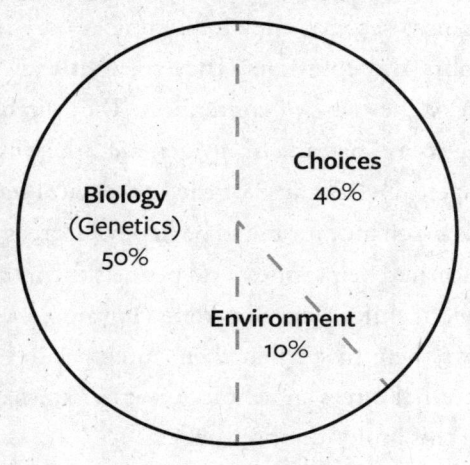

Of course, the percentages in the diagram are estimates. They differ from person to person. Nevertheless, the point that positive psychologists make with the pie chart is that people's choices significantly influence their happiness. Genes and environment cannot be blamed for all their challenges and problems. And since a person has minimal control over their environment and even less control over their genetics, their choices turn out to be the one causal factor over which people have the most control. So if students want to increase their happiness—or self-efficacy—their best option is to focus most of their energy on making better choices.

It's true that students' anxiety or depressive moods do often have genetic roots, and, yes, their environment does play a role in their positive well-being. But a significant portion of students' happiness and well-being is rooted in how they choose to live their lives. This includes their choice of friends, how they choose to spend their time, their choice of study habits, what they choose to eat, what risks they choose to take, what they choose to say no to, and so forth. Indeed, by correcting errant choices, students can have a significant impact on their happiness and overall positive well-being.

Once students see how much their choices influence their happiness, they begin to see that they have choices over how they manage their behaviors and emotions. They see that they can choose to be a peacemaker or the cause of contention. They unchain themselves from such thoughts as "Because of my genetics, there is nothing I can do about my anger." Or "Because of the bad environment I am being raised in, there is no chance for me to be happy." It frees them from living in a state of learned helplessness and propels them toward a state of *learned optimism*.[7] It shifts them toward having an *internal locus of control*, which allows them to see that their outcomes in life are strongly influenced by internal forces and choices, not by external forces such as luck or fate.[8] All this builds their self-efficacy.

So that returns us to the question: What might a teacher do to help students increase their self-efficacy? Former Stanford University professor Albert Bandura built a theory of self-efficacy that suggests four ways to help young people increase self-efficacy.[9] They are:

1. **Mastery Experiences.** Dr. Bandura declared that there is no better way to increase self-efficacy than through direct experience, or what he called *mastery experiences*.[10] Each time students experience a legitimate success, such as achieving a goal through their own efforts, it builds their self-efficacy. The key is that students see how their positive choices and efforts lead to the positive outcomes.

2. **Vicarious Experiences.** The next best way to build self-efficacy is for students to see others achieve success through effort and persistence. For example, observing a parent being successful at doing a task raises students' belief that they, too, can learn to master the skills needed to do the task and to achieve the same successful results. In other words, "I've seen Mom do this, so I can do it, too." In contrast, watching a parent fail time and again reduces a child's self-efficacy and may lead to a multi-generational pattern of learned helplessness.

3. **Verbal Persuasion.** Though less powerful than mastery or vicarious experiences, when students are told by a teacher who they trust that they possess the capability to do something difficult or achieve a challenging goal—"You can do it! I believe in you!"—that encouragement has the potential to build the students' self-efficacy.

4. **Healthy Emotional and Physiological States.** Having good health and positive emotions adds to students' confidence that they can do things on their own. It is more difficult for students to put in the necessary effort to complete a project when they feel tired, sick, lonely, fearful, or depressed than it is when they feel healthy, courageous, and optimistic.

In looking back through the skillsets and best practices in this book, most include examples of mastery experiences. So what this chapter now suggests are three additional best practices teachers can apply to help students expand their self-efficacy, and all three involve mastery experiences.

When was a time when you achieved a success that made you feel you could do things on your own?

Three Best Practices for Expanding Students' Self-Efficacy

Three best practices for empowering students to do things on their own and increase their self-efficacy are:

My teacher . . .

- gave me choice.
- gave me voice.
- supported me in achieving a goal.

Gave Me Choice

How will students learn to take charge of their lives if they are not provided opportunities to make choices and experience the consequences of those choices?

By the time Anne Sullivan took over as governess for six-year-old Helen Keller, disease had already stolen Helen's sight and hearing. It left her in a rage of mental torment and sparked violent outbursts. Some labeled Helen a wild animal. Her parents would have been thrilled if someone could merely help Helen be calm at the dinner table. Several experts tried, yet none was successful. Not until the day Anne arrived. Helen called it her soul's birthday.

Within two weeks, Helen was not only sitting serenely at the dinner table, she was also learning at previously unimaginable levels. People marveled. They began referring to Anne as "the miracle worker." But did it really take a miracle?

Years later, Helen expressed her view of what made the difference. She wrote: "A person who is severely impaired never knows his hidden sources of strength until he is treated like a normal human being and encouraged to try to shape his own life. . . . He will not work joyously unless he feels that liberty is his."[11]

Notice Helen's choice of words: "treated like a normal human being," "encouraged to try to shape his own life," and "will not work joyously unless he feels that liberty is his."

One who put a lot of importance into giving students choices, liberty, and ownership for their lives and learning was William Glasser, author of the classic *Choice Theory in the Classroom*. Dr. Glasser was a medical doctor and psychiatrist who proposed that people have five basic needs. We mentioned one of the needs in the previous chapter—fun. Another was the need for *autonomy*. Glasser noted that when parents or teachers dictate everything students must do and how they must do it, students will not feel ownership for their learning and choices. Rather, they will rely on parents or teachers to dictate what they must do and how they must do it.[12]

Dr. Angela Duckworth confirms Glasser's findings, saying, "A degree of autonomy during the early years is . . . important. Longitudinal studies tracking learners confirm that overbearing parents and teachers erode intrinsic motivation. Kids whose parents let them make their own choices about what they like are more likely to develop interests later identified as a passion."[13]

Years ago, Drs. Edward Deci and Richard Ryan conducted a study with fourth through sixth grade teachers. At the beginning of a school year, they assessed the degree to which each teacher was oriented toward controlling students versus supporting their autonomy. Two months later, they returned and assessed students' intrinsic motivation, perceived competence, and self-esteem. The students whose teachers supported autonomy turned out to be more intrinsically motivated, more curious, more willing to take on challenges, and more likely to make independent attempts at self-mastery. They felt more competent at schoolwork and had higher self-esteem than the students with the non-autonomy-supportive teachers.[14]

For students to achieve autonomy and reach a level of independence, adults must, at times, stand back and get out of their way. Yet that can be very difficult to do, especially for educators who want everything to be perfectly neat and tidy.

A principal was giving us a tour of her school one day, and we kept coming upon wall posters that students had made. Upon seeing each poster, the principal's face would cringe. She confessed that it was very hard for her not to take down the posters since they did not meet her standards for beauty and grammar. Yet the principal knew she needed to let go of such feelings if students were to be given the opportunity to grow in their art abilities and build self-efficacy.

The acclaimed British educator Thomas Huxley observed, "There is far too much of the feeding-bottle in education. Young people ought to be supplied with good intellectual food and then left to help themselves."[15] What follows are suggestions for teachers to consider when trying not to bottle-feed students and to instead empower them with more autonomy in choice making.

Keep the Responsibility for Learning with Students

A grateful set of parents shared the following tribute to a teacher who insisted on giving their son ownership for his learning:

> Mrs. Holbrook was a second grade teacher with a no-nonsense style. When our son got the news that he had been assigned to her class, he immediately began begging to be switched to the other class. He wanted to be with the "fun" teacher. That didn't happen.
>
> The first two weeks of school went by, and our son hadn't changed his feelings. Then, one day Mrs. Holbrook mentioned she was an avid fan of a certain sports team. It happened to be our son's favorite team. That fast, the two had something in common and became friends.
>
> Unfortunately, their friendship didn't increase our son's interest in schoolwork. And when the time came for the first parent–teacher conference, his progress was well below his abilities.
>
> As parents, we asked Mrs. Holbrook what we could do to help. Our son was sitting alongside us, and, in her matter-of-fact way, she let us know that she was not interested in our help. She looked directly at our son and started talking with him like she was his sports coach. She told him how confident she was in him and how she saw him as a leader. And then she put the responsibility for his learning squarely on his shoulders. "This isn't your parents' responsibility," she said. "This is your responsibility. I need you to come through for me." She asked him for his commitment to improve. He gave it to her with a look in his eye we hadn't seen before.
>
> For the remainder of the year, our son took ownership for his schoolwork. He got his homework done without our prodding. And the best news is that it became a pattern he followed through his high school years. I don't think a single year went by without one of us turning to the other and saying, "Bless you, Mrs. Holbrook."

Notice how Mrs. Holbrook didn't scold her student. She let him know that she believed in him. She asked for his commitment. She let his parents know that their son needed to accept ownership for his learning. That one conversation altered the boy's habits for life.

Contrast that story with the following story that was shared by a mother who was reflecting on her own elementary school years.

> Our father had just left our mother, so Mom took on two jobs to provide for our little family. About that time, my older sister was assigned to complete a big science fair project. Mom wasn't around to help, so my sister did it all on her own. When she turned in her project, the teacher took one look at it and said in a sarcastic tone, "Well, I can tell you did it yourself. Your parents didn't help at all, did they?"
>
> I remember my sister feeling so embarrassed. I began to worry what my teachers might think if I completed a project on my own.

Where did this teacher place responsibility for the learning? Clearly with the parent. The teacher missed a golden opportunity to applaud her student's efforts to complete the project on her own.

Robbing students of the opportunity to say "I did it myself" lessens their autonomy and dampens their self-efficacy.

Offer Choices for How to Complete Assignments

Dr. Howard Gardner proposed that there are at least nine types of intelligences, or preferred styles of learning. The learning styles include linguistic, naturalistic, musical, interpersonal, logical-mathematical, spatial, existential, kinesthetic, and intra-personal.[16]

Students are better at some of the intelligences than they are at others and prefer to show evidence of their learning according to their more natural intelligences. Similarly, teachers are stronger at some of the intelligences than they are at others, and so they tend to design assignments and exams that align with their preferred intelligences and learning styles.

What then happens when teachers' preferred intelligences and learning styles are opposite to those of some of their students? The answer is that it will likely be a very long year for those opposite students, unless, of course, teachers build some choice—some flexibility—into how they require students to complete assignments and show evidence for their learning.

Lin-Manuel Miranda had such a teacher. Adults know Miranda best from the Broadway musical *Hamilton*, for which he wrote the script, composed the music, and was the lead actor and singer. Students likely know him for having written music for the Disney movie *Encanto*, which hit No. 1 on teen pop charts.

In eighth grade, Miranda was not engaged in school. His English teacher, Mr. Herbert, tried his best to connect with him, but nothing seemed to work. Miranda was more interested in sitting in the back of the classroom, thinking about all the things he would rather be doing besides studying English.

Two-thirds through the year, Miranda submitted a writing assignment that was not completed in the format Mr. Herbert had instructed. He had written it in the form of a script for a play. Mr. Herbert could have chastised Miranda with "Why don't you follow instructions?" But instead, he told him that he thought the script was well-crafted. He said, "You could be good at this. It confirms what I have suspected about you for some time. You've been hibernating in the back of my class. Come to the front and join us. It's almost springtime."

The moment Miranda heard that his teacher believed he had the potential to become a playwright was the moment he connected with his teacher and chose to engage in the class. Years later, after accumulating all sorts of notoriety, Miranda was being interviewed live on television, and the reporter surprised him by bringing Mr. Herbert onto the show. As soon as Miranda saw Mr. Herbert's face, tears began to fall. He wept as he said, "Dr. Herbert's the reason I'm sitting here talking with you. Herbert's the one who nudged me in [this] direction. He sort of changed my life forever. I'll always be in his debt for that."[17]

Kudos to Mr. Herbert for never giving up on Miranda and for being flexible in allowing him to choose how he would complete the assignment. This does not mean that teachers must turn the instructions for every assignment over to the whims and choices of each student. And no, teachers do not need to create options to match every student's preferred intelligences. What it does suggest is that teachers can, on regular occasions, find ways to give students choices for how they will complete certain assignments. They can offer students two or three options from which to choose by saying, "You may do the assignment this way, or you may choose to do it that way." Or they can give students autonomy to propose their own preferred format for completing certain assignments.[18]

When teachers dictate the exact topics, formats, and methods for every assignment and leave students with no choice—no autonomy—over how they complete assignments, it disempowers students from learning how to do things on their own. The teacher then owns the responsibility for the students' learning and outcomes, not the students.

Teach Students How to "Fish and Hunt"

Pulitzer Prize–winning poet Mark Van Doren wrote that "the art of teaching is the art of assisting discovery."[19]

There is little adventure in learning when the teacher has already discovered all the answers and captured them in a set of slides filled with bullet points that students must copy and memorize. Students learn more and remember more when they must hunt and fish for answers rather than sitting like gullible gulls doing nearly nothing. Nearly nothing, that is, but waiting and waiting for their teachers to dole out all the answers.

Teachers empower students when they give students a challenging problem to solve and just enough of a hint about how to solve it so that the students can proudly declare in the end, "We solved it ourselves." One person we interviewed praised a former teacher by saying, "He didn't always have the answers, but he pointed us in a direction where we could go and search for them."

Socrates promoted such an approach thousands of years ago. He encouraged teachers to abandon the role of being the "sage on the stage" with all the answers, and to instead present students with open-ended questions that engage their minds in serious reflection and discussion. His questions did not have only one correct answer; rather, they sent students into introspection, where they were required to analyze, think for themselves, and become more self-aware of their beliefs. The process stretched students into being active learners, not passive learners.

Make Time for Exploring

Some of the most successful businesses empower employees with the freedom to set aside a portion of their work hours for innovating products, including products that fall outside their normal job descriptions. They call it *skunk works*.

Many teachers take a similar approach. They set aside class time for students to freely explore topics that are of interest to them and allow them to collaborate with other students to dream up possible inventions. They call it *genius hour*.

Might something innovative come out of your students if they were to be given some extra free time to explore, invent, and discover new ideas while working on their own?

Ironically, some grading systems—particularly at the secondary level—literally scare students away from exploring new ways of learning out of fear that they might get a poor grade. After all, failing a single exam or getting a low score on a project might mean that students will not receive a top grade in the class and literally might not get accepted into the university of their choice. As a result, students do not dare think outside the box. Instead, they begin interrogating their teachers from the first day of school: "Tell me exactly what you want me to do, and I will do exactly as you say." That way, when submitting an assignment they can say to their teacher, "I did exactly what you told me to do. Now give me a top score." Where in that is there autonomy for students to make choices, exercise creativity, learn from mistakes, or grow self-efficacy?

So why not offer students a few assignments where they have autonomy to explore and be creative in how they complete assignments or show evidence of their learning without all the high-stakes consequences? What they produce may surprise their teacher.

So there are a few ways teachers can empower students with more freedom of choice. What about giving students a choice of which books to read? What about giving students a choice for flexible seating assignments on various days of the week?[20] What about giving students choice over what service-learning project they will participate in? What about giving them choices for whether to work alone or in a group? And so on. Viable choices are many.

The main objective of giving students choices is to help them learn to see that they can proactively act on their environment, as opposed to reactively sitting like gullible gulls, doing nearly nothing but passively waiting for their environment to act on them. It is to help them see that their choices and efforts do influence where they go in life and who they become. It is to build their self-efficacy.

What approaches have you used or seen
other teachers use to give students choices
in how they complete their schoolwork?

Gave Me Voice

We were walking with a high school principal and passed a classroom that was loud with student chatter. We glanced in and saw students working in teams to solve a study problem. The students were actively voicing their opinions and arguing for their solutions. The principal remarked, "I absolutely love the noise of learning! That teacher is one of our best."

We then entered the classroom where our visit was expected. The desks were all pointed in a precise forward direction, as were students' eyes, noses, and feet. Students were as quiet as moonbeams on a still pond while taking notes from the teacher's slides. Everything appeared orderly and reverent.

Which students, in your opinion, were learning the most? Which students were learning best how to advocate for their opinions: the students with all the chatter or the students whose voices were being suffocated by all that silence?

Don't get us wrong. We are all in favor of moments of quiet in a classroom. But don't be surprised that learning at its best can at times sound like chaos. Teachers fight against themselves when they say they want students to learn how to be social, how to advocate for themselves, and how to get along with others, and then tell students to sit still, not talk, and not work with one another: "Just be quiet and take notes."

Thankfully, the days of teachers doing nothing more than straight lecture are passé. The mainstream has long since moved toward teachers facilitating discussions. It is a matter of teachers learning how to *talk with* students rather than how to *talk to* students.

For some teachers, this has been a difficult shift. Yet the timing for the shift couldn't be better because students are wanting more than ever for their voices to be heard. They feel their opinions matter and want to express them, discuss them, and debate them. For that to happen, teachers must provide intentional opportunities for them to express themselves. And it is worth noting that some students prefer to share their voice through writing, music, art, drama, or some means other than speaking in front of others.

The academic and non-academic benefits of giving students a voice are many. The Rennie Center for Education Research & Policy reports that when students have a voice in their learning and class decisions, they increase their academic self-efficacy, are more likely to engage in challenging academic work, and develop skills such as critical learning, creativity, communication, and collaboration.[21] Other research adds that giving students voice allows them to develop more self-awareness, self-management, social awareness, and responsible decision-making.[22]

Giving students a voice is also closely aligned with previous leadership skillsets and basic needs we have highlighted. For example, the Quaglia Institute for School Voice and Aspirations reports that when students perceive they have a voice in school, they are three times more likely to experience self-worth, five times more likely to feel a sense of purpose, and seven times more likely to be engaged academically.[23] In terms of connection, Dr. Dana Mitra of Penn State University explains, "When students believe that they are valued for their perspectives and respected, they begin to develop a sense of ownership and attachment to the organization in which they are involved."[24] So you can see how giving students a voice amplifies their feelings of connectedness, meaning, and self-worth, as well as their desire to engage in academics. All this is vital to their positive well-being.

So how do teachers go about helping students express their voice? Two general ways we have observed teachers empowering students to have more voice include:

Invite Student Voice in How the Class Is Led

When all classroom rules and plans are dictated by the teacher at the start of a year, the best it produces is year-long compliance. In contrast, when students' voices are included in setting classroom rules and consequences, students take more ownership for living the rules and accepting the consequences. As Dr. Stephen R. Covey often warned, "No involvement, no commitment."

As the year progresses, inviting students to give regular feedback on how well things are going makes the class feel more like a living, changing organism than a stagnant, unchanging learning environment. This is why some teachers reserve five to ten minutes at the end of each day or week to debrief how the day or week went. Some use graphic organizers, such as a plus/delta chart, to allow students to voice what they think went well (pluses) and what could be changed for the better (deltas).

Brainstorming is another tool teachers use to elicit student voice. Brainstorming is used to generate ideas for what activities the class will do, what service-learning projects the students will complete, what books will be read, etc. The main rule is that students cannot evaluate one another's suggestions or opinions until everyone has been given the chance to voice their thoughts. Everybody is free to share ideas and to bounce off others' ideas to come up with even better ideas without others judging them. When students know their ideas are not going to be mocked or criticized, they are more open to voicing their opinion. Of course, the brainstormed choices will eventually need to be evaluated and narrowed to a final choice, but not before everyone has had a chance to freely have their voice heard.

Of course, a handful of students will always prefer to remain silent. And that is okay. However, teachers can minimize this by having students first write their initial ideas down on paper or submit them digitally and anonymously. The class can then organize the ideas into themes using a graphic organizer such as an affinity diagram or by voting anonymously on which ideas they like best. This gets everyone's best ideas out and minimizes the chances of groupthink occurring.

Seek Opinions About Non-Classroom Matters

Sometimes things are happening at school, in the community, or in world news that are of concern or interest to students. Perhaps a natural disaster just occurred, and they want to voice their concerns about it. Maybe a popular event was attended by several students and they want to express their feelings about it. Maybe a tragedy struck one of their peers and they want time to debrief how it impacted them. If so, a teacher may set aside time for students to express thoughts freely. "Open mic" moments such as these are opportunities for students to voice what is in their minds and hearts, and will not likely happen unless their teacher creates a regular routine for them to happen.

Teachers are often surprised by the influence that students' voices can have. One teacher asked students for anonymous feedback about how things were going in the class and solicited suggestions they had for improving things. He was not surprised by the problems they identified, but he was surprised by the quality of the practical solutions they suggested.

When solutions for change come from students, students are more willing to implement them. We were in a middle school that was having issues with bullying. None of the teachers' strategies for stopping the problem had worked. So one teacher asked his students what they thought could be done about the matter. That is when a popular student stood up and voiced, "I'm tired of this bullying s*#%! We don't need the teachers to take care of it. This is our school. We can take care of it!"

We were later told how the students created a few teams, with the popular student and a few of her respected peers leading the teams. The teams went to various classrooms and started voicing their thoughts and asking for suggestions. Before long, the bullying had all but ended. Students' voices had taken over. The students' voices were more powerful than their teachers' voices—in a good way.

These are only two of many ways student voices can be used to bring about positive change in a classroom and school. It is important to note that many students will share their voice through non-vocal means, such as poetry, music, art, sports, and science, or through other talents they have developed. Other students will share their voice through their body language, so it is important for teachers to keep their eyes in listening mode. Regardless of how they make their voices heard, when students sense their voice is being listened to and that it is making a difference, their self-efficacy expands.

*What are some of the most effective ways
you have seen students being given a voice?*

Supported Me in Achieving a Goal

Few efforts build self-efficacy more than achieving a goal.

Recall that Bandura's most effective suggestion for developing self-efficacy was for students to have mastery experiences—opportunities to be successful as a result of their efforts. Achieving a goal is a mastery experience, and it is strongly associated with happiness.[25]

So why then do students not all shout for joy when a teacher announces it is time to set a goal? Why do some groan?

One reason some students groan when hearing the word *goal* is that they have failed to achieve goals in the past. They do not want to fail again. Besides that, for self-efficacy to occur, students must do more than set goals; they must achieve their goals. And that requires effort. Effort is not always fun, and yet it is an essential ingredient for building self-efficacy.

Admittedly, the people we interviewed did not always use the term *goal* when describing what a teacher did to make a difference in their lives. Some referred to a big project they completed, an important exam they passed, or an award they won. In each case, what they were saying was: "I did my best work to achieve what I achieved, and my teacher was a big support."

To highlight the role that teachers can play in helping students to achieve a goal, we'll first describe some of the theory behind goal-setting and then share a practical way to increase students' self-efficacy by helping them achieve a simple weekly goal. As you are about to discover, a key is to focus on the intangibles. Let us explain.

The Theory

Short-term goals can be motivating, fun, and rewarding in terms of building self-efficacy. That is why we recommend students make a G.A.M.E. out of it, which is a playful acronym for:

Goal—*What am I trying to achieve and why?*
Actions—*What actions must I take to achieve the goal?*
Measures—*How will I measure and track progress?*
Evaluation—*When will I assess and celebrate progress?*

All four G.A.M.E. components are common goal-setting strategies recommended by experts.[26] As we describe the G.A.M.E. components, give extra attention to the difference between the intangibles and tangibles.

Goal. A goal is the desired outcome, or *output*, that a person intends to produce through their efforts. Most students (and adults) would be better at achieving goals if they were better at setting goals. Guidelines for helping students set goals include:

1. **Ensure that the goal is important to the student.** Goals must be meaningful to students, and not just what a teacher wants them to achieve. If students feel no personal *why* associated with a goal or have no choice or voice in setting the goal, don't expect them to be committed to achieving the goal.

2. **Focus on pursuing something desirable, not avoiding something undesirable.** Goals are more likely to be achieved when focused on moving toward something desirable, such as a new "good habit," rather than breaking away from something undesirable, such as an old bad habit.

3. **Set goals that are not too difficult and not too easy.** Charles Snyder says that goals must be attainable while at the same time presenting some amount of challenge and uncertainty.[27] Daniel Pink refers to such goals as "Goldilocks goals." In other words, "This goal is not too hard. This goal is not too soft. This goal is just right."[28] If there is no challenge in a goal, self-efficacy will not result, even if the goal is achieved.

4. **Make the goal specific and measurable.** Leadership expert Peter Senge describes a leader's role as taking people from point A to point B.[29] Goals are best when they are specific enough to represent clear progress: "I will go from point A (start point) to point B (end point) by what date (due point)." The more measurable a goal is, the more likely it is that progress will be felt and self-efficacy will increase.

5. **Ensure that success is primarily due to the efforts of the student.** If a teacher sets a goal for a student and does most of the work to achieve the goal, the student may cheer and be grateful when the goal is achieved, but that student's self-efficacy will not increase. For self-efficacy to increase, the student must play a primary role in achieving the goal.

Achieving a goal produces two types of outputs: tangible and intangible. *Tangible outputs* are objective and measurable. *Intangible outputs* tend to be much more subjective and difficult to measure. Self-efficacy is one example of an intangible output, as are feelings of connection, meaning, hope, self-worth, and resilience. They are less easy to measure but are essential for enabling students to have the confidence to learn to live and to overcome challenges on their own.

Tangible Outputs	Intangible Outputs
"I got a 92 percent on the exam."	Happiness. Relief. Increased hope of getting accepted into a university.
"I lost seven pounds."	"I feel better about my appearance." "I now know I can do hard things."
"I met two new friends this week."	"I feel less lonely." "I now feel like I belong in this class." "I like school more."

Actions. Actions are a goal's *inputs*. There are also tangible and intangible inputs. *Tangible inputs* are the specific steps, processes, timelines, and resources that go into producing the desired outputs. They are relatively easy to track. Whereas the *intangible inputs* are the character traits (e.g., effort, courage, grit, positivity, sacrifice, etc.) and the competence (e.g., creativity, talent, teamwork, etc.) that students put into achieving the goal. Intangible inputs are more difficult to measure and track but are central to students feeling increased self-efficacy.

Tangible Inputs	Intangible Inputs
"To get a 92 on the exam, I will study two hours per day and give up social media on those days."	Discipline. Sacrifice. Cognitive skills.
To lose seven pounds, I will exercise for 30 minutes five times a week and eat no snacks after 6:00 p.m.	Hard work. Grit.
"To make two new friends, I will introduce myself to one new person each day this week."	Initiative. Courage.

Researchers report that it is common for students and adults to feel more happiness when pursuing a goal—being creative, overcoming barriers, working with friends, celebrating milestones, and so forth—than they do when achieving a goal.[30] As motivational speaker Zig Ziglar described it, "Success is in the doing, not the getting; in the trying, not the triumph."[31]

Measures. The *endowed progress effect* suggests that when students feel they have made even small progress toward their goal, they become more committed to continuing to pursue it.[32] As is commonly said, "Success breeds success."

But how will students know if they are making progress or have achieved their goal if they do not have a way to measure progress or know when the goal is achieved?

As with video games, students become more excited about pursuing goals when they can see their progress. They especially love seeing their progress rise to all-time-best levels.

Tangible outputs are typically much easier to measure and show progress in than intangible outputs. For example, it is easier to step on a scale and see that you are losing weight (tangible output) than to measure how you feel about losing weight and the self-efficacy you are building as a result of accomplishing the goal (intangible outputs). Similarly, it is typically easier to measure if you did your action steps ("Yes, I did them") than it is to measure how you feel about your efforts ("I worked hard, did some creative things"). Perhaps that is why most people focus solely on measuring the tangibles and don't think about measuring the intangibles.

For self-efficacy to increase, students must be able to see and feel both tangible and intangible progress. They must see and feel that their efforts are leading to positive outcomes. Sometimes the only way a teacher can tell if this has happened for students is by hearing their cheers or seeing their eyes light up or by listening to how excited they become when they achieve a goal that was sufficiently challenging and that contributed in a meaningful way. Sometimes all it takes is to hear them shout, "I did it!"

Evaluation. Drs. Edwin Locke and Gary Latham are credited with much of the original research behind goal theory.[33] They insist that for goal setting to have its highest probability of success, it must contain a system for credible feedback.

One of the best feedback systems for achieving goals is to have an *accountability partner*. People who make their New Year's resolution goals known to a partner are ten times more likely to succeed at achieving their goal than those who do not. Similarly, people who write down goals and share them with a friend are on average 33 percent more successful at achieving their goals.[34]

When evaluating progress toward a goal, it is common for accountability partners to focus solely on the tangible inputs and outputs. However, when a main objective is to build self-efficacy, it is as important that the accountability partner also emphasize the intangibles. When the accountability partner and the student meet to evaluate progress, a typical conversation might include the accountability partner asking such questions as:

1 Tangible Outputs	**Focus on the progress toward tangible outcomes.** **Examples:** "Are you seeing any progress toward the results you want?" "Are you ahead or behind in your progress?" "Did you lose any weight?"
2 Tangible Inputs	**Focus on the action steps, resources, and strategy.** **Examples:** "Were the action steps fully implemented each day?" "What went well?" "Are there adjustments you need to make to your plan?" "Is the amount of exercise enough?"
3 Intangible Inputs	**Focus on character and competence.** **Examples:** "I love your effort and initiative." "You don't give up easy." "You are very talented and creative." "How do you feel about your effort?"
4 Intangible Outputs	**Focus on the *why* of the goal and the basic needs that are being met.** **Examples:** "Well done being ahead of schedule in your progress." "You made that person feel so valued." "You can do hard things when you put your mind to it."

When students, with the help of their accountability partner, see that their tangible and intangible inputs are leading to positive tangible and intangible outputs, self-efficacy results. But what happens when students follow all the action steps with exactness and still come short of achieving their desired goals? Do they give up? No!

For starters, students deserve to be applauded for the portions they did achieve. Giving partial credit for effort and work well done is important.

Second, students need to understand that developing self-efficacy includes learning not to give up easily when facing opposition. As Kōnosuke Matsushita, founder of Panasonic, observed, "It is a kind of law of nature. The goal one aims for can rarely be reached by a direct road."[35] Students need to expect detours, roadblocks, and course corrections when pursuing a goal. If Plan A doesn't work, they need to develop the ability to adjust to Plan B or C. There is no shame in adjusting a goal or its action steps.

Third, remember to celebrate successes. Even small victories—one percent increases—are worthy of celebration. And there is no need to wait for a goal to be fully achieved before celebrating. Each milestone achieved is an opportunity to cheer and feel self-efficacy. And the celebrations themselves do not need to be elaborate to be effective. Students tend to be clever at coming up with fun, cost-effective ways to celebrate. Often all that is needed is a compliment: "I'm impressed with your effort. You did it all yourself."

Of course, teachers with multiple classes and many students cannot be expected to follow up on every student's goal, but they can establish peer-to-peer accountability partners and set aside dedicated time for the peer partners to talk about how things are progressing.

Note that even in cases where teachers cannot follow up with every student, it does help when they at least make the effort to approach individual students on occasion to ask, "How are you coming on your goal?" One former student told us about a goal she had to become a professional ice skater. She practiced every day after school. Though several teachers knew about her goal, only one teacher—her middle school English teacher—asked her on occasion how it was going. "He was the one teacher who seemed to care about me," she said. "I felt as though my life, and what I accomplished in life, was important to him."

Weekly Goals: A Simple Approach

Now, you may have reason to think, "All that theory and logic about goal setting is more complicated than it is simple."

The approach we most recommend applies the theory but keeps things simple and short by helping students achieve *weekly goals* that can be completed in a week or less. Students begin by setting one goal per week that focuses on one of the three categories of basic needs: physical, intellectual, or social-emotional. For example, suppose Sophie is lonely. She wants a friend. She has thought about trying to talk with Marsha who sits next to her in class, but Sophie is anxious about meeting new people and has never spoken to Marsha before. So for her, a challenging but doable goal for the week might be: "I will initiate a conversation with Marsha two times this week."

Next, Sophie might choose her action steps to be as simple as, "On Tuesday, I will ask Marsha a question about what she likes to do for fun. Then on Thursday, I will ask her a question about her family." Sophie knows it is best to calendar a goal, so she gets her weekly calendar and, in the time slot for when her Tuesday class meets, she writes: "Ask Marsha what she likes to do for fun." Then, in the space allotted for when her Thursday class meets, she writes: "Ask Marsha about her family." Sophie shares her plan with her mother, who she has selected to be her accountability partner.

Next, Sophie needs to follow through on her action steps. If, on Tuesday, Sophie successfully asks Marsha the first question, she can place a smiley face on her Tuesday calendar to indicate "I did it!" That's her simple scoreboard. And if she successfully asks Marsha the second question on Thursday, she can add another smiley face on her calendar for that day.

At this point, Sophie is feeling good. She has achieved her weekly goal. Her connection with Marsha has grown, as has her self-efficacy. So, when it comes time for Sophie to meet with her mother and evaluate how things went, Sophie can review and celebrate her tangible and intangible inputs and outputs. After listening to Sophie, her mother might say: "Sophie, good job asking Marsha about her family and what she does for fun. How did you feel when you approached her? Is there anything you wish you had said differently?" Her mother might conclude, "That took courage and effort, Sophie. You did it all on your own. I'm sure proud of you." Sophie will have enjoyed a mastery experience and learned: "I can do hard things on my own if I apply courage and effort."

The next week, it is not unthinkable for Sophie to set and achieve two weekly goals, such as one physical goal and one intellectual goal. If she achieves both, she will have had two successful "mastery experiences" and felt her self-efficacy increase even more.

Of course, Sophie may choose to do a more rigorous, long-term goal, such as a three-month goal to complete a project. Or she might set a goal to change a "bad" habit or to overcome an addiction. Such goals will require a more extensive series of action steps, detailed scoreboards to track progress, and extra support from an accountability partner. Or she may participate in a class, a team, or a schoolwide goal that requires more coordination and planning with multiple people. Such long-term goals or team goals can also produce feelings of self-efficacy in students, so long as the students play enough of a role in achieving the group goal and can see how their personal efforts contributed to the group goals' outputs. We have done extensive work with schools pursuing larger individual, classroom, and school goals, and those efforts are described in much more detail in the book *The 4 Disciplines of Execution for Educators.*[36]

In the end, whether pursuing a short- or long-term goal, a personal or a team goal, we agree with Zig Ziglar's observation: "What you get by achieving your goals is not as important as what you become by achieving your goals."[37]

> *What is a personal goal you can set, pursue, and model for students? What is a goal that can be achieved as a class?*

Temperance Factors

Like each of the previous leadership skillsets, empowering students to help themselves and to experience the benefits of self-efficacy can be taken too far.

Not All Students Are Ready for Independence

Expecting young students to make every important choice entirely on their own is abandonment, not empowerment. Students' voices are not always the wisest voices. So what student does not benefit, at times, from a supportive adult who gives them an assist?

We are reminded of Mr. Brown who teaches high school orchestra. One of his senior students had heard repeatedly how difficult university life can be and decided to not submit an application. Mr. Brown fully believed in the student and knew he could do well at the university level. So he literally sat down with the student, filled out the application for the local university, and even submitted it. Four years later, the student proved Mr. Brown correct. He graduated from the university and accepted an enviable position with a reputable company. It never would have happened without a nudge—a big nudge—from Mr. Brown.

No student wants to be a gullible gull. Yet there are times when even the best students need a friend to toss them a "fish." Every "one" needs some "one," on occasion.

Teach Skills for Interdependence

Independence is good, but interdependence is better.

We live in an interdependent world. People depend on others for at least some parts of our positive well-being. So, when teaching students how to become independent, also teach them how to be interdependent. Teach them how to get along with others and how to work in groups. Help them to learn how to help others and not try to do everything on their own. Help them understand that it is okay that they cannot single-handedly solve all their challenges in life, and that some challenges really are best to work on as a village.

Don't Forget the Adults!

Like students, teachers want to have choice and voice in what they do at school, including in how they teach and lead. They, too, like to feel the self-efficacy and the tangible and intangible rewards that come with achieving a challenging goal.

This is why we present the insights in this book as suggestions and insights, not as scripts that teachers must follow exactly. Teachers know their students and circumstances best, and so they deserve the autonomy to choose how they will apply the leadership skillsets and best practices with their students. Nevertheless, teachers do not want to be isolated, alone, and left to do everything entirely on their own. That, too, is abandonment, not empowerment.

Concluding Thoughts

Positive well-being takes effort. And so does self-efficacy.

Nature teaches that if a bird is not allowed to peck its way out of its shell on its own, it will be weaker throughout its life, and the impact will be passed from one generation to the next. It is no different for young humans.

Sometimes the best thing to do to build students' self-efficacy is to do nothing. That is why this chapter is as much about what teachers *do not do* for students as it is about what they *do*. It is about not turning students into gullible gulls.

Allowing students an appropriate amount of autonomy to make choices, to express their voice, and to achieve meaningful goals empowers them to help themselves and to believe in themselves. It builds their critical thinking skills, their decision-making skills, and ultimately their self-efficacy skills. So if leadership is about believing in students in a way that they come to believe in themselves, then at some point it will be essential for teachers and parents to "let go" in some instances so students can make the effort to help themselves.

The Challenge

Select one. To enable students to feel more self-efficacy, make and implement a plan or routine for how you will

- give them more choice in the things they do,
- allow them to express their voice more often, or
- support them in achieving a goal.

7

Corrected Me in a Positive Way

When the principal of another school called Muriel to warn her that a troubled fifth grade student had just moved into her school's boundaries, it was not that unusual. What was unusual was how Muriel and her staff chose to handle it.

The student's name was Jesse, and his former principal was letting Muriel know that he would be a danger to her school. She said she was sending an inch-thick file on Jesse's history that included a description of how he had knocked her unconscious.

Upon receiving such a report, most principals would have insisted on meeting with Jesse's parents to establish a strict intervention plan. Yet Muriel and her team took a different approach. As Muriel recalls, "I never read Jesse's file, which may not have been the wisest choice. But it was a choice from the heart to give him a new chance."

When Jesse got off the bus for the first day of school, there was no mistaking who he was. He walked with an attitude. Muriel went up to him with a smile and said, "You must be Jesse." The school counselor was beside her and added, "We're so happy you are here."

Jesse gave them a puzzled look before responding, "Who the f*#* are you? And get the s*^t out of my face."

Muriel said, "We don't use that kind of language here. We use a different kind of language. We're happy you're here nonetheless."

The school's culture and philosophy was to look for and utilize the strengths of all students, and Muriel and her team were determined to treat Jesse no differently. They began by giving him small assignments to help in his classroom. They let him know how his efforts were valued. They pointed out what they saw as his strengths. They also found ways to tell Jesse they loved him every day. At first, when they used the words *We love you*, he would sometimes curse at them. Other times he looked at them like they had two heads.

Weeks went by before they could see Jesse's tough exterior starting to fade. After two months, he began to tell them he loved them.

At one point, Jesse ran for student body president. He didn't win, but it was a positive experience for him. And by the end of the year, he made the honor roll, something he had never heard of before. He still walked and talked with an attitude, but it was a positive attitude.

Jesse had some setbacks during the year, but when he did, Muriel and his teachers could involve him in coming up with a corrective plan of action. In most cases, he corrected the problem on his own.

When it came time for Jesse to move on to middle school, Muriel felt it her duty to call the principal and let her know: "I can't wait for you to meet a student named Jesse." She told of all the hurdles he had overcome in life. She shared his strengths.

When Jesse's eighth grade year came around, he decided to run again for student body president. That time he won.

From there, Jesse was relocated out of state to live with a relative. Muriel lost track of him. She only hopes that, wherever he is, he knows there are people who love him and still believe in him.

The Need for Growth

As a result of the teachers and staff making consistent efforts to believe in Jesse, he was coming to believe in himself and growing in beyond ordinary ways. That is leadership.

When seeing this chapter's title, "Teacher Corrected Me in a Positive Way," teachers might assume that its main focus is on managing students' inappropriate behaviors in a kind way. But this is not a chapter on positive discipline strategies. We are not focused on *managing* students' behaviors for a day or two, we are focused on *leading* students in ways that will change the trajectory of their lives for a lifetime. Isn't that what Muriel and her staff did for Jesse?

We have chosen such a lofty focus because no one we interviewed about a teacher who made a difference in their life ever said anything like "She had the most amazing discipline strategies!" Or "The way he punished me was inspiring!" Rather, they said things like "I was messing up my life and she helped me turn it around." Or "I wasn't a troublemaker. I just had no idea of where I was going in life. He pointed me in a positive direction."

Such comments, and stories like Jesse's, remind us of the poem "Crossroads." Written years ago by an unknown author, it reads:

He stood at the crossroads all alone,
The sunlight in his face.
He had no fear for the path unknown,
He was set for a grueling race.
But the road stretched east, and the road stretched west,
And there was no one to tell him which road was best.
So, he took the wrong road and it led him down,
Till he lost the race and the victor's crown.
He fell at last in an ugly snare,
Because no one stood at the crossroads there.

Another boy on another day,
At the selfsame crossroads stood.
He paused a moment to choose the way,
That would lead to the greater good.
For the road stretched east and the road stretched west,
And there was one there to show him which road was best.

So to the right he turned and went on and on,
Till he won the race and the victor's crown.
He walks today the highway fair,
Because one stood at the crossroads there.[1]

We could argue that this entire book is a guide for how to meet students at their crossroads. We have shared several stories about students whose teachers have stood at their crossroads and helped them to elevate their self-beliefs. It is not merely a matter of stopping students from going in wrong directions. It is not just a matter of managing their behavior. It is a matter of leadership—leading students toward new and better ways of believing.

Each story we have shared models what Dr. Jane Nelson encourages teachers to do, which is to "connect before you correct." In her blog she writes, "Extensive research shows that we cannot influence children in a positive way until we create a connection with them. It is a brain (and heart) thing. Sometimes we must stop dealing with the misbehavior and first heal the relationship. Connection creates a sense of safety and openness. Punishment, lecturing, nagging, scolding, blaming, or shaming create fight, flight, or freeze."[2]

How do teachers "connect before you correct"? They connect with students by meeting their basic needs for connection, meaning, hope, self-worth, resilience, self-efficacy, and growth. They call them by name, get to know their stories, voice respect for them. They teach them about life, help them see their strengths, give them opportunities to be a leader, let them know they appreciate them. They listen to them, give them voice, help them achieve a goal. And so forth.

Dr. Robert Marzano notes, "When teachers have a good relationship with students, then students more readily accept classroom rules and any consequences that follow the breaking of rules."[3] It makes things easier for teachers. But the primary motive behind correcting students in positive ways is to help them to grow.

Numerous experts on human motivation have researched the basic human need for growth. One of the earliest was Clayton Alderfer, who was a professor at Cornell, Yale, and Rutgers universities. Dr. Alderfer took the top levels of Maslow's hierarchy of needs and collapsed them into what he called *growth needs*. He described people's growth needs mostly in terms of their self-esteem, self-actualization, and self-transcendence, each of which is geared toward enabling people to become their best self.[4]

Other experts use other terms to describe the need for growth. Dr. David McClelland refers to people's need for growth as the need for achievement.[5] Daniel Pink refers to the need for growth as *mastery*, which he defines as the desire to get better and better at doing something that matters.[6] Jim Collins describes growth in terms of progressing from "good to great."[7] Whichever term or phrase or definition is used, it reflects people's earnest belief that their best self is yet ahead.

Harvard Business School's Teresa Amabile and colleagues recently published a study that highlights people's need for growth and progress in the workplace. They gave 238 employees from seven companies a daily journal and asked them to record at the end of each workday how their day had gone. More than 12,000 journal entries were collected and analyzed. The results indicated that the greatest source of motivation for people on the job is "making progress in one's work." The days the employees reported making progress were the same days they reported feeling the most engaged in their work. On the other hand, the days they reported making no progress were the same days they reported feeling the least engaged. The results only held true, however, when the employees perceived that the work they were doing was meaningful. Dr. Amabile concluded, "The power of progress is fundamental to human nature, but few managers understand it or know how to leverage progress to boost motivation."[8] To which we might comment that that is because they are acting as "managers" and not "leaders."

Dr. Amabile's observations apply as much to students as they do to employees, if not more so. Students are motivated by the desire to progress, so long as they perceive that what they are doing is meaningful. That said, we join Dr. Amabile in wondering if teachers truly understand how to leverage students' need for growth in ways that boost their motivation to learn. Some teachers might even push back and ask: "If the need for growth is such a strong source of motivation, why then is it so difficult, at times, to motivate students to pursue their need for growth at school?"

One answer is that students do not always view what they are learning and doing at school as meaningful. What matters to adults does not always matter to students.

A second answer is that many students feel their needs for growth are being satisfied elsewhere. Just ask them, and they will tell you about the great progress they made the night before on their video game—"I jumped three levels!"—or how they just added a mass of new friends to their social media account. So not all students arrive at school feeling a huge hunger or need for progress. As Maslow observed, "A satisfied need is not a motivator."

A third reason why some students are not more aggressive in pursuing their growth needs at school is that they perceive that they do not have the capability for growth. Stanford professor Dr. Carol Dweck has studied young people's thought processes for more than 40 years. She claims that students generally operate from either a "fixed" or a "growth" mindset.[9] Students with fixed mindsets hold the self-belief that there is little or nothing they can do to get smarter or to progress. They say things like "I'm not good at art, so I give up!" Or "I'm lousy at math, so why try?" They perceive that their efforts have no effect on the outcomes of their learning, so they do not put in the necessary effort to learn and grow.

In contrast, students with growth mindsets operate from the belief that their intelligence can grow. They say things like "With effort, I can improve my art skills." They view feedback, mistakes, and criticism as opportunities to learn and grow, which makes them more resilient and more likely to achieve academically. They understand that their brains can literally physically expand when they learn.[10] This is why students with growth mindsets are inclined to pursue growth more than students with fixed mindsets.

These three explanations make clear that there is more to correcting students in positive ways than for teachers to casually stand at the crossroads and point students in a positive direction. So, as you explore the following best practices, look for specific things teachers can do to inspire students and give them insights into what they can *start*, *continue*, and *stop* doing to enhance their growth.

Do you recall a specific class or school year
where you felt a lot of growth?
What made it such a time of growth for you?

Three Best Practices for Correcting Students in Positive Ways

According to research and the people we interviewed and surveyed, three best practices teachers use to correct students in positive ways and help them grow are:

My teacher...

- provided me with encouragement.
- gave me constructive feedback.
- held me self-accountable.

Provided Me with Encouragement

Recall Muriel's comment to Jesse, "We don't use that kind of language here. We use a different kind of language."

Muriel learned the importance of language when she was in elementary school. As a child, she frequently doubted herself. Her self-doubts were made worse when she was assigned to a teacher who often started sentences with phrases such as "You can't . . ." or "You won't. . . ." She literally said things like "You come from a small town and a poor family, so your chances of doing big things in life are slim." She spoke the language of despair.

The following year, Muriel was assigned to Miss Rose's class. Miss Rose spoke the language of hope. She started sentences with "You can . . ." and "You will. . . ." She told students, "It doesn't matter how much money you have in your pocket. What matters is how much belief you have in your heart." Muriel recalls, "Miss Rose made me feel special. She told me I would make a great teacher someday if that was what I wanted. I am indebted to Miss Rose. I cried when I heard she died."

Whether a teacher uses discouraging language of despair or encouraging language of hope can make a world of difference. Change a word, and you may change a student's world.

Consider four examples of discouraging language that is bound to lead students in the direction of despair:

Buts

Perhaps you have heard a teacher say something like "I'm glad you came to class on time, *but* I wish you would . . ." Or, "I think you are a great student, *but* if only you would . . ." "I'm glad you are in my class, *but* . . ." When teachers communicate with *but* when correcting students, it negates anything positive the teacher may have said prior. Students come away feeling more discouraged than they do motivated to change.

If your desire is to correct students in positive ways, it may be time to *kick your buts*.

Comparisons

As the saying goes, "Comparison is the thief of joy."

Students already over-compare themselves with their peers, and they are often very self-effacing. They see friends at school or on social media and think, "She's thin, I'm not." "He's smart, I'm not." "They have friends, I don't." Students do not need teachers to add to their existing pile of negative comparisons with comments such as "Why don't you pay attention like all the other students?" Or "Why don't you turn in your homework on time like your sister always did?"

If you are trying to correct students in positive ways, it may be time to *skip the comparisons*.

Criticism

A sign posted on a patch of new grass at a school read: I'M TRYING HARD TO GROW. PLEASE DON'T WALK ON ME. Isn't that essentially what students are saying to teachers and parents?

When all things that have been said to a young person are combined at the end of a day, it is often the case that adults have bombarded them with a stream of negative messages: "You're late." "Don't play your music so loud." "Get off that device." Each instance may be only a small criticism, yet when all are combined, they make for a rather discouraging message and day.

Some criticisms leave wounds that heal with time, others leave scars. Therefore, consider the words of Dr. Stephen R. Covey: "As long as we are in the role of judge and jury, we rarely have the kind of influence we want. Be a light, not a judge; a model, not a critic."

If your intent is to correct students in positive ways, it is time to *cease the criticisms*.

Shaming

Some teachers use cynicism, sarcasm, or shaming to try to correct students. Some do it in front of other students to get a laugh. They may get the laugh, but what they don't get is the loyalty of the student they just mocked. It is not motivating. It is not leadership.

A college student recalled:

> I suffered a traumatic brain injury as an infant. It required me to get extra help throughout my school years. My teachers were sensitive to my situation, though I remember one very discouraging moment.
>
> I had studied hard and managed to get the highest score in the class on a math test. It may have been the only time in my life that happened. When the teacher announced to the class that I had received the highest score, I wanted to dance for joy.
>
> But then the teacher proceeded to scold the rest of the class. She told them that I never should have gotten the highest score because I had learning disabilities. She told them they should be ashamed.
>
> I went from feeling total joy to total embarrassment. I doubt the other students felt motivated by the teacher shaming them either.

What could have been a grand opportunity to celebrate the student's remarkable achievement was turned into a public shaming of all students. Shaming encourages students to want to hide, not to shine. It creates ill will, not the will to change. The path to growth is meant to be a joyful journey, not a guilt trip.

Effective teachers do not humiliate students. If your intent is to correct students in positive ways, it is time to *halt the shaming*.

So there are four types of language that discourage. As Martin Seligman notes: "I cannot say this too strongly. . . . There is not a shred of evidence that strength and virtue are derived from negative motivation."[11] Or as parenting expert Pam Leo puts it, "You cannot teach children to behave better by making them feel worse. When children feel better, they behave better."[12]

What follows are three types of language that encourage students to "start" improving the trajectory of their lives.

Language of Connecting

In his research on choice theory, Dr. William Glasser described two sets of language that teachers use when attempting to correct students: (1) *disconnecting language* and (2) *connecting language*.[13] Based on the descriptions below, how might the two sets of language differ in how they make students feel?

Disconnecting Language	Connecting Language
Criticizing	Supporting
Blaming	Encouraging
Complaining	Listening
Nagging	Accepting
Threatening	Trusting
Punishing	Respecting
Bribing to control	Navigating Differences

Disconnecting language gives students the feeling of being controlled, manipulated, coerced, or managed. At best, it leads to mere compliance, though it may also lead to resistance or rebellion. Connecting language encourages and inspires. It gives students the feeling that they are being trusted, valued, and respected. It is leadership language.

In an intriguing study, Dr. David Yeager and colleagues took the essays of 50 students and had their teacher grade them. They then randomly put half the essays into one pile and half into a second pile. On each essay in the first pile, they had the teacher write, "I'm giving you these comments so that you will have feedback on your paper." On each essay in the second pile, they had the teacher write, "I'm giving you these comments because I have very high expectations and I know you can reach them." All the students were then given the chance to revise their papers in hopes of getting a better grade. Only 40 percent of the students from the first pile revised and resubmitted their essays compared to a full 80 percent of the students from the second pile. Thus, the simple act of the teacher inserting connecting language into the feedback had a significant impact on the students' desire to improve.[14]

Language of the Mind and Heart

Teachers and parents will often try to correct a student's behavior by trying to convince them that there is a better way using facts or personal experiences to reason with them. They are appealing to their minds and logic. Sometimes it works, often it does not. Sometimes they forget that students' brains are not fully developed at that point. And so they go on trying to reason. When reasoning doesn't work, they may turn to making threats: "Do this, or else!"

When basic reasoning with students' minds does not work, rather than turning to force or threats, consider appealing to their hearts. In other words, try reaching their minds and their hearts—both.

To encourage means to put courage into another person. The word *courage* itself comes from the Latin *cor* or the French *coeur*. Both translate to *heart* in English. So it can be said that to encourage students means to put heart into them. In fact, teachers must often figure out how to first reach students' hearts before they have any chance of reaching their minds.

Aristotle used the Greek terms *logos*, *pathos*, and *ethos* to describe such methods of persuasion. *Logos* appeals to students' logic—their minds. *Pathos* appeals to students' emotions—their hearts. *Ethos* appeals to students' sense of what is the "right" or "wrong" thing to do—their ethics. Aristotle knew that all three were viable methods of persuading or encouraging people, and not always in any particular order. Some students will be persuaded more by messages to the mind, others will be more easily persuaded by messages of the heart. Most often, however, they will best respond to persuasive messages that contain both mind and heart.

Language of a Higher Level

Students like to be treated as older, wiser, and better than they are. They like to be spoken up to, not down to. One man recalled a high school experience with Mr. Jarman:

> One day, our class was taking turns reading out loud. Afterwards, Mr. Jarman approached me and said, "I like it when you read. You go slow and pronounce your words so very clearly."
>
> Hearing Mr. Jarman say that left me feeling proud. From then on, whenever we read out loud in class, I was careful to read slowly and pronounce every word clearly. I knew Mr. Jarman would be listening.
>
> A few years went by before I recognized that I had a problem with reading too fast and mumbling my words. Mr. Jarman had been trying to get me to slow down and say things more clearly. But he was doing it in a positive way, not in a critical way. It worked.

By speaking to the student as if he were a better reader and speaker than he was, Mr. Jarman lifted the young man to a higher level. As Johann Wolfgang von Goethe observed: "If you treat a man as he is you make him less than he is. If you treat a man as he can and ought to be you make him better than he is."[15]

So, there are three examples of the types of language that encourage students to grow: the language of connection, the language of mind and heart, and the language of a higher level. Again, change a word and you just may change a student's world.

*What positive language have you found
to be most helpful in encouraging students?*

Gave Me Constructive Feedback

The biggest difference between *destructive* feedback and *constructive* feedback is the intent. Is the intent to tear down or to build up? Teachers feel the difference when they speak it, students feel the difference when they hear it. The intent is important because it impacts how students feel about themselves—and about their teachers.

Constructive feedback comes in two forms: *praise* and *reprimands*. There is something of a general understanding among teachers that for every one positive reprimand teachers give students, they need to give five praises. Whether the exact ratio is correct or not, there seems to be some validity to the value of giving more praise than reprimands. Researchers from the University of Kansas and Brigham Young University found that when middle school teachers praised students more than they reprimanded them, the on-task behaviors of students improved 60 to 70 percent. Academic scores and classroom behavior also improved. This held particularly true for students who were dealing with depression, anxiety, and anger.[16]

Praise is well known as a reinforcer or reward for good behavior, but it can also be used as a strategy for correcting poor behavior and inspiring new growth. That is because students will often try to match their behaviors and outcomes to what they hear being praised. What gets praised gets repeated.

Throughout the book, we have provided multiple examples of the power of praise. We have written about praise in terms of voicing respect for students, communicating their strengths, expressing appreciation for their contributions, celebrating their goal achievements, and encouraging them to use positive self-talk. Each is an example of constructive feedback and praise.

Five types of praise teachers use to provide constructive feedback and inspire new growth are found in the five P's:

- **Product praise:** "Your art is incredible!" "You got the top score on the exam." "Your science project was outstanding."
- **Process praise:** "I admire the techniques you used." "I love how you made a clear plan and timeline."
- **Purpose praise:** "How you mentored Sherry truly helped her confidence to blossom." "The kind words you spoke to Rick changed his entire view of himself."
- **Person praise:** "You are so reliable." "You're always thinking of others." "You're so patient." "Thanks for being honest."
- **Progress praise:** "Your art skills have improved tremendously." "You went from averaging 60s to 80s on your quizzes."

All five forms of praise motivate students to "continue" doing what they are doing and to progress toward further growth. As one person said of her former teacher: "Her words made me want to be a better me." Another former student said of his teacher, "He was a man of few words, but those few words of praise meant a lot to me."

Offering students praise makes "deposits" in students' emotional bank accounts.[17] When praise is genuine, it strengthens connections and increases students' positive well-being.

As for reprimands, reprimands are meant to let students know what they must "stop" doing to more fully progress and grow. Some teachers, however, use negative reprimands as emotional "whipping sticks" to motivate students, only to find it does not work so well. Negative reprimands are what we described earlier: criticisms, comparisons, shaming, nagging, threatening, and so forth. They do not inspire growth.

In contrast, positive reprimands are done with the full intent to build and inspire students. They are constructive. They encourage growth. They are not harsh, offensive, accusatory, or combative—just the opposite. When done with positive intent, reprimands can be very inspiring and even life changing. They can be one of the best ways to tell a student, "I believe in you. This is what I see in you and your potential."

Though they are meant to be positive, positive reprimands can still be tough conversations. This is why some teachers avoid them. After all, it is not always easy to approach a student at a critical crossroads and say, "Hey, you and your path are headed in a wrong direction. Things need to change if you are going to arrive at the potential I see in you." But we have never said that teachers who make a difference were the "easy" teachers. In fact, numerous people we surveyed talked about a teacher who was very stern and had high expectations. They weren't afraid to reprimand a student when appropriate.

Again, however, we are not so much talking about reprimands that are meant to stop a certain behavior for a day or two; we are talking about positive reprimands that change the trajectory of students' lives for a lifetime. What follows are our Top Ten Tips for keeping reprimands positive and lasting.

Tip 1: Show genuine care and interest in students' growth.

"The dream begins," says Dan Rather, "most of the time, with a teacher who believes in you, who tugs and pushes and leads you on to the next plateau, sometimes poking you with a sharp stick called truth."[18]

We chuckled when a man shared that he never knew how much his former teacher cared about him until the day he started yelling at him for not taking school more seriously. The man said he could hear the teacher's intent and tell by his teacher's tone of voice how much he cared about him. "I'd never had anyone care for me that much before," he said.

No, we do not condone the yelling. But it appears in this situation that the man's former teacher had previously built a connection with the student and exhibited a volume of caring that was louder than his yelling. He had connected before he corrected. When students know a teacher cares about them and is genuinely interested in their growth, they become more open to accepting teachers' corrections.

Tip 2: Pick your battles.

A man needed three medical operations. So on the same day, his efficient doctors removed his gallbladder, replaced his knee, and extracted his tonsils. All three operations were a grand success. The patient, however, died of shock.

At the end of a day, some students appear to go into shock due to all the corrections they have received from adults. "Don't play your music so loud!" "Get off that device!" "Why didn't you tell me?" "Your pants have holes!" None of these corrections are overly harsh but combined they are emotionally deafening.

There is no need to correct every student's every flaw, and especially not within the same conversation or day. So before reprimanding a student, pause and ask: What is the one most important piece of feedback I can offer this student? What will be the end result if I say something? Is this just an ego battle that I intend to win, or a true battle that will impact the future growth of this student?

Be picky when you pick your battles.

Tip 3: Set reasonable growth expectations.

Teachers who make a difference in students' lives set inspiring—but achievable—expectations.

Data from 20,000 American, Canadian, and British college students indicates that parents have increased both the level of expectations they have for their children and the amount of criticism they give their children. The combination of higher expectations and higher criticism is pushing students to strive for perfection. That push for perfection has been linked to depression, anxiety, obsessive-compulsive disorders, self-harm, and eating disorders. The study's lead author, Dr. Thomas Curran of the London School of Economics and Political Science, notes that parents' excessive expectations can be more damaging than their criticisms.[19] Imagine what additional pressures or harm might result when teachers also set expectations too high or offer too much criticism.

Teachers are at their best when they engage students' choices and voices to establish expectations, and when they put the focus on growth, not perfection. As Britain's former prime minister Winston Churchill warned, "Perfection is the enemy to progress."[20]

Tip 4: Be patient.

Aristotle added a fourth Greek term to *logos*, *pathos*, and *ethos* as a strategy of persuasion. That term is *kairos*. *Kairos* means "the right time or season."[21]

To positively reprimand a student, wait for the right time or season. It may not be when the student is in the middle of an already rough day or is in front of peers. It may not be when the teacher is angry and not in control of their emotions.

Sometimes students use their choices to make decisions that stunt or delay their growth. Sometimes students use their choices to do things that hinder their teachers' efforts to make a difference. Therefore, for growth to happen, sometimes teachers must exhibit a full season's worth of patience before expecting any signs of a fruitful harvest.

Correcting students often requires the patience of an orthodontist. Small corrective actions made over a long time may be required before the desired smile is achieved.

Tip 5: Use "I feel" statements.

Dr. David Burns suggests that when teachers correct students, it is best to use *"I feel . . ." statements* in place of *"You . . ." statements.*[22] "You" statements attack, criticize, and accuse students. "You need to change!" "You shouldn't have done that!" "You" statements put students into defensive mode.

In contrast, "I feel" statements state feelings without attacking students. Instead of saying "You are rude for talking during my lesson," "I feel" statements describe teachers' feelings: "When students talk during my lessons, I feel I am being ignored, and I worry that other students will miss the instructions." There is no direct attack in those statements, just teachers voicing feelings and observations.

Tip 6: Discern between emotional issues and behavioral issues.

Ruby Payne suggests that many teachers try to address social or emotional issues as if they are strictly behavioral issues, and it doesn't work very well.[23] There is a difference between students who are intentionally disrespectful, rebellious, or disruptive versus students who are dealing with underlying emotional health issues. When underlying emotional health issues are involved, teachers are best to use empathic listening and seek professional advice to determine what basic needs are not being met for the student before taking corrective action.

Tip 7: Use growth mindset language.

Dr. Carol Dweck suggests that teachers use growth mindset language when giving students corrective feedback. This can be as simple as adding "yet" or "not yet" to the end of a sentence. For example, when a student in an art class exclaims, "I'm no good at art. I cannot even draw a circle!," the teacher might respond, "You mean you cannot draw a circle yet?" The addition of "yet" or "not yet" represents the teacher's confidence in the student's ability to learn, progress, and eventually draw a circle.

Consider additional examples of how to replace fixed mindset language with growth mindset language:

Fixed Mindset	Growth Mindset
You should give up.	Try a different strategy.
Drawing is not your talent.	Keep trying until you get it how you want it.
This is too hard for you.	You will improve with effort.
This is your weakness.	This isn't a strength, yet.

Tip 8: Turn mistakes into opportunities for growth.

Bob Ross taught oil painting lessons to millions of television viewers. Whenever he made a mistake with his brush, or whenever the painted object didn't turn out as he wanted, he smiled and called it a happy accident. He then figured out a way to turn his happy accident into something beautiful in his painting.

A third grade teacher shared how she has several students with perfectionistic tendencies. They become stressed whenever they make the slightest mistake. She has taught them to say to themselves when they make a mistake, "It's okay. You're still cool." She then models it herself. If she misspells a word when writing on the whiteboard, she says, "It's okay, Miss Barnes. You're still cool."

Failure is an inevitable part of growth. Students who are not failing at times or making occasional mistakes are likely not being sufficiently challenged. They are stuck in their comfort zones and not moving toward their growth zones. They need opportunities to learn how to learn from failure. Leadership expert John Maxwell describes such opportunities to learn from failures and mistakes as "stepping stones to success." Some describe it as "failing forward."[24]

Tip 9: Forgive and forget.

Sailor Sam returned to his ship drunk one night, and the captain noted it in the ship's log: "Sailor Sam was drunk tonight!" This offended Sailor Sam. It was the only time in all his years of sailing that he ever returned drunk, and the only time his name appeared in the ship's log.

Sailor Sam did not want that to be the only record kept in the ship's log about him. So he pleaded with the captain to strike the entry. The captain not only refused, he continued to mock Sailor Sam. Eventually, Sailor Sam had had enough and decided it was time for revenge.

That night Sailor Sam wrote in the ship's log in large letters: "Captain was sober tonight!"

Of course, there are times when teachers do need to keep a "log" of students' misbehaviors, such as the thick folder Jesse's former principal had kept. Nevertheless, students want the comfort of knowing that their teachers will not define them by one mistake. Therefore, teachers may at times need to forgive and forget a mistake or two. That is what Muriel and her team did when they intentionally chose to give Jesse a clean start.

Tip 10: Always preserve the relationship.

If we were forced to give only one tip for keeping reprimands positive, it would be to follow the advice of the wise teacher who said: "Always preserve the relationship." In other words, when correcting students, always refrain from saying or doing anything today that will prevent you from having influence with the student in the days or months ahead.

Do students view you as their constant accuser
or as their constant advocate who corrects
them because you care?

Held Me Self-Accountable

Encouraging students helps them know what to "start" doing. Praising them helps them know what to "continue" doing. Reprimanding lets them know what to "stop" doing. Each has the intent to help them grow.

But when do students start taking on the responsibility for holding themselves accountable?

Drs. Richard DuFour and Michael Fullan declare that "autonomy must be balanced by accountability."[25] One barrier to holding students accountable is that the word *accountability* often has a negative connotation for students. If a teacher says, "I'm going to hold you accountable," students might expect to be confronted with a list of things they did wrong or ways they must change. And they might expect their teacher to be fully in charge of the accountability.

Professors Simon Borg of the University of Leeds and Saleh Al-Busaidi of the Sultan Qaboos University in Oman say that to become autonomous learners, students must develop the ability to evaluate their own learning.[26] This requires shifting accountability from a teacher-led experience to a student-led experience.

In *Leaders of Their Own Learning*, Ron Berger and colleagues note that student assessments are more than a tool to measure growth, they are also a tool to stimulate growth. They say, "The root meaning of the word *assess* is 'to sit beside.' When schools adopt student-engaged assessment practices, teachers and parents will find themselves sitting beside students, discussing with them the quality of their work and thinking, and their plans for growth and development."[27]

The image of a teacher, parent, and student sitting beside one another, assessing the student's growth, is powerful. Even more powerful—and more positive—is when the student takes the lead in the assessment and the teacher and parent do more listening than talking.

One parent shared two contrasting experiences with parent-teacher conferences at her son's elementary school:

> Our son had a teacher who did student-led conferences where our son did almost all the talking. We, as parents, could ask questions of the teacher, but mostly got what we needed from our son.
>
> The next year, the same son had a teacher who had her Ph.D. She seemed most interested in making sure we knew how smart she was. She did all the talking. Our son scarcely said a word. Neither did we.

The name "parent–teacher conference" itself takes away accountability from a student, whereas the name "student-led conference" places the responsibility where it belongs. After all, the most important student assessments are not those that take place inside a classroom but those that take place inside a student's mind and heart. As Dr. Berger notes, "These internal assessments govern how much [students] care, how hard they work, and how much they learn. . . . In the end, these are the assessments that really matter."[28]

Young students tend to know more about what they can do to improve than many parents or teachers give them credit for. We were observing a colleague, Dana Penick, discuss with a group of elementary teachers how to set academic goals with students. At one point she asked, "Do you have a few fourth grade students who we can invite into this discussion?" Within minutes, three students entered the room. They had no idea why they had been pulled out of class. Dana asked them: "If you were to do one thing that would most improve your academics, what would that one thing be?"

With little hesitation, the three students began giving answers. "I need to spend less time watching television and get my homework done before dinner," said one. "I need to do the assigned online readings so I can improve my comprehension," said another. It wasn't a teacher imposing the "one thing" or the solutions onto the students. Granted, the one thing the students identified may not have been the most important thing they needed to do to improve, but the students had choice and voice in selecting it, which meant they were certainly more committed to act on it.

One reason to encourage students to be self-accountable is that they are going to self-assess anyway. Students are constantly self-evaluating their progress and grading themselves. Unfortunately, they often choose poor measuring sticks and give themselves unreasonably poor scores. Their self-assessments are frequently nothing more than a self-comparison: "I'm not as good as others."

The day after a concert, a middle school choir teacher gave her students the chance to self-assess. She showed videos of them singing each song and asked them to identify what went well and what went not so well. To her surprise, the students only critiqued what they did not do well. They made no mention of their strengths or their growth. The teacher would have never recognized the need to help them improve their self-assessment skills had she not given them the chance to self-assess.

Indeed, when helping students to be self-accountable, one of the most important things teachers can do is to provide students with more accurate and positive tools to self-assess. Some teachers find that to be difficult because it is so ingrained in them to diagnose and "fix" students' performance issues instead of patiently asking such questions as:

- What have you already done to address the matter?
- What is your next step?
- Have you considered trying . . . ?
- How can I help to support you to . . . ?
- Who else can you involve?
- What strengths do you have that can help you improve what you do not do well yet?

Notice that none of the questions involves teachers taking over ownership of the assessment process.

What makes self-accountability a positive experience for students is that it gives them a chance to account for not only their mistakes and stretches, but also their achievements, their strengths, and their progress—their growth.

Muriel was visiting an elementary school, and a third grade student persisted in asking the principal if he could meet Muriel. He insisted that it was "important." The principal granted his wish, and when he entered the room where Muriel was working, he was surprised to see a handful of his former teachers also present. He introduced himself to Muriel and began to tell his story.

"I used to be 'bad,'" he said, while looking over at the teachers for confirmation. "Wasn't I?"

He went on to tell Muriel how the principal had invited him to give a speech at an open house. It had gone well. "I started feeling 'good' about myself again," he said. "I never want to feel 'bad' again now that I know how 'good' feels."

The boy was taking ownership for his past poor behavior. Yet his real desire was to advocate for his new self, to be validated for his progress. His life had taken on a new positive trajectory, and he wanted Muriel to know about it.

What student does not want to self-advocate for the "good" they have done and the exciting possibilities that lie ahead in their future?

Allowing students to self-account for their progress may take time, patience, and leadership. That is why we admire a high school counselor who was asked to take corrective action with a student named Jake. Jake had been sent to the counselor for repeatedly disrupting class. However, before the counselor began talking with Jake about his behavior, he felt a hunch: "Jake needs a friend."

The counselor said that when he entered his office, Jake appeared emotionally beaten down. "This guy has no one believing in him," the counselor thought. "His parents don't believe in him. His teachers don't believe in him. Even his few friends don't really believe in him." The counselor didn't want to be added to the crowd of non-believers, so he chose to try to connect with Jake before making any attempt to correct his classroom behavior.

The counselor asked Jake to tell him about what was going well in his life. Jake thought it was an odd request but proceeded to share a few things that were going well. After listening to a few examples, the counselor smiled and said, "That's great, Jake. Now I want you to come back next week and update me on what else is going well in your life. As for now, I need you to get back to class."

Jake looked suspiciously at the counselor as he exited the office. "What trick is he up to?" he wondered. "No lecture? No punishment?"

Jake did return to the counselor's office the next week. He continued to be suspicious of the counselor's motives as he shared a few things from the current week that had gone well. It started a series of near weekly visits. The counselor eventually began to ask Jake about his life plans and ambitions. To the counselor's surprise, Jake did have plans and ambitions. When the counselor asked Jake how he was progressing toward his plans, Jake admitted that he was not doing well. He was letting himself get distracted by less important things.

When the counselor asked if there was anything he could do to support him, Jake responded, "No, I just need to start taking life more seriously." Jake was self-assessing and self-correcting. In fact, the counselor never did get around to "managing" Jake's classroom misbehaviors because he was too busy "leading" Jake in a way that was changing the trajectory of his life. Jake was managing his own classroom behaviors.

Renowned education researcher John Hattie insists that in classrooms where there are positive teacher–student relations, there is greater non-directivity, which means that students are more likely to initiate corrective actions on their own and self-regulate.[29] Isn't that what happened with Jake?

Self-accountability will look different depending on the student and the circumstances. More self-accountability is expected as students mature. However, self-accountability can start when students are very young. Over the past 20 years, we've watched numerous students, some as young as kindergarteners, set goals, track their progress, and report to adults on how they are doing during student-led conferences. We have seen them collect their best work in notebooks that they happily share. They truly seem to enjoy being held self-accountable when the main focus is on self-advocating for their strengths, their successes, and their growth.

What effective strategies have you seen
teachers use to hold students self-accountable?

Temperance Factors

When attempting to correct students in positive ways:

Be Realistic with the Amount of Encouragement and Feedback

Just as gardeners can overwater when trying to grow plants, classroom leaders can over-encourage, over-praise, and over-correct when attempting to nurture and grow students. When students feel they are too closely monitored or over-assessed, they may become nervous and disengage from learning.

Likewise, if teachers fill students with excessive, exaggerated, or undeserved affirmations, such as "You can do anything!," while the students actually lack the skills and knowledge they need to get a job or to be accepted to a university, then when it comes time to graduate, those students will feel the adults have deceived them. A graduating student may be a very nice person, but without some academic rigor to their credit, they will feel anxiety.

In short, teachers must be both genuine and realistic when it comes to the amount and content of the encouragement and feedback they give students and balance the amount of accountability they pass on.

Classroom Management Remains Important

Some teachers think that to be popular, they must be every student's best friend, bend the rules, and tolerate misbehavior. That is neither good classroom management nor good leadership.

There are times when teachers must take decisive action to manage students' behaviors and implement restorative practices. Violence, bullying, and behaviors that cause constant distractions cannot be left unmanaged, especially when doing so risks putting other students in harm's way. Yet, by taking a leadership approach first, the hope is that the need for more stringent classroom management strategies will be lessened or reduced.

Don't Forget the Adults!

Adults also want to feel they are growing and progressing. They, too, like to receive encouraging words and constructive feedback. They, too, like to self-account for their positive progress.

Most teachers are doing better than they give themselves credit for. If anything, they need to be more self-compassionate when holding themselves self-accountable. They do so many positive things inside their classrooms, and yet seldom do they get appropriately acknowledged by parents, peer teachers, administrators, or students. So why not give them opportunities to self-advocate for their successes? Why not let them share how they have made connections with students and made a difference in their positive well-being?

As teachers grow to believe in students and find ways to help students to believe in themselves, one of the best outcomes is that they also grow to believe in themselves.

Concluding Thoughts

One person said of his former teacher, "He was a man of few words, but those words meant the world to me."

Students want to feel they are progressing and growing, and to be acknowledged for it. A timely word of encouragement or praise, or a constructive word of feedback, might be the key that unlocks students' hearts and minds and alters the trajectory of their life. But it takes the gentle nurturing of a teacher to make it happen with proper timing.

For as in nurturing a tender plant, teachers cannot force students to grow. They can only create the best natural conditions and the systems to encourage growth. And when their efforts to correct students in a positive way do not go as hoped, they know when to pause and preserve the relationship in hopes of having the opportunity to make a difference at a future time—a later growing season.

The Challenge

Select one. To help students see more growth and progress in what they are learning and doing at school, create and implement a plan or routine for how you will

- use encouraging language to inspire them;
- provide them with constructive feedback, either praise or a positive reprimand; or
- empower them to be more self-accountable.

8

Crafting a Sustainable Plan

Aesop, whose life itself may have been a fable, provided some of the most instructive fables of all time. Our favorite tells the story of "The Man, the Boy, and the Donkey," and our version goes like this.

Once upon a time, a father and son faced a harsh fate on their farm. The rent on their farm was due and their money was spent.

In desperation, they decided to take their prized donkey to a distant farmer's market and sell it for cash. And off they set on their journey. But as they passed through the first village, they encountered a series of jeers from some cranky old bystanders. "How silly," shouted one. "Ridiculous!" called out another. "Why do the father and son both walk when they have a donkey to ride?"

Embarrassed, the father heaved his son on the back of the donkey and off again they went. Yet, as they came upon the next village, they were met by another set of hecklers. "The son makes his father walk while he rides," mocked one. "What a disrespectful son!" sneered another.

Reacting to the crowd of opinions, the father and son switched places. Now, the father sat upon the donkey's back while the son walked. Yet, as they entered the next village, again the critics were out. "The father makes the son walk while he sits comfortably in the saddle," cackled one. "Shameful man!" scoffed the onlookers.

With that, the only option left for the father and son duo was to mount the donkey together. Both would ride.

But as the journey stretched on and the sun rose to noon high, the combined weight of the father and son bent the donkey's back and stole away its stamina. Within view of the market, the donkey collapsed and died.

Never again did the father and son set foot on the farm.

Even Simple Needs a Plan

To the father and son's credit, they had a clear *vision*. They would sell the donkey, use the money to pay the rent, and stay on the farm. It was as simple as that. So what went wrong?

What the father and son lacked was a clear *plan* for getting the donkey to market in a way that would sustain its stamina and retain its value. Had they had a plan, they could have ignored the hecklers, stayed with their plan, sold the donkey, paid the rent, and returned to the farm. Instead, they learned the hard way that "even simple needs a plan."

Recall that our purposes—our *vision*—for writing this book are twofold:

1. to enable students from all corners of the world to increase their positive well-being and readiness to learn; and
2. to inspire, or re-inspire, teachers' passions for making a difference in young people's lives.

While the need to fulfill the two purposes in schools is urgent, it requires a plan. A simple plan.

So how do teachers make a plan for implementing all seven leadership skillsets and keep it simple?

The best way we know for teachers to make a simple, sustainable plan is to create a set of simple, sustainable routines and systems. Systems and routines provide continuity, retain quality, and remove the need for teachers to constantly "re-create the wheel." They are meant to make things easier for teachers, not more difficult.

When attempting to address students' mental health and school connectedness, the Centers for Disease Control and Prevention (CDC) recommends that educators create routines and systems that

- ensure that every student feels a close, trusting connection with at least one supportive adult at school;
- dedicate time for teachers to explore students' interests and give personalized attention to their social and emotional needs;
- establish a stable, positive network of peers to improve students' perceptions of school; and
- provide a physical environment that inspires positive student perceptions at school.[1]

What follows are four approaches that teachers and administrators can consider when creating a plan for their classroom or school. Each approach is aligned with the CDC's recommendations. The first three can be implemented by teachers on their own. The fourth is a whole-school approach.

Approach 1: Connect Teachers with Students

The first approach connects teachers with students. It addresses the seven leadership skillsets and their basic needs over a stretch of time, perhaps over an entire year. As a review, the seven leadership skillsets and their matching basic needs are brought together in the following table.

Leadership Skillsets		Basic Needs
Accepted Me as I Was	→	Connection
Taught Me About Life	→	Meaning
Inspired Me to See My Strengths	→	Hope
Entrusted Me with Responsibility	→	Self-Worth
Helped Me Through a Hard Time	→	Resilience
Empowered Me to Do It Myself	→	Self-Efficacy
Corrected Me in Positive Ways	→	Growth

This approach for implementing the seven skillsets and their best practices uses what we refer to as the *Power of 10*, which is a series of three routines. The routines optimize the first 10 days of school, the first 10 minutes of class, and the first and last 10 seconds of each day or class period.

The First 10 Days

The impact that the first 10 days of school has on teacher–student connections, and on school connectedness in general, must never be underestimated.

Our colleague Dr. Lesley Eason has been a high school teacher, a school administrator, a district administrator, and an education consultant for years. So, when we asked her to identify a teacher who made a significant difference in her life, we found it interesting that she returned to her first-ever day of school. In her words:

> I remember my first-ever day of school like it was yesterday. I was so excited about starting school, but I was also very nervous. It was one of the scariest times of my young life. Then, I turned a corner and saw

Mrs. Fountain standing outside her classroom. She was extending her arms towards me, greeting me by name, and welcoming me to her classroom. She was the epitome of a teacher who makes students feel like they belong. To this day, I continue to give her credit for the deep love I have for education.

Mrs. Fountain not only helped Dr. Eason feel welcomed in the first minutes of a school year, she also put her on a trajectory that would lead her to enjoy school and the gift of learning for the rest of her life. What a difference she made in Dr. Eason's life.

Welcoming students during the first day of a new school year is like opening a gifted box of assorted chocolates. You never quite know what to expect. Students come in all shapes and sizes. It is hard to tell from their outsides what they are like on their insides. Some will melt under the least bit of heat. Others might even be a little "nutty." But we do like to assume that all have something sweet about them.[2]

Much of what is inside of students can be discovered during the first 10 days of a school year. In fact, for decades Rosemary and Harry Wong have promoted the benefits of teachers dedicating the first days of a school year to getting to know something about each student and establishing a positive classroom culture. Teachers who apply the insights from the Wongs' book, *The First Days of School*, know the value of optimizing the first 10 days.[3]

We strongly suggest that the first 10 days be focused on applying the first leadership skillset, "Teacher Accepted Me as I Was." It is a time for teachers to begin calling students by name, taking an interest in students' stories, and voicing respect for students. When done well during the first 10 days (or less), these best practices will enable teachers to make important connections with students and, at the same time, begin the process of enabling students to feel a sense of connection throughout the rest of a school year. Insights and best practices for how to use the first 10 days to build connections are found in Chapter 1, "My Teacher Accepted Me as I Was."

The First 10 Minutes

The second routine is what happens after the first 10 days. It involves optimizing the first 10 minutes of each day for the remainder of the school year.

We were visiting a high school in Kentucky and we kept hearing students rave about the choir teacher, Mrs. Conley. We were taken to see her class in action. The choir room looked like it was meant to hold 50 students but was packed with what looked like 70. The students were all engaged and singing with full hearts. Afterward, we spoke with a few students and asked what drew them to Mrs. Conley. They gave all kinds of great answers, but one specifically caught our attention. One student said, "She knows and cares about each one of us individually." We thought, "How could that be with 70 students?" When we asked the student what Mrs. Conley did to connect with that many students individually, she responded, "She takes about 10 minutes at the start of each class to ask us about what's going on and how we are doing."

At a high school in Missouri, Lexi's mother described to us how Lexi was a colorful butterfly in elementary school. She was a leader in all kinds of events. But when she arrived at middle school, she almost instantly began to shut her wings. She was intimidated by the larger number of students and anxious that they were more talented than she was. By the time she got to high school, her wings were nearly closed entirely. In Lexi's mind, the high school was so, so big, and the students were so, so much more talented. Her wings closed nearly entirely. All this was much to the great chagrin of her mother, who saw Lexi as such a talented, capable, bright student with much to give. She only wished she could help Lexi see it in herself.

But then in her junior year Lexi was enrolled in Mr. Wood's English class. Her mother described how Lexi would come home from school excited and start talking about an inspiring quote Mr. Wood had shared that day. Lexi wanted to discuss it with her mother. It turned out that

Mr. Wood would take the first 10 minutes of each class to get to know students and to chat with them and talk about life. His goal was to inspire them, and with Lexi it was working. When he invited her to join a team of students who were assigned to make life easier for new students, Lexi took on the challenge. Her mother was thrilled. Lexi's wings were once again open and in full color.

In both of these cases, it was interesting that the teachers took 10 minutes at the start of each class to connect with the students. By connecting first, the teachers put themselves in a position to influence the students academically—and in life.

This has been a theme throughout the leadership skillsets. Teachers have dedicated routines to connect with students. We like to think of the dedicated time as being in the first 10 minutes, so they do not get crowded out by other tasks or lost in the commotion of the day.

The main priorities of these first 10 minutes are to connect, engage, and lead.

Connect. This is dedicated time for teachers to connect with students before jumping into academics. Many teachers and schools already have dedicated time set aside. They call it a morning meeting, advisory period, academy, circle time, homeroom, clubs, or some other fitting name. This can be a perfect time for teachers to be intentional in their efforts to connect with students.

What might teachers do to connect with students during these 10 minutes? For starters, they can apply the skillsets and best practices found in this book over an extended period of time. For example, they can apply one best practice per week in the order they are presented in this book. Or they can choose to go in any order they want based on what they see as the immediate needs of their students. Or they can focus on their own professional development by choosing one strength or one stretch from the *Leadership Skillsets Self-Assessment* (see next page) and then work on applying it for a week or two before selecting a new stretch or strength to work on. Or teachers can use the time to share a personal story of a "mountain" they have climbed and overcome in life, or to share their joy of learning. The aim is building connections and making progress. It is not about seeking perfection.

Leadership Skillsets Self-Assessment

	As a teacher, I . . . (Mark "X" if a strength or stretch.)	Stretch	Strength
1	**Accept Students as They Are (Connection)**		
	Call students by name.		
	Take an interest in students.		
	Voice respect for students.		
2	**Teach Students About Life (Meaning)**		
	Connect academic lessons with life.		
	Share motivational thoughts and life hacks.		
	Live an inspiring life.		
3	**Inspire Students to See Their Strengths (Hope)**		
	Communicate students' strengths and potential.		
	Turn students' stretches into strengths.		
	Views students' differences as strengths.		
4	**Entrust Students with Responsibility (Self-Worth)**		
	Give students a chance to lead.		
	Involve students in service learning.		
	Express appreciation for students' contributions.		
5	**Help Students Through a Hard Time (Resilience)**		
	Listen to students with empathy.		
	Help students see the good in their world.		
	Make time for relaxation and fun.		
6	**Empower Students to Do it Themselves (Self-Efficacy)**		

	Give students choices.		
	Give students voice.		
	Support students in achieving goals.		
7	**Correct Students in Positive Ways (Growth)**		
	Provide students with positive encouragement.		
	Give students constructive feedback.		
	Hold students self-accountable.		

Engage. Not all students arrive at school calm and ready to learn. Turmoil at home, bus noise, bullying, hallway chaos, loneliness, anxiety, and so forth can lead students to arrive in an unsettled state. So a second priority of the first 10 minutes is to engage students by giving them a few moments at the start of a day or class to re-connect with school and with their peers, and to become more ready to learn. It is time for "calming the sailors." This might include discussing a positive quote, listening to inspiring music, providing a few free minutes to relax, laugh, and have fun. It can include allowing time to do "Monday highs and lows" or time to chat about life or school events. It could be time to plan a service learning project.

Lead. Portions of the 10 minutes are intended to be dedicated to teaching positive skills for positive well-being. This might entail teaching a skill for personal, interpersonal, or team effectiveness, or for discussing a positive character trait. It is an excellent time for discussing one of the best practices from one of the seven leadership skillsets. These brief teaching moments are best received by students when they are facilitated as conversations rather than as formal lessons, especially with secondary students.

It is not intended that all three priorities be met in the first 10 minutes of every day of every week, as if it is a daily checklist. That is not the spirit of the first 10 minutes. The larger intent and spirit of the daily 10 minutes is to enable every student to have at least one teacher who takes a focused interest in them and whose sincere intention is to let no student go unnoticed or fall through the gaps. Ten minutes is not a lot of time, yet when aggregated over a school year, much can happen in those 10 minutes to help students feel connected, to start their days off in a positive tone, and to learn positive skills for positive well-being.

Some educators prefer to combine the daily 10 minutes into fewer days, such as blocking out 30 minutes twice a week, or whatever best fits their schedule. And though we suggest the 10 minutes be done first thing each day, if "first thing" does not work, choose another time. And if more time is desired, take more time. We work with a school that takes the first 45 minutes of each day to address these purposes due to the heavy social and emotional needs of its students. Regardless of when it is scheduled, or the amount of time that is allotted, it is most effective when the time is turned into a consistent routine and kept simple.

Granted, some teachers may feel they cannot give up 10 minutes of precious class time. However, a typical school day contains approximately six hours, or 360 minutes, of class time. What we are suggesting is that 350 minutes be dedicated to academics and 10 minutes to positive well-being. We view it as a small investment with rich returns. It may require teachers to eliminate something from their usual list of daily tasks. Management guru Peter Drucker calls this *planned abandonment*, or giving up something important to do for something even more important.[4] Artist Hans Hofmann refers to it as "eliminating the unnecessary so the necessary may speak."[5] We simply refer to it as leadership.

The First and Last 10 Seconds

The third *Power of 10* routine is actually two very short routines. It uses the first and last 10 seconds of each class period (or day) to start and end on a positive note.

Suppose friends come to your home for dinner. When you greet them at the door, your first words wouldn't be, "All right. Let's get started. Everyone sit down and be quiet so I can talk." Of course not.

And when it comes time for your friends to depart, you would not say, "Well, there's the bell. That's it for today!" and then just walk away and let them find their way out the door. Of course not.

Nor would you do that with students at the end of each school day or class period. Would you? Of course not.

From researchers like Solomon Asch, we learn about the *primacy effect* and the *recency effect*.[6] People remember most what they hear, see, and experience first (the primacy effect) and what they hear, see, and experience last (the recency effect). So what would happen if students were to base their opinions of you as a teacher entirely on what they hear, see, or experience from you in the first and last 10 seconds of each class or day? Would their assessments be positive?

Recall how Mr. Rogers always ended his show with the words, "I like you just the way you are." Those words took less than 10 seconds for him to express, but they were the final words children heard from him each day. It was his routine for ending every program in a positive, "I believe in you" manner.

What teachers say in the first or last 10 seconds might be a favorite motto, an inspiring quote, a life hack, or a voice of respect. It could be a word of appreciation or a mention of something good teachers see in the world. It could be a piece of humor, a line from a song, a word of encouragement. It could be the same words each day or a variety of expressions, such as "Thanks for being on time and ready to learn." Or "I enjoy being with this class." Or any other simple gesture that starts and ends classes on a positive note.

Positive words spoken at the start and end of each day or class period can set the tone for how students feel about themselves and how they treat each other throughout the remainder of a day. The key is to turn it into a routine so that it happens consistently.

So, there are three routines that make up the *Power of 10*: optimizing the first 10 days of school; mastering the first 10 minutes of each day; and making the first and last 10 seconds positive. It is important to note, however, that teachers can apply the leadership skillsets and their best practices at any time of day and within any subject matter lesson.

The best practices are not limited to being applied for only 10 minutes in any given day. They are meant to be a relevant, meaningful part of any classroom or school culture.

Approach 2: Connect Students with Students

Whereas Approach 1 is focused on enabling teachers to connect with students, Approach 2 focuses on teachers facilitating opportunities for students to connect with one another.

The simplest plan we know for doing this is to involve students in the *Power of 10*. Instead of the teacher being the only one connecting with students, the first 10 days, the first 10 minutes, and the first and last 10 seconds can be used to involve students connecting with each other. For example, during the first 10 days, involve students in fun activities where they call each other by name, provide opportunities for them to learn about each other's stories and voice respect for each other. By the end of the first 10 days, every student should know each other's name, know something about each other, and have voiced respect for each other. The hope is that each student will feel connected with other students in their class. No student should go home from that class feeling that no one knows or cares about them. The bonus is that as students participate in the activities, teachers will also be participating, listening in, and making small connections. So in essence, Approaches 1 and 2 will be happening simultaneously.

Beyond the first 10 days, the first 10 minutes can also involve students in making connections with each other, in starting days on a positive note, and in learning positive skills for positive learning. Teachers and students can work together to discuss all seven leadership skills and their best practices. Let's say that one week a teacher chooses to focus on the best practice, "Shared a memorable life hack." The teacher might start the week by sharing one of their personal favorite life hacks, how it has helped them in their life, and how it can benefit students. Then, during the remaining days of the week, four or five students each day can share one of their favorite one-sentence life hacks or an inspiring quote, so that each student has a chance to share. Each student might even write their one-sentence life hack on an individual large piece of paper and post it on a classroom wall for all students to see. The next week, the teacher can choose a different best practice to discuss with students during the first 10 minutes of one or more days of that week before moving on to a different best practice the next week. As teachers follow a one-best-practice-per-week pattern for the remainder of the year, teachers and students will connect with each other and basic needs will be met.

As for the first and last 10 seconds of each day or class period, students can also be involved in starting or ending a day or class with a positive message or thought. The intent again is not to conduct a scripted set of lessons or activities, but for teachers and students to find opportunities for connecting, for starting each day on a positive note, and for students to learn positive skills for positive well-being. How exactly that happens is up to the artistry of the teacher. But it needs a plan. A simple plan.

Approach 3: Connect with Adults

According to Roland S. Barth, "The nature of relationships among the adults within a school has a greater influence on the character and quality of a school and on student accomplishment than anything else."[7] We agree.

We have never seen a school create a great social and emotional environment for students without first delivering a great social and emotional environment for the adults in the school. So why would it not be just as important, if not more important, for the adults to feel connected with the other adults in the school?

This is why Approach 3 focuses on teachers and other adults connecting with each other. Teacher-to-teacher, adult-to-adult connections cannot be minimized in a school. After all, students are not alone in their day-to-day struggles or their desires for positive connections. So a safe strategy to apply when connecting with the other adults in a school is to always look out for each other. Apply the seven leadership skillsets to your interaction with one another.

Whether you are a teacher, an administrator, or some other adult in a school, when you see a new teacher in the hallway, call them by name. Ask about their story. Voice respect.

When you see the media specialist, language specialist, or office worker, let them know how meaningful their role is for students. Share a favorite life hack. Be a positive role model.

When you see a specialty teacher in the staff lounge, acknowledge their unique strengths. Compliment them for turning a student's stretch into a strength. Let them know you view their differences as strengths.

When you pass the school counselor or nurse in the office, express thanks for their leadership and service. State specific reasons why you appreciate their contributions and the impact they have on students . . . on you.

When you see the principal or an assistant administrator having a crazy or difficult day, pause and listen. Empathize. Help them to see the good in their world. Help them to relax and enjoy a little fun.

When you see the safety officer, bus driver, physical facilities crew, a parent, or other adults in the school, ask them to voice their opinion on how to connect with students, or congratulate them on achieving a goal.

When you see the cafeteria or custodial staff hard at work, encourage them. Praise them. Let them self-advocate for the good they do.

If you happen to be a school administrator, we hope you glean from this that every leadership skillset and best practice in this book applies equally to an administrator working with the teachers and other adults in a school.

In short, whatever your role, put all the seven leadership skillsets and their best practices to work in helping the adults in the school feel connection, meaning, hope, self-worth, resilience, self-efficacy, and growth. Everyone in a school deserves to know that there are people believing in them.

Don't forget the adults!

Approach 4: Connect the Whole School

The fourth approach is our preferred approach. It is to involve all teachers, all adults, and all students in implementing the *Power of 10*. It is a whole school approach.

Think about it. Teachers can apply each of the first three approaches independently.

However!

Wouldn't it be better if all teachers and all students in a school worked together to apply the leadership skillsets and create a school culture in which all students, teachers, and staff are applying the best practices? Wouldn't it be better if every student in a school has at least one stable and committed teacher calling them by name, taking an interest in them, voicing respect for them, and so forth?

We were visiting with Dr. John Shepard, a high school principal whose students have some of the top academic scores in his state. He and his administrative team have set aside 30 minutes twice a week for what they call Lead Time. The time is used for working with students on goals and teaching them life skills, such as *The 7 Habits of Highly Effective People*, and other leadership skills. But what Dr. Shepard says is the highest priority of that timeframe is for teachers to connect with students. To get to know them. To identify any special needs. To take an interest in their futures. And for Dr. Shepard, he wants that to happen with all of his students, not just a handful. And he wanted all of his teachers doing it, not just the ones who do it naturally. So they built it into a schoolwide system that they have been doing for about 10 years, and Dr. Shepard says he would not have it any other way.

And what about all the support staff? They, too, can be applying the skillsets in their roles. They, too, can have it built into their routines.

We knew a custodian who stood at the arrival drop-off spot each morning cheerfully greeting students by name. It was his daily routine. He did the same when passing students in the hallways throughout the day. And what about the office staff? They have a front-row seat to students coming and going. What impact would it have if they were to have routines built into their work with students to help the students feel connected? The cafeteria crew serves students one-by-one every day. What if each cafeteria crew member saw a big part of their role and a part of their routine to contribute to a more positive culture?

The key to a whole-school approach starts with an effective principal—the teacher of teachers. We are so impressed with the principals and assistant principals we have met on our journeys. But they cannot do it all alone. It takes everyone contributing and a team to oversee it.

Therefore, a vital part of a whole-school approach is to entrust a small team of teachers and other adults with the responsibility to plan and oversee the implementation of the leadership skillsets throughout the school and to build school-wide connections. Such a team might include the principal (or assistant principal), a school counselor, a few teachers, a non-teaching staff member, and a parent or two. The team coordinates activities and creates routines to ensure that teachers and staff experience connection, meaning, hope, self-worth, resilience, self-efficacy, and growth throughout a school year. The team also oversees the placement of inspiring quotes or life hacks on murals located at key crossroads throughout the school. They also identify opportunities for students to take on schoolwide leadership responsibilities, such as planning and leading assemblies or creating motivational videos to inspire students. And they oversee the training of new teachers and staff in the leadership skillsets. But they, too, do not need to do it all themselves. They can assemble adult action teams and delegate responsibilities to them.

If school counselors are available, be sure to utilize their expertise. Counselors make excellent members of the adult team and excellent mentors in working with students. They may know of specific students or adults who can truly benefit from taking on an action team responsibility at the school level. They can also be very helpful in providing sage advice for students and adults.

Ideally, a team of students can also be entrusted with building connections and applying the leadership skillsets throughout the school. The student team works with the adult team to plan and carry out events and activities at the school level. Trust us, students can do much of what the adult team might normally do, with the adult team lending support. For instance, students can take on responsibilities for planning service-learning opportunities. They can act as peer mentors to new or struggling students. They can identify, utilize, and celebrate students' talents. They can help identify students who may be lonely or distressed and in need of being a part of something meaningful. They can offer suggestions on how to create and lead action teams of students to create a more positive school culture. Indeed, by the time they get to high school, there is little students cannot do when given the chance to take the lead.

In some secondary schools, student team members are invited to register for a class that is dedicated to implementing the leadership skillsets throughout the school. This gives them an intentional block of time to plan and carry out activities on a near-daily basis without having to meet before or after school.

In our work with *Leader in Me* schools, we name these adult and student teams "Lighthouse Teams" because they provide stable guidance and positive role models for the whole school. Your school might call your student or adult teams "The Believe Team," or some other appropriate name. They can take on an enormous role in building connections in the school, setting positive tones for each school day, and even for teaching some of the positive skills for positive living. We have spoken with numerous educators who have been stunned by the impact these students can have on a school.

So there are four general approaches to implementing all seven leadership skillsets and best practices in simple ways. Teachers can choose to implement one or more of the approaches, whereas administrators can work with staff to decide if a whole-school approach is well matched for their students and circumstances.

Approach 1	Connect Teachers with Students		
Approach 2		Connect Students with Students	
Approach 3			Connect Adults with Adults
Approach 4	Connect Teachers with Students	Connect Students with Students	Connect Adults with Adults

When making a plan for implementing the leadership skillsets, there are two additional stakeholders—or support groups—to consider: families and communities.

Connect with Families

Perhaps you have seen a daring act being performed on a stage and, beforehand, the commentator says, "Do *not* try this at home!" Well, this is a case where we say, "*Do* try this at home!"

Though this book is meant for professional teachers, we indicated from the start that we hope it will also reach other important teachers who work with students, "especially parents." After all, parents are students' first teachers.

We also noted from the start that what strengthens teens' mental health is for them to feel connected to school and family—both.[8] While a school may not have a specific focus to build connections with students and their families, there are ways educators can connect with families, and perhaps even strengthen them.

Social and emotional challenges hit all families, and families of all types. No family is fully immune. Nevertheless, research shows that students with strong families are more likely to experience positive well-being. For example, Robert Whitaker of Columbia University led a team of researchers in a study of 37,000 students across Europe, Africa, Asia, and South America. Students who reported having a strong bond with their family were 49 percent more likely to flourish socially and emotionally than were the students who reported low levels of family connection.[9]

Indeed, when students feel both strong family connectedness and strong school connectedness, they are less likely to struggle with mental health challenges, as illustrated below.

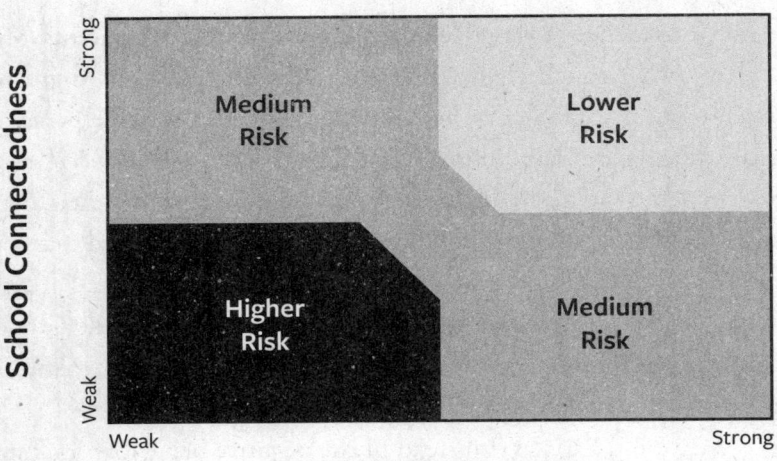

The words *lower risk* in the diagram are a reminder that even when students feel both strong connectedness in their family and strong connectedness at school, they may still be at risk of mental health challenges due to factors beyond parents' or teachers' control. Parents can be superheroes and still not be able to prevent all the social and emotional challenges their child encounters.

Nevertheless, it is hard to imagine students who do not feel better and do better when they have a parent (or parents) who accept them as they are, who teach them about life, and who see their strengths (not just their weaknesses). Parents who entrust them with meaningful responsibilities and express appreciation. Parents who listen and help them through difficult times. Parents who empower them to do things on their own. Parents who correct them in positive ways.

Let's be real. Even under the best of conditions, parenting is not easy. One teacher shared a story about standing in line at a store to pay for a few items. In front of her was a mother whose children were running around being raucous. The teacher was thinking, "Why doesn't this mother do something about her children?" Just then, the mother said to the clerk, "I need help." She proceeded to have a panic attack. She grabbed her chest and slid to the floor. The teacher rushed in and did her best to calm the mother as the children stared in stunned silence.

For the teacher, it was a vivid reminder not to judge parents. She wondered what tough challenges and parental meltdowns might be happening in the families of her students. Indeed, a sizeable percentage of students are raised under conditions known as *childhood emotional neglect*. Their parents are ill-prepared to deal with their own emotional stress or relationship difficulties, let alone prepared to teach or model for their children how to deal with such challenges. Parents' lack of skills for positive well-being often ends up being cascaded down through their children and on to their children's children. It is a multi-generational downward spiral.

What would happen if instead of the negative behaviors trickling downward from parent to child to grandchild, students were to take the seven leadership skillsets home and pass them upwards to their parents and grandparents? This could happen through teachers sending a weekly message home with students to let parents know what positive skills for positive living their child is learning each week. Parents could then discuss the leadership skillsets with their child, perhaps during a mealtime. In that way, the entire family is being strengthened. Better yet, a parent could model the skillsets for their child.

When training these leadership skillsets and best practices to teachers in a workshop setting, we nearly always get a teacher or a principal who comes up to us during a workshop and says, "Can we teach these skillsets to parents?" Our answer is "absolutely." We even had a principal say to us as she was leaving the workshop, "Thank you. This is great! You have just given me the basic messages to put in the weekly newsletters that we send home to parents."

As author and educator Barbara Coloroso observed: "If kids come to us from strong, healthy, functioning families, it makes our jobs easier. If they do not come to us from strong, healthy, functioning families, it makes our job more important."[10] Families are vital to the success of students and schools. Schools are strengthened when families are strengthened, and families are strengthened when schools are strengthened. It is a nice partnership. So why not make an effort to share these leadership skillsets and best practices with parents?

It is important to remember, however, that a parent does not need to be flawless to be a strong parent. In fact, some parents try to be superheroes, and that, by itself, can create problems. Parents who try to be perfect parents and try to raise perfect children, are often the same parents who produce perfectly stressed-out children, and that, in turn, produces perfectly stressed-out parents. As with teachers, the aim for parents must be for progression, not perfection.

At a minimum, it is important for teachers to model and apply the seven leadership skillsets with parents. Parents will not feel they belong or are connected when they are at school when teachers do not know their names, do not take an interest in them, or do not voice respect for them. Parents will not fully relax when teachers view them only through their weaknesses, not their strengths. Parents, like students, prefer to be led, not managed.

Perhaps the best way to begin modeling the leadership skillsets is for teachers to model them with their immediate and extended family members. They can think of a family member who might be struggling with an issue or perhaps of a family relationship that seems to be somewhat broken. Then review the seven leadership skillsets and see if there are any of the best practices that would benefit that relationship. For example, we know a lot of parents who wish they had connected better before they corrected. However, rather than focusing on what a relationship "should have been" in the past, they can focus ahead on what the relationship can become. Dwelling on the weaknesses of the past is never as effective as working on the strengths that will happen in the future.

So when making a plan for implementing the leadership skillsets in a school or classroom, also consider a plan for connecting with parents and sharing with them the leadership skillsets, so they, too, can apply them in leading their families.

Patience Is a Proactive Choice

For school connectedness to have its greatest impact on students, on teachers, and on the culture of a school, it takes the combined efforts of everyone.

So when making a plan—a simple plan—for how you will increase connectedness at school, be sure to build in routines and systems that will have the potential to connect all of the school's stakeholders: teachers, students, administrators, and parents. And for extra support, why not connect with community leaders? Community members, leaders, businesspeople, and heroes are all interested in students' positive well-being and readiness to learn. Why not enlist their talents and knowledge in your plan for increasing students' positive well-being and readiness to learn? Why not enlist their help in acknowledging the great work that teachers do as a way of sustaining teachers' passions for making a difference in students' lives? Why not enlist the whole village? Everyone can contribute, as illustrated below.

School Connectedness

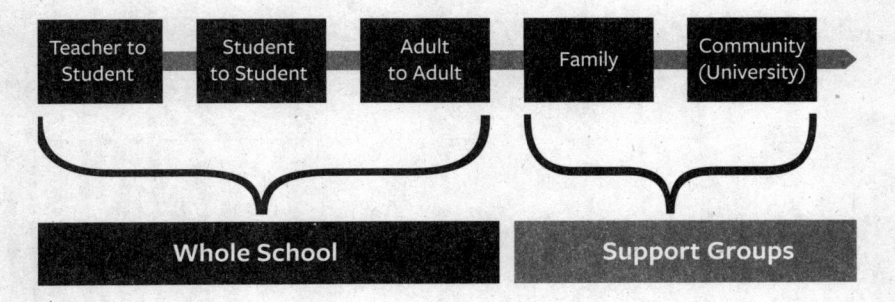

As teachers believe in students and create positive classroom environments with the help of the village, the promising news from research is that most social or emotional interventions in schools do increase students' positive well-being and are even cost-effective. They also make schools safer.[11] And the bonus is that the behavioral and academic outcomes of students also improve.[12] And while teaching social and emotional effectiveness skills provides benefits for all students, it particularly benefits students who have experienced trauma or who come from families facing income insecurities.[13]

But it takes a plan. A simple plan.

Of course, the success of any school plan or intervention is dependent upon the quality of the plan and the fidelity of the implementation. This may take time and some trial and error. Don't give up if plans to implement the skillsets of this book do not all work out as you hoped on your first try. Accept in advance that you will not connect with every student, and not every approach will go exactly as planned. As the saying goes, "Life is what happens when you are making other plans."[14] Accept in advance that you will not connect with every student.

Be prepared to adapt more than once. Be ready to practice proactive patience. The aim, again, is for progress, not perfection. Celebrate even the small successes. Recognize that, as James Clear declares in *Atomic Habits*, "Changes that seem small and unimportant at first will compound into remarkable results if you're willing to stick with them for years."[15]

The Challenge

Select all of the following:

- Choose one of the approaches suggested in this chapter.
- Make a plan to implement the approach. Keep it simple. Pursue it in bite-sized pieces.
- Celebrate victories, even small successes.

9

Just Love 2.0 Them!

The following recollection comes from Muriel's days as principal:

We knew there was a kind young man inside nine-year-old Jaden. He would be helpful for days and show signs of real progress. Then, in a matter of seconds, he would explode. He would kick and yell. He would rip items off walls. This pattern persisted for some time, which meant occasional calls to his mother. Each time we reached out to her, the tone of her voice let us know she did not want to be bothered.

The one trigger we detected with Jaden was that if he ever felt like a failure, then it was at those times when he would lose control of his temper. We tried to prevent such moments by pointing out to Jaden his strengths and the times when he was successful.

One day, everything clicked for Jaden. He did well on a quiz. He got his assignments done. He helped his teacher. And so forth. His teacher brought it to my attention, and we decided to call Jaden's mother with a "good news" report.

When his mother picked up the phone, we felt her usual "I-don't-have-time-for-this!" So I jumped right in with the good news. "Jaden has had his best day ever!" I said. "He's here in my office and I want him to tell you what a great day he's had!"

I then handed the phone to Jaden. Instead of being excited, he seemed nervous. His teacher and I stood by.

"I've had a good day, Momma," Jaden started slowly. "I got my work done. I helped my teacher. I did well on a test."

Jaden sheepishly shared a few more items and then paused. We could hear his mother's voice but could not detect what she was saying. Jaden listened intently.

"Okay, Momma. Okay, Momma," Jaden said as the call ended. But then, as he handed the phone back to me, tears appeared. We couldn't imagine what his mother had said to upset him.

"What did she say?" we asked.

Burying his little head into my side, Jaden responded, "She told me she loved me. That is the first time she's ever told me she loved me." His tears puddled on my sleeves.

Hearing his mother say she loved him made a significant difference in Jaden's daily countenance, confidence, and behavior. It also helped us to be more sensitive to Jaden's need for love.

Pulling It All Together

Teacher and reformist Nicholas Ferroni observed, "Students who are loved at home come to school to learn. Students who aren't loved at home come to school to be loved."[1] But before we make a case for students' need to be loved, let's re-highlight a few core learnings from the book as a way of pulling it all together.

For starters, we learned that students across the globe are experiencing tumultuous times. The difficult times are causing unprecedented levels of mental health challenges that interfere with students' learning and living.

We learned from the Centers for Disease Control and Prevention that what works to support students' mental health is to help them feel school and family connectedness. For the purposes of this book, we have focused on school connectedness, though the importance of family connectedness is never to be underestimated.

We learned that teachers are in a prime position to influence students' feelings of school connectedness. In fact, we learned that one of the single most significant factors that enables students to get through times of unrest is to have a connection with a stable, committed, and supportive adult, such as a teacher.

We learned that this book is as much about igniting, or reigniting, teachers' passions for making a difference in students' lives as it is about benefitting students. While it is not expected that every teacher make a significant difference in every student's life, students connect best with teachers who

1. accept them as they are,
2. teach them about life,
3. inspire them to see their strengths,
4. entrust them with meaningful responsibilities,
5. help them through hard times,
6. empower them to help themselves, and
7. correct them in positive ways.

If you question any of the seven leadership skillsets, try thinking of their opposites, such as: "My teacher did not accept and respect who I was, didn't connect school with life, never saw my strengths, didn't trust me with responsibilities, ignored me in hard times, did everything for me, and corrected me in negative ways." That is no recipe for making a difference in a student's positive well-being.

We learned that all people have in common three basic categories of needs: intellectual, physical, and social-emotional. When all three categories of needs are being adequately satisfied, students are said to enjoy positive well-being. This book's primary focus is on students' social-emotional needs for connection, meaning, hope, self-worth, resilience, self-efficacy, and growth. As those needs are satisfied, students' physical and intellectual needs are strengthened.

We learned that there are two general approaches to helping students face social or emotional challenges: one is to remove the negatives from their lives; two is to increase the positives in their lives. Both approaches are important. This book emphasizes best practices that are designed to create the conditions that develop and nurture students' strengths. They are each positive, build connections, and are relatively simple to apply. And they apply to all students, all teachers, and all corners of the world.

We learned that leadership and management are both important roles of teachers, and that many classrooms are over-managed and under-led. Classroom leadership believes in students in such a way that students come to believe in themselves and resolve to do something special as a result.

A Model for Personal Change

Another important lesson we learned is woven throughout the book and deserves more explanation. It is that people's *beliefs* drive what they *believe*, which ultimately leads to who they *become*.

The relationship between beliefs, believe, and become is illustrated in the following model of personal change that we have used for years in *Leader in Me* schools. We call it the *See-Do-Get cycle* because another way of saying it is: How students *SEE* themselves, others, and life drives what they *DO*, including their behaviors, words, and habits, which ultimately influences the results they *GET*, including who they become in life, what they achieve, and what feelings they experience.[2]

So what does this cycle look like in real life?

In *The Biology of Belief*, Dr. Bruce Lipton describes a child who frequently hears his parents communicating to him negative messages like "You are a stupid child," "You will never amount to anything," or "You are a weak person." Dr. Lipton concludes, "During early development, the child's consciousness has not evolved enough to critically assess that those parental pronouncements were only verbal barbs and not necessarily true characterizations of 'self.' Once programmed into the subconscious mind, however, these verbal abuses become defined as 'truths' that unconsciously shape the behavior and potential of the child through life."[3]

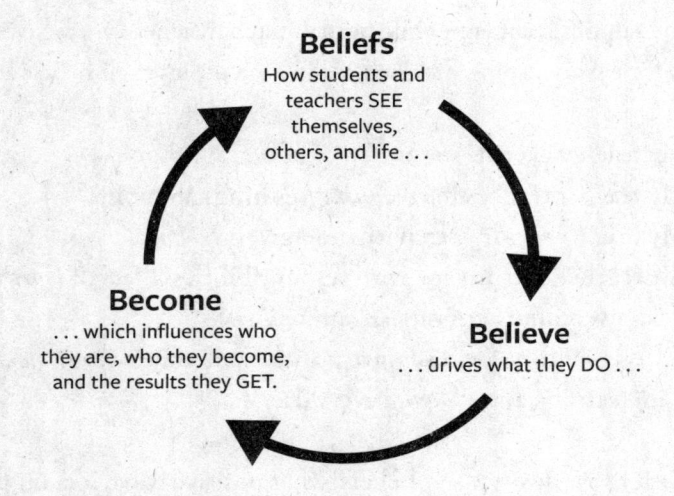

Beliefs
How students and
teachers SEE
themselves,
others, and life . . .

Become
. . . which influences who
they are, who they become,
and the results they GET.

Believe
. . . drives what they DO . . .

Now, suppose that same child goes to school and receives more negative messages from his teachers and peers. He returns home from school each day holding the following additional beliefs:

"I don't *belong* at school."
"I do nothing of *meaning* at school."
"I have no strengths, no *hope*."
"I am never given responsibilities of worth. I am not of *worth*."
"Life is hard and I have little *resilience*."
"I lack *self-efficacy* to do things on my own."
"I am making no *growth*."

With all those negative beliefs developed at home and at school, what behaviors might you expect the child to exhibit at home and at school? What type of person might you expect the child to become?

Can you see how the See-Do-Get cycle is negatively impacting the child's life? When students "see" themselves in mostly negative ways, it is nearly impossible for them to see school or life in positive ways, which, of course, impacts what they "do" in school and ultimately who they "become" in life.

Now suppose that same child has a different teacher. One who believes in him. One who inspires him to develop such positive self-beliefs as:

"My teacher accepts me as I am. I *belong* at school."
"My teacher teaches me *meaningful* things about life."
"My teacher sees my strengths and gives me *hope*."
"My teacher entrusts me with responsibilities. I feel of *worth*."
"I can overcome hard times. I am *resilient*."
"Through effort, I can achieve positive outcomes *on my own*."
"I am learning and *growing* every day."

With those positive self-beliefs, what positive behaviors might you expect from the child? How might those positive behaviors influence who the child becomes?

So how then might teachers use the See-Do-Get cycle to increase students' positive well-being? The answer is that they can start anywhere on the cycle.

Start with Beliefs. Communicate positive messages to students. As teachers call students by name, take an interest in their stories, voice respect for them, share positive life hacks, communicate their strengths, express appreciation for what they do, and start and end each day with positive messages, teachers elevate students' beliefs about themselves, about school, and about life. That, in turn, has the potential to improve what they believe—do.

Start with Believe. For many students, it takes more than positive words to enhance their self-beliefs. They want to experience it for themselves—to have mastery experiences. To offer students such experiences, teachers can entrust students with opportunities to be a leader or participate in service-learning. They can help students turn a stretch into a strength. They can give students choice and voice. They can provide opportunities for students to express gratitude and use positive self-talk. They can support students in achieving a goal. When students successfully experience positive outcomes from these types of behaviors, their self-beliefs will also in turn increase. In other words, by being given opportunities to apply the seven leadership skillsets and the best practices, students can be expected to enjoy improved outcomes in life, including increased positive well-being.

Start with Become. Not all students recognize their day-to-day progress or positive outcomes. They don't always see their positive qualities. They don't always see how their positive efforts lead to positive outcomes. In such cases, it is helpful for teachers to praise students and to find ways to celebrate their efforts. They can give students chances to self-advocate for their strengths and achievements. As students experience that their efforts are leading to positive outcomes, their beliefs about self will increase, which will in turn enhance what they do in life. And so the cycle continues and so students' positive well-being continues to increase.

And when applying the See-Do-Get cycle, "Don't forget the adults!" The See-Do-Get cycle applies equally to teachers. Teachers cannot keep the same *beliefs* they've always held, continue to "do" (*believe*) the same routines they've always used, and expect to *become* better at connecting with students and making a greater difference in their lives. So, to improve their outcomes, some teachers may need to follow the example of Winnie-the-Pooh, who said, "I always get to where I'm going by walking away from where I have been."[4] In other words, teachers may need to *see* and *do* different if they want to *get* different results when connecting with students. In the words of Abraham Lincoln: "The dogmas of the quiet past are inadequate to the stormy present. The occasion is piled high with difficulty, and we must rise to the occasion. As our case is new, so must we think anew."[5]

Micro-Moments of Warmth and Connection

Something else we learned that deserves extra attention returns us to the topic of love, or what Abraham Maslow described as the need "to love and to be loved."

Carol Rodgers and Miriam Raider-Roth declared: "Schools need to be safe houses for love, not only for the sake of the children they temporarily house, but also for the teachers who are their long-term residents."[6] Making a difference does not typically happen by happen-chance. It happens by intentional design. More often than not, it takes love and caring. In fact, in our search of the research literature and our interviews, we were surprised at how often the words *love* and *caring* were voiced. Consider just a few examples, starting with Mrs. Clark:

> My first teaching assignment was in a pre-K classroom. I was deter-mined to make mine the best classroom in the entire school.
>
> The first three days I went home in tears. The children did not want to do any of the activities I had planned. I felt unqualified.
>
> I unloaded all my woes on my husband. He listened until I was able to get out all my feelings. Then he responded: "Forget your lesson plans. Just go back tomorrow and love those children."
>
> I took his advice. The next day I greeted each child and told them something specific that I liked about them. I put my lesson plans on pause and took time to connect with the students.
>
> Did mine turn out to be the best classroom in the entire school? Maybe not. But what a difference that made in how my days went from that point on.

After decades of studying the best practices of excellent teachers, Rosemary and Harry Wong concluded, "Structure, mixed with care and love, is what every student needs in the classroom."[7]

Similarly, Dr. Daggett and colleagues at the International Center for Leadership in Education asserted: "We know that if a child is suffering with anxiety, depression, or low self-worth, she cannot begin to climb out of this if she feels uncared for and unseen by the adults in her life. The need for caring connections in schools has grown only more critical and for reasons that extend beyond rigor and relevance and into our students' wellbeing and capacity to engage in school in the first place."[8]

Those examples are just a few of the many usages of the words *love* and *caring* that appeared in our research and interviews. Indeed, there were several times when we asked teachers to share advice on how to make a difference in students' lives and their first response was a big shrug of the shoulders, followed by, "Just love them!"

And yet we have also encountered some heavy eye-rolling from teachers who literally squirm when they hear the words *Just love them!* associated with the role of a teacher. "That's not what I am hired to do!" they say. "I'm not their mother!"

The difference between the teachers who say "Just love them" and the teachers who want the word *love* taken out of schools is largely due to the different ways they define or perceive the term *love*. For some, the word *love* is reserved solely for matters of romance, intimate relations, or the unconditional love of a parent–child relationship. And indeed, those types of love may feel awkward, if not inappropriate, in school settings.

Barbara Fredrickson of the University of North Carolina refers to those types of love as *Love 1.0*. But she proposes that a different kind of love—*Love 2.0*—is perhaps a better fit for schools. She defines Love 2.0 as "micro-moments of warmth and connection that are shared with another living being."[9] The emphasis is on the "micro," the small moments. Jim Collins, who has studied great leaders of all types and industries for over 30 years, made a similar conclusion: "Big things happen because you do a bunch of little things supremely well that compound over time."[10] In other words, teacher–student connections do not need to be large or dramatic to make a difference. Teachers do not need to build deep relationships with students in order to make a connection and a difference in students' positive well-being and readiness to learn.

When it comes to making a difference in students' positive well-being, the consistent micro-moment acts of caring really do turn out to be the big things. As a highly cited meta-analysis of school interventions concludes: "Seemingly 'small' social-psychological interventions in education—that is, brief exercises that target students' thoughts, feelings, and beliefs in and about school—can lead to large gains in student achievement and sharply reduce achievement gaps even months and years later. These interventions do not teach students academic content but instead target students' psychology, such as their beliefs that they have the potential to improve their intelligence or that they belong and are valued in school."[11]

You might recall from the opening, "Setting the Context," the woman who had scars on her arms from inflicting self-harm, and who said her high school teacher prevented her from ending her life. When we asked what the teacher had done to save her life, the woman responded, "She always smiled at me." Believing in students does not get much more micro than that.

So no, teachers do not need to use the words *I love you*, and do not need to hug or touch students to communicate that message. But without a sense that their teachers care about them, students might easily view the seven leadership skillsets as manipulative techniques. It goes back to the old adage, "Students don't care how much you know until they know how much you care."

Honor to the Teachers!

Perhaps the most remarkable thing we learned in this book is that people in their 60s, 70s, 80s, and even 90s are still thinking about the teachers who made a difference in their lives. Because their teacher believed in them, they are still believing in their teachers, and are still benefitting from what their teachers did to make a difference in their lives.

Indeed, when it comes to making a difference in students' positive well-being, it is not about the school building, it is not about the latest technology, and it is not about the curriculum. It is about the teachers.

Are modern school buildings beneficial? Absolutely! Do we thrive on the latest technology? Undeniably! Are well-designed curriculums vital? No doubt! But when it comes to making a difference in students' positive well-being and readiness to learn, nothing compares with the influence of a stable, committed, and supportive teacher.

In fact, while writing this book, a very visual image has kept reappearing in our minds. It is an image that comes from South Sudan, where civil war has raged for years. Thousands of refugees have been forced into dire circumstances. Many are children who have known nothing but fear, hunger, disease, and poverty their entire lives. Hope is absent from their vocabularies.

Seeing the despair in young people's eyes, parents and other caring adults have organized classrooms beneath the shade of trees. There, young people gather to learn under the guidance of a teacher. There are no walls. No technology. No formal curriculum. Imagine teaching under those conditions. Just you and the students beneath a tree. Each student looks to you for hope of a better life.

How might you bring those students feelings of connection, meaning, hope, self-worth, resilience, self-efficacy, and growth—positive well-being? If you could teach those students only one life hack, what would it be? How might the way you lead your life inspire them?

Our hearts go out to those young people of South Sudan. We also feel for millions of young people in the world who receive no formal education. We feel for the students whose mental health challenges go well beyond what the pages of this book are intended to handle.

More than anything, however, we have such great respect for teachers who do have students to teach. No matter where we go in the world, we find teachers who—given a tree and some shade—will do wonders to make a difference in students' lives.

Teachers are part of a global and noble community. Whenever the sun sets on teachers in one part of the world who are closing their day, elsewhere on the planet are teachers who are opening their days and opening the minds of their students to a world of learning. The joy of making a difference in students' lives continues non-stop around the clock.

And so we concur with Rosemary and Harry Wong, who declared, "Decade after decade of educational theories, innovations, and fads have not increased student achievement. The only factor that significantly increases student achievement is an effective teacher."[12] The same applies to increasing students' positive well-being. So much of students' engagement and success in school relies on the connections students have with their teachers and their ability to lead students in practical, positive ways.

The Best Is Yet Ahead

If you are a teacher, a school administrator, a parent, or other influencer of today's students, we hope that something in these pages has inspired—or re-inspired—you with a renewed sense of passion for making a difference in students' lives. We hope that something in these pages will enable you to better connect with students in ways that will increase their positive well-being and readiness to learn.

Times may be tough, teaching may be difficult. Yet these are the very times when it is so vital to be making a difference in students' lives. As Rita Pierson, a teacher of 40 years, declared, "Is this job tough? You betcha! Yet it is not impossible! We can do this! We're educators! We're born to make a difference!"[13] So, as the Dutch author Alexander Den Heijer says it, "Be bold enough to know that you can make a difference, and humble enough to know that you are a limited being."[14]

Do we expect you or the insights of this book to eliminate every challenge students face? No! Are teachers responsible for preventing or solving all emotional and social challenges? No! Will the best practices in this book cure students' mental illnesses? No! Do we anticipate every student will leave school each day enjoying positive well-being? No! Do we expect students will always be ready to learn? No! But, we do expect that when the storms of life arise—when adverse winds blow fiercely—there will be stable, committed teachers to help calm the sailors.

Please accept our best wishes for the positive well-being of your students, your peer teachers, your loved ones, and you personally in the days and years to come. We like to believe the best is yet ahead. And so we conclude by expressing our trust in your ability to believe in students in such a way that they come to believe in themselves and resolve to do something special as a result.

And that, again, is what we call leadership.

The Challenge

Identify a student, a peer teacher, or a family member who might most benefit from a slight increase in feelings of connection, meaning, hope, self-worth, resilience, self-efficacy, or growth as a result of a micro-moment of caring from you. Make that moment happen. Make a difference in someone's positive well-being today.

Acknowledgments

Writing a book of this magnitude is a tortuous endeavor. Thankfully, the days of chisels and stone tablets have been replaced by digital tablets.

Writing this book has had its invigorating parts. Most notable has been the joy of interacting with teachers and former students across the globe. We thank them for their insights.

We also acknowledge the more than 250 researchers and thought leaders whose insights are cited in this work. They lend credibility to each page.

Furthermore, we extend special thanks to numerous colleagues, school administrators, teachers, and counselors, who have given careful review and support of this work. They include:

Sean Covey	Meg Thompson
Gina Tanner	Evett Barham
Lonny Moore	Logan Pettit
Dr. Lesley Eason	Mary Ann Hatch
Dana Penick	Sarah Farnsworth Hatch
Ebony Lofton	Adam Merrill
Jodee Gupton	M. J. Fievre Logan
Gary McGuey	Dr. David Ansbacher
Chad Smith	Meg Hackett

Laney Hawes	Zac Cheney
Dr. Kim Cummins	Aaron Ashby
Brett Shelby	Joshua Covey
Jessica Oberto	Dr. Jill Scheulen
Banks Spicer	Sarah Noble Flokstra
Annie Furches	Catherine DiGioia-Weinfeld
Keli Sare	Debra Lund
Dr. Kim Fisenne	Christine Eisenhauer
Vickie Brown	Don Zegler
Dr. Aaron Allen	Thom Cochran
Dylan King	Dr. Tommy Schmolze
Cris Edwards	Juley Sexton
Erin Hardy	Molly Garcia

Special thanks to Simon & Schuster for their professionalism in guiding us through the various publishing stages. They and the professionals at Dupree Miller & Associates have proven to be exceptional.

Thanks also to Qualtrics, the world's technology leader in collecting and analyzing survey feedback, for supplying quality insights from hundreds of adults in 12 countries regarding how to make a difference in students' lives.

Above all, we extend extra, extra thanks to our families for supporting us on this journey.

This was truly a synergistic work.

Notes and References

Setting the Context—The Why

1. Odham, D. (Host), & Schmolze, T. (Guest). (2024, August 20). Leading with courage [audio podcast episode]. In *Change starts here*. FranklinCovey Education.

2. The distinctions between a job, career, and calling are cited in several references, including Wrzesniewski, A., McCauley, C., Rozin, P., & Schwartz, B. (1997). Jobs, careers, and callings: People's relations to their work. *Journal of Research in Personality*, *31*(1), 21–33.

3. The song "For Good" was composed by Stephen Schwartz for the musical *Wicked* and released on Broadway in 2003.

4. United Nations International Children's Education Fund (2021). The *Changing Childhood* Project. UNICEF. Gallup interviewed people by telephone in two groups, ages 15–24 and 40 and older.

5. The research of Dr. Jack Shonkoff and others was summarized by Bari Walsh in Harvard's Graduate School of Education's *Usable knowledge* (2015, March 23). The science of resilience: Why some children can thrive despite adversity. See https://www.gse.harvard.edu/news/uk/15/03/science-resilience .

6. See https://www.cdc.gov/healthyyouth/mental-health/index.htm and the CDC Youth Risk Behavior Survey Data Summary and Trends Report (2009–2019).

7. For the last 15-plus years, we have been fortunate to work with teachers across the globe as part of the *Leaders in Me* process. See Covey, S. R., Covey, S. M., Summers, M. T., & Hatch, D. K. (2008). *The leader in me* (2nd ed.). Simon & Schuster.

8. We partnered with Qualtrics, the world's leading survey and customer feedback company, to survey 750 respondents in North America, Asia, Southeast Asia, South America, the South Pacific, and Europe about teachers who made a significant difference in their lives.

9. Cited in Wong, A. (2021, April 11). Students crushed by stress, depression are back in class. Here's how schools are meeting their needs. *USA Today*. For further details, see *Youth Truth student survey 2022: Insights from the student experience, part 1, emotional & mental health*. Youth-Truth.

10. *Positive well-being* is a broad term for which there is no agreed-upon definition. Greeks as far back as Aristotle referred to overall well-being as eudaimonic well-being. Current research uses several overlapping definitions, terms, and synonyms to describe well-being. For example, University of Rochester psychologists Drs. Edward Deci and Richard Ryan describe well-being as having three dimensions: autonomy, competence, and positive relatedness. Dr. Martin Seligman suggests five elements of well-being: positive emotion, accomplishment, engagement, meaning, and positive relationships. Drs. Felicia So and Timothy Huppert of the University of Cambridge assembled ten features of well-being: competence, emotional stability, engagement, meaning, optimism, positive emotion, positive relationships, resilience, self-esteem, and vitality. Positive psychologists use terms such as *gratitude*, *kindness*, *growth*, *forgiveness*, *grit*, *mindfulness*, *goals*, and *flow* to describe elements of well-being. The World Health Organization says that well-being occurs when individuals can realize their abilities, cope with the normal stresses of life, work productively, and make contributions to their community. See Deci, E. L., & Ryan, R. M. (2008). Self-determination theory: A macro-theory of human motivation, development, and health. *Canadian Psychology*, *49*(3), 182–185; Seligman, M. E. P. (2013). *Flourish*

(p. 16). Atria Paperback; Huppert, F. A., & So, T. T. C. (2013). Flourishing across Europe: Application of a new conceptual framework for defining well-being. *Social Indicators Research*, *110*(3), 837–861; World Health Organization (2001). The world health report 2001: Mental health: New understanding, new hope.

11. Richards, M., & Huppert, F. A. (2011). Do positive children become positive adults? Evidence from a longitudinal birth cohort study. *Journal of Positive Psychology*, *6*(1), 75–87.

12. For those familiar with a Multi-tiered System of Supports (MTSS), or the three-tiered Response to Intervention (RTI) model, this book describes a Tier 1 level of support, which means it universally applies to all students. Tier 2 is for students at risk, while Tier 3 is for students at high risk. For Tier 2 and 3 needs, teachers are encouraged to seek assistance from counseling professionals.

Tiered System of Support

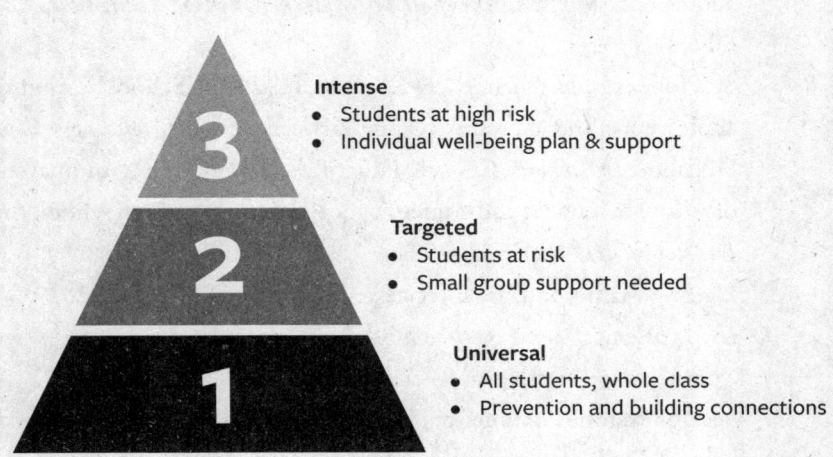

Intense
- Students at high risk
- Individual well-being plan & support

Targeted
- Students at risk
- Small group support needed

Universal
- All students, whole class
- Prevention and building connections

13. Keller, H. A. (1985). *Teacher: Anne Sullivan Macy*. Reprinted by Greenwood Press. Additional opportunities to explore Helen Keller's legacy can be found at www.afb.org/HelenKellerArchive.

14. "Management is doing things right; leadership is doing the right things" is found in Drucker, P. (2016). *People and performance*. Routledge. (Originally published in 1959.)

15. DuFour, R., & Marzano, R. J. (2011). *Leaders of learning: How district, school, and classroom leaders improve student learning*. Solution Tree Press.

16. Pierson, R. (2013, April). *Every kid deserves a champion*. TED Conference, New York.

1: Accepted Me as I Was

1. Rogers, F. (1967, October 8). From the television documentary series *The creative person*, episode 70.

2. Goodenow, C., & Grady, K. E. (1993, July). The relationship of school belonging and friends' values to academic motivation among urban adolescent students. *The Journal of Experimental Education*, *62*(1), 60–71.

3. See, for example, Allen, K., & Kern, M. L. (2017). School belonging in adolescents: Theory, research and practice. *SpringerBriefs in psychology*. Singapore. Also Neel, C. G., & Fuligni, A. (2013). A longitudinal study of school belonging and academic motivation across high school. *Child Development*, *84*(2), 678–692.

4. Darling-Hammond, L., interviewed as part of Edutopia. (2019). *Fostering belonging with classroom norms* [Video]. YouTube. https://www.youtube.com/watch?v=oRXYc4xmvwg

5. See, for example, Baumeister, R. F., & Leary, M. R. (1995). The need to belong: Desire for interpersonal attachments as a fundamental human motivation. *Psychological Bulletin*, *117*(3), 497–529. https://doi.org/10.1037/0033-2909.117.3.497

6. These outcomes are compiled from numerous studies. See, for example, Allen, K., & Kern, P. (2019). *Boosting school belonging: Practical strategies to help adolescents feel like they belong at school*. Routledge. Also

Newman, B. M., Lohman, B. J., & Newman, P. R. (2007). Peer group membership and a sense of belonging: Their relationship to adolescent behavior problems. *Adolescence, 42*(166), 241–263.

7. Waldinger, R., & Schulz, M. (2023). *The good life: Lessons from the world's longest study of happiness*. Simon & Schuster.

8. Sonja Lyubomirsky, for example, has been a leading pioneer in the study of happiness for 30-plus years, and she for one has concluded, "Connections are the key to Happiness." See https://www.youtube.com/watch?v=5_Yc1p2db-E

9. Organization for Economic Cooperation and Development (2020). Sense of belonging at school. Found in *PISA 2018 results (Vol. III): What school life means for students' lives*. OECD Publishing. Note: A more recent PISA (Programme for International Student Assessment) survey has since been conducted, but the results were negatively influenced by the Covid pandemic and tainted the trends, so we stayed with the earlier PISA survey report.

10. Hodges, T. (n.d.). *Why a best friend at school matters for students and teachers*. https://www.gallup.com/education/231758/why-best-friend-school-matters-students-teachers.aspx#:~:text=In%20all%20of%20our%20research,the%20student's%20daily%20school%20experience

11. Murthy, V. H. (2020). *Together: The healing power of human connection in a sometimes lonely world* (pp. xix–xxiii, 14). HarperCollins. For further health risks, see also Centers for Disease Control and Prevention (2023). Health risks of social isolation and loneliness. https://www.cdc.gov/emotional-wellbeing/social-connectedness/loneliness.htm

12. The World Health Organization says that depression alone is a multibillion-dollar cost to society. Some countries, such as the U.K., have appointed Ministers of Loneliness to find ways to combat the loneliness epidemic. See https://www.who.int/news/item/30-03-2017--depression-let-s-talk-says-who-as-depression-tops-list-of-causes-of-ill-health.

13. Brown, B. (2008). *I thought it was just me (but it isn't)*. Gotham Books.

14. Darling-Hammond, L. (2018, August). Arming teachers and expelling students is not the answer to school shootings, and it's dangerous. The Learning Policy Institute.

15. Numerous articles bemoan the negative impacts of social media and smartphones on young people, and even governments calling for restrictions on social media. For insights, see Haidt, J. (2024). *The anxious generation: How the great rewiring of childhood is causing an epidemic of mental illness*. Penguin Press.

16. Kay Tye quoted in Piore, A. (2022, November 9). I feel invisible: As teen loneliness rates soar, schools may be making it worse, scientists say. *Newsweek*. https://www.newsweek.com/2022/11/18/teen-lone liness-rates-soar-schools-may-making-it-worse-scientists-say-1758 013.html

17. Allen, K., Kern, M. L., Vella-Brodrick, D., Hattie, J., & Waters, L. (2018, March). What schools need to know about fostering school belonging: A meta-analysis. *Educational Psychology Review, 30* (1), 1–34.

18. Springtide Research Institute (2020). *Belonging: Reconnecting America's loneliest generation*. Springtide Research Institute.

19. See for example: Carmody, D. P., & Lewis, M. (2006). Brain activation when hearing one's own and other's names. *Brain Research, 1116* (1), 153–158. https://doi.org/10.1016/j.brainres.2006.07.121

20. Mapp, K., Carver, I., & Lander, J. (2017). *Powerful partnerships: A teacher's guide to engaging families* (pp. 17–18). Scholastic.

21. Carnegie, D. (1936). *How to win friends and influence people*. Gallery Books.

22. Rogers, F. (1969, May 2). Testimony given before the Senate Commerce Committee's communications subcommittee.

23. Payne, R. (2018). *Emotional poverty in all demographics: How to reduce anger, anxiety, and violence in the classroom*. aha! Publications.

24. *Time* (1975, December 29). Saints among us: The work of Mother Teresa.

25. Winfrey, O. *AWAKENING*, Oprah's SuperSoul Conversations. https://podcasts.apple.com/us/podcast/oprah's-supersoul-conversations/id1264843400?i=1000501802728

26. Blanchard, K. (1982). *The one minute manager*. William Morrow and Company.

27. DuFour, R., & Eaker, R. (1998). *Professional learning communities at work*. National Education Service.

28. Dykstra, P. A. (2009). Older adult loneliness: Myths and realities. *European Journal of Aging, 6*(2), 91–100.

29. Hodges, T. (n.d.), p. 11.

30. Yeager, D. S., & Walton, G. M. (2011). Social-psychological interventions in education: They're not magic. *Review of Educational Research, 81*(2), 267–301. https://doi.org/10.3102/0034654311405999

31. YouthTruth (2023). Student survey: Students weigh in, part IV: Learning and well-being after COVID-19, p. 6.

32. Hattie, J. A. C. (2009). *Visible learning for teachers: Maximizing impact on learning*. Routledge.

2: Taught Me About Life

1. The story of the *Italian Sculptor* is a re-created version of a story Dr. Hatch was told while in Europe more than 40 years ago.

2. Nietzsche, F. (2008). *Twilight of the idols (Die Gotzen-Dammerung)*, in "Maxims and Arrows" section. Oxford University Press.

3. Frankl, V. E. (1984). *Man's search for meaning*. Washington Square Press.

4. Daggett, B., & Jones, S. M. (2019, June). *Addressing whole child growth through strong relationships: The evidence-based connections between academic and social-emotional learning*. https://leadered.com/wp-content/uploads/AddressingtheWholeChildSEL.pdf

5. Csikszentmihalyi, M. (1990). *Flow: The psychology of optimal experience* (pp. 214–240). Harper & Row.

6. Duckworth, A. (2016). *Grit: The power of passion and perseverance* (p. 145). Scribner.

7. Fredrickson, B. (2009). *Positivity: Discover the upward spiral that will change your life* (p. 17). Oneworld.

8. Sinek, S. (2009). *Start with the why: How great leaders inspire everyone to take action*. Portfolio/Penguin.

9. Silver, L., Van Kessel, P., Huang, C., & Gubbala, S. (2021, November 18). What makes life meaningful? Views from 17 advanced economies. Pew Research Center. https://www.pewresearch.org/global/2021/11/18/what-makes-life-meaningful-views-from-17-advanced-economies/

10. See Kasser, T., Rosenblum, K. L., Sameroff, A. J., Deci, E. L., Niemiec, C. P., Ryan, R. M., Árnadóttir, O., Bond, R., Dittmar, H., Dungan, N., & Hawks, S. (2014). Changes in materialism, changes in psychological well-being: Evidence from three longitudinal studies and an intervention experiment. *Motivation and Emotion, 38*(1), 1–22. Also Kasser, T. (2002). *The high price of materialism*. Bradford Books.

11. See https://www.youtube.com/watch?v=qv8VZVP5csA.

12. Lin, G. (2016, January). The windows and mirrors of your child's bookshelf. TEDxNatick, Natick, MA. https://www.youtube.com/watch?v=_wQ8wiV3FVo. See also Kidd, D. C., & Castano, E. (2013, October 3). Reading literacy fiction improves theory of mind. *Science, 342*(6156), 377–380. DOI:10.1126/science.1239918

13. Twain, M. (2010). *The innocents abroad, or, the new pilgrim's progress*. Wordsworth.

14. Angelou, M. (2011). *Wouldn't take nothing for my journey now*. Bantam.

15. See, for example, Immordino-Yang, M. H., & Knecht, D. R. (2020). Building meaning builds teens' brains. *Educational Leadership, 77*(8), 36–43. And Gotlieb, R. M., Yang, X-F., & Immordino-Yang, M. H. (2022). Concrete and abstract dimensions of diverse adolescents' social-emotional meaning-making, and associations with broader functioning. *Journal of Adolescent Research, 39*(5), 1224–1259.

16. Quoted in *Inc.* magazine's online newsletter: Zetlin, M., 21 inspiring quotes from the mentor who taught personal performance expert Tony Robbins how to be Tony Robbins. See https://www.inc.com/minda-zetlin/21-inspiring-quotes-from-the-mentor-who-taught-tony-robbins-how-to-be-tony-robbi.html

17. Spurgeon, C. (2009). *Essential works of Charles Spurgeon* (p. 1411). Barbour Publishing. Spurgeon was an English minister who was known for humorous sermons.

18. The Commission on Children at Risk (2003). *Hardwired to connect: The new scientific case for authoritative communities*. Broadway Publications.

19. "The Next Right Thing" is a song from the 2019 animated Disney movie *Frozen II*. Songwriters: Robert Lopez and Kristen Jane Anderson, Wonderland Music Company Inc.

20. Martin Luther King quote was retrieved from "The Power of Education," found in Carson, C., Luker, R., & Russell, P. A. (Eds.). *The papers of Martin Luther King, Jr.*, Vol. 1: *Called to serve, January 1929–June 1951*.

21. Angela Duckworth quoted in Seligman, M. E. P. (2011). *Flourish* (p. 103). Atria Paperback. See also her book *Grit* (2016, p. 274).

22. Daniel Goleman played a leading role in promoting such skills, and even demonstrated that emotional intelligence (EQ) is a better predictor than IQ of academic performance and leadership potential. See Goleman, D. (2004, January). What makes a leader? *Harvard Business Review*.

23. Covey, S. R. (1989). *The 7 habits of highly effective people*. Simon & Schuster. Student-friendly versions of the seven habits are available through Sean Covey's bestsellers, *The 7 habits of highly effective teens*, *The 7 habits of happy kids*, and *The 6 most important decisions you'll ever make*, also from Simon & Schuster.

24. Ben-Shahar, T. (2007). *Happier*. McGraw-Hill.

25. Lyubomirsky, S. (2008). *The how of happiness: A new approach to getting the life you want*. Penguin Books.

26. Fredrickson (2009).

27. Santos, L. podcast, *The happiness lab.*

28. Yeager, D. S., & Walton, G. M. (2011). Social-psychological interventions in education: They're not magic. *Review of Educational Research, 81*(2), 267–301. https://doi.org/10.3102/0034654311405999

29. See, as an example, Leonhardt, D. (2021, March 24). Bad news bias. *The New York Times.* https://www.nytimes.com/2021/03/24/briefing/boulder-shooting-george-segal-astrazeneca.html. Also Baumeister, R. F., Bratslavsky, E., Finkenauer, C., & Vohs, K. D. (2001). Bad is stronger than good. *Review of General Psychology, 5*(4), 323–370.

30. Charles Kuralt (1934–1997) was an American television, newspaper, and radio journalist.

31. Covey (1989).

32. McKnight, K., Graybeal, J., Yarbro, J., & Graybeal, L. (2016). *The heart of great teaching: Pearson global survey of educator effectiveness.* Pearson Education, Inc.

33. Bill Gates quote in Covey, S. R., & Hatch, D. K. (2006). *Everyday greatness: Inspiration for a meaningful life.* Rutledge Hill Press.

34. Gehlbach, H., Brinkworth, M. E., King, A., Hsu, L., McIntyre, J., & Rogers, T. (2016). Creating birds of similar feathers: Leveraging similarity to improve teacher–student relationships and academic achievement. *Journal of Educational Psychology, 108*(3), 342–352.

35. Nichols, M. H. (2019). From her Facebook post, April 29, 2019.

36. Aspen Institute (2019). *From a nation at risk to a nation at hope: Recommendations from the National Commission on Social, Emotional, & Academic Development,* 13–14.

37. *Harvard Business Review* reported, "Helping others find the meaning in their own work magnifies the meaning one experiences personally." See Achor, S., Kellerman, G. R., Reece, A., & Robichaux, A. (2018, March 19). America's loneliest workers, according to research. *Harvard Business Review.* https://hbr.org/2018/03/americas-loneliest-workers-according-to-research#:~:text=In%20a%20breakdown%20of%20loneliness,prevalence%20of%20depression%20among%20lawyers

38. Keller, H. (1903). *The story of my life.* Doubleday, Page & Co.

3: Inspired Me to See My Strengths

1. Rath, T. (2007). *StrengthsFinder 2.0* (p. i), Gallup Press. See also Buckingham, M., & Clifton, D. O. (2001). *Now, discover your strengths.* The Free Press.

2. Seligman, M. E. P. (2002). *Authentic happiness: Using the new positive psychology to realize your potential for lasting fulfillment* (p. 27). The Free Press.

3. Seligman (2002), p. 28.

4. James, W. (1890). *The principles of psychology* (chap. 11). Dover Publications.

5. See, for example, Hammond, W. (2010). Principles of strength-based practice. In *Resiliency initiatives* (p. 13). Retrieved from http://www.ayscbc.org/Principles%20of%20Strength-2.pdf

6. Georgia State University professor Pauline Clance and psychologist Suzanne Imes studied high-achieving women who were in positions of authority in their organizations. Though the women had diplomas, experience, and other accolades to prove their readiness to lead, they doubted their qualifications. They felt like impostors, or frauds. See Clance, P. R., & Imes, S. A. (1978). The impostor phenomenon in high achieving women: Dynamics and therapeutic intervention. *Psychotherapy: Theory, Research & Practice, 15*(3), 241–247.

7. Buckingham & Clifton (2001).

8. Oxford English Dictionary (2006 ed.).

9. Snyder, C. R., Irving, L. M., & Anderson, J. R. (1991). Hope and health. In C. R. Snyder & D. R. Forsyth (Eds.), Pergamon general psychology series, Vol. 162. *Handbook of social and clinical psychology: The health perspective* (pp. 285–305). Pergamon Press.

10. Rand, K. L., & Cheavens, J. S. (2012). Hope theory. In S. J. Lopez & C. R. Snyder (Eds.), *The Oxford handbook of positive psychology.* Oxford University Press.

11. Lazarus, R. S., & Launier, R. (1978). Stress related transactions between person and environment. In L. A. Pervin & M. Lewis (Eds.), *Perspectives in interactional psychology.* Plenum Press.

12. Zakrzewski, V. (2012, November). How to help students develop hope. *Greater Good Magazine*. https://greatergood.berkeley.edu/article/item/how_to_help_students_develop_hope

13. Conti, R. (2000). College goals: Do self-determined and carefully considered goals predict intrinsic motivation, academic performance, and adjustment during the first semester? *Social Psychology of Education*, *4*(2), 189–211.

14. Snyder, C. R., Shorey, H. S., Cheavens, J., Pulvers, K. M., Adams III, V. H., & Wiklund, C. (2002). Hope and academic success in college. *Journal of Educational Psychology*, *94*(4), 820–826.

15. Roesch, S. C., & Vaughn, A. A. (2006). Evidence for the factorial validity of the Dispositional Hope Scale. *European Journal of Psychological Assessment*, *22*(2), 78–84.

16. Hammond (2010).

17. Jackson, J. (1984, July). Keynote speech given at the 1984 Democratic National Convention, San Francisco, often referred to as his "Rainbow Coalition" speech.

18. Peter Drucker quote is found in Buckingham & Clifton (2001).

19. Cited at https://robertjohnmeehan.blogspot.com/

20. Seligman, M. E. P., & Csikszentmihalyi, M. (2000). Positive psychology: An introduction. *American Psychologist*, *55*(1), 5–14.

21. Pierson, R. (2013, April). *Every kid deserves a champion*. TED Conference, New York.

22. This is a common refrain that journalist and political commentator David Brooks uses in his writings and speeches. See, for example, his editorial in *The New York Times* (2017, 3 March).

23. Pink, D. (2009). *Drive: The surprising truth about what motivates us* (pp. 198–199). Riverhead Hardcover.

24. This popular quote is often misattributed to Henry van Dyke. The first known use is from *The Ladies Repository: A Monthly Periodical, Devoted to Literature, Arts, and Religion* (1874, September, p. 231).

25. Collective intelligence has been discussed from the 1700s under various titles, such as group intelligence, symbiotic intelligence, and collective wisdom.

26. Janis, I. L. (1982). *Victims of groupthink* (2nd ed.). Houghton-Mifflin.
27. The ability to work well with others and in teams is always one of the top qualities employers seek with recruiting job candidates. See, for example, Cunningham, W., & Villasenor, P. (2016). Employer voices, employer demands, and implications for public skills development policy connecting the labor and education sectors. (World Bank Policy Research Working Paper No. 7582, World Bank Group).
28. Floyd's statements cited in Demp, B. (2014). *The quotable coach: Daily nuggets of practical wisdom.* Kindle ed.
29. Kroc, R., & Anderson, R. (1977). *Grinding it out: The making of McDonald's.* St. Martin's Paperback.
30. Angelou, M., cited in #TeameBONY (2014). *10 life lessons from Maya Angelou.* https://www.ebony.com/10-life-lessons-from-maya-angelou-302/
31. Peters, T. J., & Waterman, R. H. (1982). *In search of excellence: Lessons from America's best-run companies.* Harper & Row.
32. "The One and Only One," in the DVD classic *Sing a Song with Pooh Bear* (1999), with Harry Arends as producer, writer, and director.
33. Festinger, L., Pepitone, A., & Newcomb, T. (1952). Some consequences of deindividuation in a group. *Journal of Abnormal and Social Psychology, 47*(2 Suppl.), 382–389.
34. See, for example, Cannavale, F. J., Scarr, H. A., & Pepitone, A. (1970). Deindividuation in the small group: Further evidence. *Journal of Personality and Social Psychology, 16*(1), 141–147.

4: Entrusted Me with Responsibilities

1. Oprah Winfrey's favorite teacher. See https://www.oprah.com/oprahshow/meet-oprahs-favorite-teacher-mrs-duncan-video.
2. These words were spoken at The Cotton States and International Exposition in Atlanta, Georgia, on September 18, 1895.
3. *Oxford English Dictionary* (2006 ed.).

4. For more on learning by doing, see DuFour, R., DuFour, R., Eaker, R., & Many, T. (2016). *Learning by doing: A handbook for professional learning communities at work*. Solution Tree.

5. Crocker, J., Luhtanen, R. K., Cooper, M. L., & Bouvrette, A. (2003). Contingencies of self-worth in college students: Theory and measurement. *Journal of Personality and Social Psychology, 85*(5), 894–908.

6. Clark-Jones, T. (2012). The importance of helping teens discover self-worth. *Michigan State University–MSU Extension.* http://www.canr.msu.edu/news/the_importance_of_helping_teens_discover_self-worth

7. See early references to self-worth theory at Covington, M. V., & Beery, R. G. (1976). *Self-worth and school learning*. Holt, Rinehart & Winston; and also Covington, M. V. (1984). The self-worth theory of achievement motivation: Findings and implications. *The Elementary School Journal, 85*(1), 5–20.

8. Clark-Jones (2012).

9. Seligman, M. E. P. (2013). *Flourish* (p. 20). Atria Paperback.

10. Lyubomirsky, S. (2008). *The how of happiness: A new approach to getting the life you want* (p. 205). Penguin Books.

11. Barth, R. S. (2013, October). "The time is ripe (again)." *Educational Leadership, 71*(2), 10–16.

12. The Pygmalion effect refers to situations where students perform better or worse based on how their teacher expects them to perform. See Rosenthal, R. J., & Jacobson, L. (1968). *Pygmalion in the classroom: Teacher expectation and pupils' intellectual development*. Holt, Rinehart & Winston.

13. Annie E. Casey Foundation cited in https://www.deseret.com/2019/9/18/20871271/toxic-childhood-experiences-poor-health-byu-study-neighbors-teachers-cure

14. See https://www.mayoclinichealthsystem.org/hometown-health/speaking-of-health/3-health-benefits-of-volunteering

15. Lander, J. (2016, December 20). Students as teachers. Harvard Graduate School of Education. https://www.gse.harvard.edu/uk/blog/students-teachers

16. Hope Squads are found in K–12 schools in various parts of the world. A group of students are trained to identify peers who might be enduring personal crises.

17. As an example of a superordinate goal, see Sherif, M., Harvey, O. J., White, B. J., et al. (1961). *Intergroup conflict and cooperation: The robbers cave experiment*. University of Oklahoma Press.

18. James, W. (1890). *The principles of psychology*. Dover Publications.

19. Heath, C., & Heath, D. (2017). *The power of moments: Why certain experiences have extraordinary impact* (chap. 4). Bantam Press.

5: Helped Me Through a Hard Time

1. See National 4-H Council (2020, June 17). New survey finds 7 in 10 teens are struggling with mental health. PRNewswire, at https://www.prnewswire.com/news-releases/new-survey-finds-7-in-10-teens-are-struggling-with-mental-health-301078336.html.

2. Astrid Tuminez quoted in https://www.deseret.com/2021/11/12/22776537/the-many-paths-to-success-astrid-tuminez-utah-valley-university-higher-ed-diversity-inclusion.

3. Research reported in Aspen Institute (2019). *From a nation at risk to a nation at hope: Recommendations from the National Commission on Social, Emotional, & Academic Development*.

4. These are common percentages reported over the past few years by the U.S. Centers for Disease Control and Prevention, as well as other research institutions. They may not match your students.

5. See Bethell, C. D., Carle, A., Hudziak, J., Gombojav, N., Powers, K., Wade, R., & Braveman, P. (2017). Methods to assess adverse childhood experiences of children and families: Toward approaches to promote child well-being in policy and practice. *Academic Pediatrics*, *17*(7), S51–S69. http://www.academicpedsjnl.net/article/S1876-2859(17)30324-8/abstract

6. Chartier, M. J., Walker, J. R., & Naimark, B. (2010). Separate and cumulative effects of adverse childhood experiences in predicting adult

health and health care utilization. *Child Abuse & Neglect, 34*(6), 454–464. Retrieved from https://www.sciencedirect.com/science/article/pii/S0145213410000955. See also Chapman, D. P., Whitfield, C. L., Felitti, V. J., Dube, S. R., Edwards, V. J., & Anda, R. F. (2004). Adverse childhood experiences and the risk of depressive disorders in adulthood. *Journal of Affective Disorders, 82*(2), 217–225. https://www.ncbi.nlm.nih.gov/pubmed/15488250

7. See Ghandour, R. M., Jones, J. R., Lebrun-Harris, L. A., Minnaert, J., Blumberg, S. J., Fields, J., Bethell, C., & Kogan, M. D. (2018). The design and implementation of the 2016 National Survey of Children's Health. *Maternal Child Health Journal, 22*(8), 1093–1102. https://doi.org/10.1007/s10995-018-2526-x

8. Sege, R., Bethell, C., Linkenbach, J., Jones, J. A., Klika, B., & Pecora, P. J. (2017). *Balancing adverse childhood experiences (ACEs) with HOPE: New insights into the role of positive experience on child and family development.* Casey Family Programs. Retrieved from https://www.cssp.org/publications/documents/Balancing-ACEs-with-HOPE-FINAL.pdf

9. American Association of Suicidology (2006). *USA suicide: 2003 final data.* http://www.suicidology.org/associations/1045/files/2003datapgb.pdf

10. Joiner, T. E. (2005). *Why people die by suicide.* Harvard University Press.

11. Brown, G., Beck, A. T., Steer, R., & Grisham, J. (2000). Risk factors for suicide in psychiatric outpatients: A 20-year prospective study. *Journal of Consulting and Clinical Psychology, 68*(3), 371–377.

12. For more, see Fredrickson, B. L. (2013). *Love 2.0: How our supreme emotion affects everything we feel, think, do, and become* (p. 78). Hudson Street Press.

13. Darling-Hammond, L. (2019, January 14). Quoted in Getting started with trauma-informed practices. *Edutopia.* Video found at https://www.edutopia.org/video/getting-started-trauma-informed-practices/. The video is part of Edutopia's *How Learning Happens Series* and was

developed in collaboration with the National Commission on Social, Emotional, and Academic Development, with support from the Chan Zuckerberg Initiative.

14. Duck syndrome is not a formal mental health diagnosis nor is it meant to be limited to Stanford students.

15. Psychologist Carl Rogers was one of the early promoters of empathic listening as a means of counseling people during therapy.

16. Dr. Burns's steps for empathic listening are often cited in counseling journals and textbooks. For some of his original work on it, see Burns, D. D. (1999). *The feeling good handbook* (rev. ed.). Plume.

17. Peters, T. J., & Waterman, R. H. (2006). *In search of excellence: Lessons from America's best-run companies*. Collins Business Essentials.

18. Longfellow, H. W. (1849). *Hyperion: A romance* (p. 154). John W. Lovell Company.

19. Rosenberg, M. B. (2015). *Nonviolent communication: A language of life*. PuddleDancer Press.

20. Schultz, J. (2018, June). Your child is sending you signals. Are you ignoring them. *Attitude Magazine*. See https://www.additudemag.com/why-do-children-act-out-reducing-negative-adhd-behaviors.

21. Deming, W. E. (2018). *Out of the crisis*. The MIT Press.

22. Smith, E. E. (2013, March 1). The benefits of optimism are real. *The Atlantic*. https://www.theatlantic.com/health/archive/2013/03/the-benefits-of-optimism-are-real/273306/

23. Seligman, M. E. P. (1995). *The optimistic child: How learned optimism protects children from depression*. Houghton Mifflin Company.

24. Fredrickson, B. (2009). *Positivity: Groundbreaking research to release your inner optimist and thrive*. Oneworld.

25. See Emmons, R. A., & Shelton, C. M. (2002). Gratitude and the science of positive psychology. In Snyder, C. R., & Lopez, S. J. (Eds.). *Handbook of positive psychology* (pp. 459–471). Oxford University Press.

26. Mayo Clinic (2022, December 6). Can expressing gratitude improve your mental, physical health? https://www.mayoclinichealthsystem

.org/hometown-health/speaking-of-health/can-expressing-gratitude
-improve-health

27. Wood, A. M., Froh, J. J., & Geraghty, A. W. (2010). Gratitude and well-being: A review and theoretical integration. *Clinical Psychology Review, 30*(7), 890–905. See also Lyubomirsky, S. (2008). *The how of happiness: A new approach to getting the life you want* (pp. 90–95). Penguin Books.

28. Crandall, A. Miller, J. R., Cheung, A., Novilla, L. K., Glade, R., Novilla, M. L. B., Magnusson, B. M., Leavitt, B. L., Barnes, M. D., & Henson, C. L. (2019, October). ACEs and counter-ACEs: How positive and negative childhood experiences influence adult health. *Child Abuse and Neglect, 96,* 104089.

29. Paraphrasing the song "I Have Confidence," from *The Sound of Music* (1965), produced by 20th Century-Fox, music and lyrics by Richard Rodgers and Oscar Hammerstein.

30. The earliest reference for Oscar Hammerstein's quote is from a speech he gave at the 1953 Theatre Guild Awards.

31. For more details and examples of why asking "What went well today? And why?," see Seligman, M. E. P. (2013). *Flourish* (p. 33). Atria Paperback.

32. Glasser, W. (1998). *Choice theory: A new psychology of personal freedom.* HarperCollins.

33. Payne, R. (2018). *Emotional poverty in all demographics: How to reduce anger, anxiety, and violence in the classroom.* aha! Publications.

34. Payne (2018).

35. See Haidt, J. (2024). *The anxious generation: How the great rewiring of childhood is causing an epidemic of mental illness* (pp. 7, 251–265). Penguin Press.

36. Robinson, L., Smith, M., Segal, J., & Shubin, J. (n.d.). The benefits of play for adults. HelpGuide.org, https://www.helpguide.org/mental-health/wellbeing/benefits-of-play-for-adults

37. For more on the topic, see Ginsburg, K. (2007, January). The importance of play in promoting healthy child development and maintaining

strong parent-child bonds. *Pediatrics*, *119*(1), 182–191. http://pediat rics.aappublications.org/content/119/1/182

38. Bibliotherapists help people recover from mental health issues by finding them books to read that soothe them, help them to feel more empathy, or help people to see how others have overcome similar challenges in life. The American Library Association suggests resources and booklists in this area. See https://www.ala.org/tools/atoz/bibliotherapy

39. Lyubomirsky (2008), p. 254.

40. Duckworth, A. (2016), *Grit: The power of passion and perseverance* (p. 190). Scribner.

41. Center on the Developing Child at Harvard University (2016). 8 things to remember about child development. Retrieved from www .developingchild.harvard.edu

6: Empowered Me to Do It Myself

1. Re-created in alliterative fashion from The fable of the gullible gulls, *Reader's Digest*, October 1950.

2. See American Psychological Association's website: https://www.apa .org/pi/aids/resources/education/self-efficacy#:~:text=Self%2Def ficacy%20refers%20to%20an,%2C%20behavior%2C%20and%20 social%20environment

3. For more benefits see Bandura, A. (1986). *Social foundations of thought and action: A social-cognitive view*. Prentice-Hall. Dr. Hatch had the privilege of spending a day with the late Dr. Bandura. If one character- istic stood out, it was his humility.

4. Britt Frank quoted in Collins, L. M. (2019, November 29). For teens and college-age kids to thrive, parents need to stop doing this. *Deseret News*. https://www.deseret.com/indepth/2019/11/29/20966851/he licopter-parenting-teens-college-age-kids-thrive-parents

5. Years before he launched positive psychology, Martin Seligman pro- posed the concept of "learned helplessness" and scores of research

papers have since followed. See Seligman, E. P. (1972). Learned helplessness. *Annual Review of Medicine*, *23*, 407–412. Dr. Seligman later turned to writing about "learned optimism." See Seligman, E. P. (1990). *Learned optimism: How to change your mind and your life*. Vintage Books.

6.   The happiness pie chart is presented in Lyubomirsky, S., Sheldon, K. M., & Schkade, D. (2005). Pursuing happiness: The architecture of sustainable change. *Review of General Psychology*, *9*(2), 111–131. We have added the dashed lines to indicate that all three sources interact with one another.

7.   Seligman, M. E. P. (1995). *The optimistic child: How learned optimism protects children from depression*. Houghton Mifflin Company.

8.   Locus of control has been studied by many researchers. Some people perceive that they have an internal locus of control, where their actions are determined by their choices. Others have an external locus of control, where they perceive that their behaviors are determined by factors outside themselves, including fate and luck. The construct was originally proposed by Julian Rotter. See, for example, Rotter, J. B. (1966). Generalized expectancies for internal versus external locus of control of reinforcement. *Psychological Monographs*, *80*(1), 1–28.

9.   See Bandura, A. (1977). Self-efficacy: Toward a unifying theory of behavioral change. *Psychological Review*, *84*(2), 191–215; and Bandura, A. (1997). *Self-efficacy: The exercise of control*. W. H. Freeman.

10. Bandura, A. (2008). An agentic perspective on positive psychology. In S. J. Lopez (Ed.), Praeger perspectives. *Positive psychology: Exploring the best in people*, *1*, 167–196.

11. Keller, H. (1903). *The story of my life: With her letters (1887–1901)*. Double-day, Page & Co.

12. Glasser, W. (1998). *Choice theory: A new psychology of personal freedom*. HarperCollins.

13. Duckworth, A. (2016). *Grit: The power of passion and perseverance*. Scribner, 107.

14. Deci, E., & Ryan, R. (2008). Facilitating optimal motivation and psychological well-being across life's domains. *Canadian Psychology*, *49*(1), 14–23.

15. In Bibby, C. (1971). *T. H. Huxley on education: A selection from his writings*. Cambridge University Press.

16. Gardner, H. (2006). *Multiple intelligences: New horizons in theory and practice*. Basic Books.

17. See cbsnews.com/video/lin-manuel-miranda-reacts-to-message-from-8th-grade-teacher-who-changed-my-life-forever/#x.

18. This is the expertise of our good friend Dr. Elizabeth Murphy. See Murphy, E. (2021, November 18). Type development in childhood and beyond. *Journal of Advanced Analytical Psychology*, *66*(5), 1074–1093.

19. Mark Van Doren cited in Byrne, J. (2018, April 24). The world's 40 best under-40 MBA professors. *Forbes*.

20. See Prodigy (2018, April 3). Flexible seating: 21 awesome ideas for your classroom. https://www.prodigygame.com/main-en/blog/flexible-seating-classroom-ideas/

21. Rennie Center for Education Research & Policy (2019). *Student voice: How young people can shape the future of education*. Rennie Center for Education Research & Policy.

22. See Elevate Student Voice. https://schoolguide.casel.org/focus-area-3/school/elevate-student-voice/

23. Quaglia, R., Corso, M., & Lande, L. (2016). *School voice report 2016*. Developed by the Quaglia Institute for School Voice and Aspirations in partnership with the Quaglia Institute for Student Aspirations, Teacher Voice and Aspirations International Center, and Corwin Press. https://quagliainstitute.org/dmsView/School_Voice_Report_2016

24. Mitra, D. L., & Serriere, S. C. (2012, August). Student voice in elementary school reform: Examining youth development in fifth graders. *American Educational Research Journal*, *49*(4), 743–774.

25. See Lyubomirsky, S. (2008). *The how of happiness: A new approach to getting the life you want* (pp. 206–207). Penguin Books.

26. The G.A.M.E. components are consistent with Malcolm Baldrige criteria and the Six Sigma quality movements that have been around in organizations for years.

27. Snyder, C. R., Ilardi, S., Michael, S. T., & Cheavens, J. (2000). Hope theory: Updating a common process for psychological change. In C. R. Snyder & R. E. Ingram (Eds.), *Handbook of psychological change: Psychotherapy processes & practices for the 21st century* (pp. 128–153). John Wiley & Sons, Inc.

28. Pink, D. (2009). *Drive: The surprising truth about what motivates us* (p. 116). Riverhead Hardcover.

29. Senge, P. M. (2006). *The fifth discipline: The art & discipline of the learning organization*. Random House Business.

30. Lyubomirsky (2008), pp. 224–225.

31. Ziglar used the quote in his motivational speeches. One of his main messages was that the most rewarding part of being successful is the process itself.

32. Nunes, J. C., & Drèze, X. (2006). The endowed progress effect: How artificial advancement increases effort. *Journal of Consumer Research*, *32*(4), 504–512. https://doi.org/10.1086/500480

33. See Locke, E. A., & Latham, G. P. (2019). The development of goal setting theory: A half century retrospective. *Motivation Science*, *5*(2), 93–105.

34. Norcross, J. C., Mrykalo, M. S., & Blagys, M. D. (2002). Auld lang syne: Success predictors, change processes, and self-reported outcomes of New Year's resolvers and nonresolvers. *Journal of Clinical Psychology*, *58*(4), 397–405.

35. Retrieved from Kōnosuke Matsushita Quotes, www.quoteswise.com /konosuke-matsushita-quotes.html

36. For detailed guidance on how to set and achieve team, classroom, or schoolwide goals, see Covey, S. M., Kosinski, L., & Thompson, M. (2022). *The 4 disciplines of execution for educators: Achieving your wildly important goals*. FranklinCovey.

37. Ziglar, Z. (1974). *Biscuits, fleas, and pump handles*. Update.

7: Corrected Me in a Positive Way

1. This version of "Crossroads" is adapted from a poem credited to Laura Soper entitled "To Your Chum and My Chum," which appeared in G. F. Rowell (Ed.) (1919). *Guide posts on the highways and byways of education: The public schools of America, the hope of democracy.* It has also been credited to Sadie Tiller Crawley and named "The Upward Reach."

2. See Connection before correction in Dr. Jane Nelsen's blog at https://www.positivediscipline.com/articles/connection-correction-0. Also Nelsen, J. (2006). *Positive discipline: The classic guide to helping children develop self-discipline, responsibility, cooperation, and problem-solving skills.* Ballantine Books.

3. Marzano, Robert J., Pickering, D. J., & Pollock, J. E. (2001). *Classroom management that works* (p. 41). ASCD.

4. Alderfer, C. P. (1969). An empirical test of a new theory of human needs. *Organizational Behavior and Human Performance, 4*(2), 142–175. doi:10.1016/0030-5073(69)90004-X

5. McLelland, D. C. (1975). *Power: The inner experience.* Irvington.

6. Pink, D. (2009). *Drive: The surprising truth about what motivates us.* Riverhead Hardcover.

7. Collins, J. (2001). *Good to great: Why some companies make the leap . . . and others don't.* HarperBusiness.

8. Amabile, T. M., & Kramer, S. J. (2011). The progress principle: Using small wins to ignite joy, engagement, and creativity at work. *Harvard Business Review Press.* https://hbr.org/2011/05/the-power-of-small-wins

9. Dweck, C. S. (2006). *Mindsets: The new psychology of success.* Ballantine Books.

10. Blackwell, L. S., Trzesniewski, K. H., & Dweck, C. S. (2007). Implicit theories of intelligence predict achievement across adolescent transition: A longitudinal study and an intervention. *Child Development, 78*(1), 246–263. 10.1111/j.1467-8624.2007.00995.x

11. Seligman, M. E. P. (2002). *Authentic happiness: Using the new positive psychology to realize your potential for lasting fulfillment* (p. xi). Free Press.

12. Retrieved from Tait, V. (2019, January 5). Authoritative parenting examples through John Gottman's emotion coaching. https://veroni katait.com/posts/2019-01-05-emotion-coaching.html

13. Glasser, W. (1999). *Choice theory: A new psychology of personal freedom*. HarperPerennial.

14. Yeager, D. C. (2014). Breaking the cycle of mistrust: Wise interventions to provide critical feedback across the racial divide. *Journal of Experimental Psychology, 143*(2), 804–824.

15. The quote from Goethe was published originally in German and has since come out in various translations including Goethe, J. W. (2024). *Wilhelm Meister's Apprenticeship* (E. A. Blackall & V. Lange, Eds.). Princeton University Press.

16. Caldarella, P., Larsen, R. A. A., Williams, L., & Wills, H. P. (2020, January). Effects of middle school teachers' praise-to-reprimand ratios on students' classroom behavior. *Educational Psychology, 40*(2), 1–17. doi: 10.1080/01443410.2020.1711872

17. Covey, S. (2014). *The 7 habits of highly effective teens*. Simon & Schuster.

18. Rather, D. (1984). *The camera never blinks*. Ballantine Books.

19. Curran, T., & Hill, A. P. (2022). Young people's perceptions of their parents' expectations and criticism are increasing over time: Implications for perfectionism. *Psychological Bulletin, 148*(1–2), 107–128.

20. This quote is attributed to Winston Churchill and is believed to be a variation on Voltaire's words, "The good is the enemy of the best."

21. Aristotle recorded this in his work *Rhetoric*, which has been republished in multiple commentaries.

22. Burns, D. (2008). *Feeling good together: The secret to making troubled relationships work*. Broadway Books. See also Burns, D. (1999). *Feeling good: The new mood therapy*. Quill.

23. Payne, R. (2018). *Emotional poverty in all demographics: How to reduce anger, anxiety, and violence in the classroom*. aha! Publications.

24. Maxwell, J. C. (2007). *Failing forward: Turning mistakes into stepping stones for success*. Thomas Nelson.

25. DuFour, R., & Fullan, M. (2013). *Cultures built to last: Systemic PLCs at work*. Solution Tree Press.

26. Borg, S., & Al-Busaidi, S. (2012). *Learner autonomy: English language teachers' beliefs and practices*. British Council.

27. Berger, R. (2014). *Leaders of their own learning: Transforming schools through student-engaged assessment* (p. 5). Jossey-Bass.

28. Berger (2014), p. 6.

29. Hattie, J. (2009). *Visible learning: A synthesis of over 800 meta-analyses relating to achievement* (p. 119). Routledge.

8: Crafting a Sustainable Plan

1. See the Centers for Disease Control and Prevention (2009). *School connectedness: Strategies for increasing protective factors among youth*. U.S. Department of Health and Human Services.

2. This is a spin on a scene from the movie *Forrest Gump*, where Forrest is on a bench contemplating life. He is enjoying a box of assorted chocolates when he turns to a stranger and sighs: "My mamma always said that life is like a box of chocolates. You never know what you're going to get." Zemeckis, R. (1994). *Forrest Gump*. Paramount Pictures.

3. Wong, H. K., & Wong, R. T. (1998). *The first days of school: How to be an effective teacher*, 5th ed. Wong Publications.

4. Drucker, P. (n.d.). Planned abandonment: Out with the old, in with the new. https://drucker.institute/wp-content/uploads/2018/08/Reading_Drucker-on-Planned-Abandonment-1.pdf

5. Becker, J. (2024). Hans Hofmann on minimalism. See https://www.becomingminimalist.com/hans-hofmann-on-minimalism/.

6. The primacy and recency effects are typically credited to Solomon Asch, as far back as Asch, S. E. (1946). Forming impressions of personality. *Journal of Abnormal and Social Psychology*, 41(3), 258–290.

7.   Barth, R. S. (March 2006). Improving relationships within the school-house. *Educational Leadership*, *63*(6), 8–13.

8.   See https://www.cdc.gov/healthyyouth/mental-health/index.htm and CDC Youth Risk Behavior Survey Data Summary and Trends Report (2009–2019).

9.   The data was extracted from the International Survey of Children's Well-Being, funded by the Zurich-based Jacobs Foundation. The Dr. Whitaker comments were cited in: Marples, M. (2022, May 20). Children are more likely to succeed if they live in this type of environment. CNN. See https://www.cnn.com/2022/05/20/health/family-connections-flourish-parenting-study-wellness/index.html

10.   Barbara Coloroso is the author of Coloroso, B. (2002). *Kids are worth it!: Giving your child the gift of inner discipline*. William Morrow Paperbacks. Her quote is cited in azquotes.com/quote/1265601.

11.   Aspen Institute (2019). *From a nation at risk to a nation at hope: Recommendations from the National Commission on Social, Emotional, & Academic Development*. See also Durlak, J., Weissberg, R., Dymnicki, A., Taylor, R., & Schellinger, K. (2011). The impact of enhancing students' social and emotional learning: A meta-analysis of school-based universal interventions. *Child Development*, *82*(1), 405–432. See also Berkowitz, R., Moore, H., & Benbenishty, R. (2016). A research synthesis of the associations between socioeconomic background, inequality, school climate, and academic achievement. *Review of Educational Research*, *20*(2), 1–45.

12.   Taylor, R. D., Oberle, E., Durlak, J. A., & Weissberg, R. P. (2017, July/August). Promoting positive youth development through school-based social and emotional learning interventions: A meta-analysis of follow-up effects. *Child Development*, *88*(4), 1156–1171. Based on a meta-analysis of 82 studies on social-emotional learning programs.

13.   Aspen Institute (2019). *From a nation at risk to a nation at hope: Recommendations from the National Commission on Social, Emotional, & Academic Development*. See also Durlak et al. (2011). See also Berkowitz et al. (2016).

14. The "Life is what happens . . ." quote is often attributed to John Lennon, but there are several earlier sources in various forms.

15. Clear, J. (2018). *Atomic habits: An easy & proven way to build good habits & break bad ones*. Avery.

9: Just Love 2.0 Them!

1. Nicholas Ferroni is a high school history teacher and reform advocate. He was quoted in Curtis, C. (2019, July 26). Teacher role models: How to help students who need it the most. CU/Online. See online.camp bellsville.edu/education/teacher-role-models/.

2. We recognize that the See-Do-Get Cycle is oversimplistic when considering all the factors that go into personal change. However, we have used it for years and found that people appreciate its simplicity in thinking about how to go about personal change.

3. Lipton, B. H. (2016). *The biology of belief: Unleashing the power of unconsciousness, matter and miracles*. Hay House.

4. Uttered in Foster, M. (2018). *Christopher Robin*. Walt Disney Studios Motion Pictures. The original author behind the character of Pooh is A. A. Milne.

5. Lincoln, A. (1862, December 1). Records of the U.S. Senate, RG 46: Page 85 of President Abraham Lincoln's Second Annual Message to Congress, SEN37A-F1.

6. Rodgers, C., & Raider-Roth, M. (2006). *Presence in teaching. Teachers and Teaching: Theory and Practice, 12*(3), 265–287. doi:10.1080/13450600500467548

7. Wong, H. K., & Wong, R. T. (1998, January). *The first days of school: How to be an effective teacher*, 5th ed. (p. 15). Wong Publications.

8. Daggett, B., & Jones, S. M. (2019, June). *Addressing whole child growth through strong relationships: The evidence-based connections between academic and social-emotional learning*. International Center for Leadership in Education.

9. Fredrickson, B. (2013). *Love 2.0: How our supreme emotion affects everything we feel, think, do, and become* (see pp. 10, 12, & 67). Hudson Street Press.

10. From Jim Collins's website in reference to his flywheel concept in Collins, J. (2001). *Good to great: Why some companies make the leap . . . and others don't*. HarperBusiness.

11. Yeager, D. S., & Walton, G. M. (2011). Social-psychological interventions in education: They're not magic. *Review of Educational Research, 81*(2), 267–301. https://doi.org/10.3102/0034654311405999

12. Wong & Wong (1998), p. 10.

13. Pierson, R. (2013, April). *Every kid deserves a champion*. TED Conference, New York.

14. den Heijer, A. (2018). *Nothing you don't already know: Remarkable reminders about meaning, purpose, and self-realization*. CreateSpace.

Index

Note: Page references in *italics* refer to figures.

About the Authors

Writing this book has been a synergistic effort. As authors, we are very diverse in our backgrounds and skillsets, but our passions for making a difference in students' and teachers' lives can pass as twins.

Dr. David K. Hatch earned a bachelor's in psychology from California State University, Long Beach, and a doctorate in social-organizational psychology from Brigham Young University. His work in schools began at a public school for students with special learning needs. He then taught for the University of Maryland's European Division in Germany, prior to working in corporate education with Dr. Stephen R. Covey. His consulting work has taken him to over 40 countries, and his leadership workshops and assessments have been utilized by more than a million leaders.

Dr. Hatch was consulting on a project for the United Nation's Development Program in New York City when the attacks of September 11, 2001, erupted. While walking among the smoke and screaming sirens, he resolved to do his part to enable young people to experience a more positive world. He re-directed his career back into the field of education and co-authored *The Leader in Me* with Dr. Covey and others. For the past 15 years, he has consulted with hundreds of schools and authored leadership curriculum and learning resources that are being used by over two million K–12 students and thousands of teachers worldwide.

Muriel Summers, from the minute she stepped into the classroom, has always viewed teaching as a *calling*. As a principal, she twice guided her school, A.B. Combs Elementary in Raleigh, North Carolina, to being named the top magnet school of America. The school also became the original leadership school featured in FranklinCovey's *Leader in Me*. The vision and strategies she and her remarkable staff developed are now being replicated in over 8,000 schools in more than 60 countries.

Muriel has received several honors, including teacher of the year, principal of the year, and an honorary doctorate. She was awarded the William and Ida Friday award for Leadership in Innovation, The Order of the Long Leaf Pine given by the Governor of North Carolina (the state's highest honor given to a North Carolinian), the University of North Carolina at Chapel Hill Award for Leadership in Education, and the Ralph Kimmel Award, North Carolina's highest honor for principals. She now serves as the Global Ambassador for *The Leader in Me* and keynotes at conferences across the United States and abroad.

Muriel's career reflects her teaching motto—*Just luv'em*. She says, "Just as I have learned that my journey has less to do with a particular destination, and more to do with the adventures and miracles along the way, so too I have learned that my work will *not* ultimately be judged by some singular, lofty contribution, but rather by simple day-to-day gestures that improve a student's life." While never compromising academic standards or the intellectual integrity of solid learning strategies, it has always been her quest that children leave her schools with a "diploma of the heart"—a strong sense of self-worth, an understanding of true citizenship, and a style of communication that has its origins in kindness, compassion, and mutual respect.

Together, we are thrilled about the positive potential this book presents for teachers and students. We are truly grateful and pleased to acknowledge the contributions of so many others who have offered their insights and feedback to this work.

About FranklinCovey Education

For over three decades, FranklinCovey Education, a division of FranklinCovey and a global leader in education solutions, has been one of the world's most prominent and trusted providers of educational-leadership solutions. FranklinCovey's programs, books, and content have been utilized by thousands of public and private primary, secondary, and post-secondary schools and institutions, including educational service centers and vocational schools in all 50 states within the United States and in over 60 countries.

Our Mission

To enable greatness in students, educators, and school communities everywhere.

Our Vision

Our vision is to profoundly impact education across the globe by enabling missions of educators and students to achieve their own great purposes and potential.

Our PK–12 Solutions

- **Leader in Me:** A comprehensive PK–12 model designed to build leadership in students, create a high-trust culture, and improve academic achievement.
- **Professional Development:** Such as The 7 Habits of Highly Effective People®, The 4 Essential Roles of Leadership®, and Teacher Believed in Me.
- **Coaching:** Optimize productivity, personal effectiveness, and leadership skills in your school and district leaders.
- **Strategy Execution:** Use The 4 Disciplines of Execution® process to achieve success in your strategic priorities.

LEARN MORE
franklincovey.com/education

Developing
Life-Ready Leaders®

Every student possesses inherent greatness and unique potential. They deserve opportunities to develop leadership and life skills that prepare them for success in the future, but many schools are not set up to unleash that potential.

100+
independent research studies demonstrate our impact

8,000+
Leader in Me Schools

60+
countries served

20 million+
students reached

Leader in Me is FranklinCovey Education's comprehensive, evidence-based PK–12 model. It provides schools and districts with:

- A leadership and life-readiness framework for all students.
- The tools to create a high-trust school culture.
- A system for increasing academic achievement.

GET STARTED

Teacher Believed in Me

Through this professional development experience, educators ignite or re-ignite their passions for making a difference in students' lives through actionable, evidence-based practices that:

- Build connections with students.
- Teach meaningful life lessons that resonate beyond the classroom.
- Inspire students to discover and develop their unique strengths.
- Entrust students with responsibilities that build self-worth.
- Support students with empathy and optimism when they face challenges.
- Empower students to take ownership of their learning and growth.
- Provide correction and feedback in positive, constructive ways.

Teacher Believed in Me is complementary to Leader in Me, FranklinCovey's flagship whole-school leadership model. For more information, visit LeaderinMe.org.

GET STARTED

FranklinCovey
Education

Books that Shape Leaders at Every Age

Bestselling books from FranklinCovey that have helped millions grow — at home, at school, and at work.

- *The Leader in Me*
- *Teacher Believed in Me*
- *The 7 Habits of Highly Effective Teens*
- *The 7 Habits of Happy Kids*
- *The 7 Habits of Happy Kids* Boxed Set
- *The 7 Habits of Highly Effective People: 30th Anniversary Edition*
- *The 6 Most Important Decisions You'll Ever Make*
- *The 4 Disciplines of Execution*

Available wherever books are sold.

SHOP NOW

FranklinCovey
Education